Henry Sebastian Bowden

The Religion of Shakespeare

Chiefly from the Writings of the late Mr. Richard Simpson, M.A

Henry Sebastian Bowden

The Religion of Shakespeare
Chiefly from the Writings of the late Mr. Richard Simpson, M.A

ISBN/EAN: 9783337063108

Printed in Europe, USA, Canada, Australia, Japan

Cover: Foto ©Thomas Meinert / pixelio.de

More available books at **www.hansebooks.com**

THE RELIGION OF
SHAKESPEARE

CHIEFLY FROM THE WRITINGS OF THE

LATE MR. RICHARD SIMPSON, M.A.

BY

HENRY SEBASTIAN BOWDEN
OF THE ORATORY

LONDON: BURNS & OATES, Limited

NEW YORK, CINCINNATI, CHICAGO: BENZIGER BROTHERS

1899

PREFACE

THE following work has little claim to originality, the greater portion of it being based on manuscripts of the late Mr. Richard Simpson. From his singular acquaintance with Elizabethan literature, these writings offer a sound foundation for the study of Shakespeare in relation to the religious thought of his day. The State Paper documents, the Harleian, Ashmolean, Sloane, and Lansdowne collections, the Rutland and Salisbury Papers, Visitation Returns, the libraries of Paris and Lille, the archives of the English College at Rome, the Douay Registers, the Registers of the Jesuit Colleges of Malines and Bruges, the Stonyhurst MS., were all within the range of his research. It must be remembered also that many of these documents, now printed, indexed, and ready to hand, existed in Mr. Simpson's time only in manuscript, and thus their contents could only be acquired by laborious personal investigation. His note-books are an abiding memorial of his exploring zeal. They contain autograph copies of every rare play, tale, or ballad, cognate to his subject, and abound with varied and recondite data and references.

But Mr. Simpson was not merely a collector of rare or curious material. As Shakespeare's plays

were professedly composed under " the pressure
of the time," Mr. Simpson's object was to inquire
what contemporary event may have furnished the
political motive of the play, or at least suggested
some of its incidents and characters.   The political
allegory, did it reflect on the Government, would
be necessarily veiled, and would pass unheeded by
the ignorant or the inattentive, but would have
spoken clearly to the wise.   Doubtless this desire
of solving the dramatic riddles of the past may
lead to merely fanciful and arbitrary assertions,
but the art of the interpreter, soberly exercised,
discovers in a play a real though hidden motive,
which would otherwise be lost, and is of genuine
historic value.   Thus Professor Gardiner, from his
intimate knowledge with the times of James I.
and Charles I., has been able to trace the political
element in the plays of Massinger.   In these
dramas, Mr. Gardiner says, " Massinger treated of
the events of the day under a disguise hardly less
thin than that which shows off the figures in the
caricatures of Aristophanes or the cartoons of
Punch.[1]   Now Mr. Simpson's political interpretation
of " Richard II." and " Measure for Measure " rests
on evidence as sound, we think, as that produced
by Mr. Gardiner in his solution of "The Emperor
of the East," or "The Maid of Honour."   In any
case Mr. Simpson's power to decipher the political,
religious, and dramatic allusions in Shakespeare can
be gauged by his writings published in the New
Shakespeare Society, *Transactions*, 1874–1875, and

---

[1] "Political Element in Massinger," New Shakespeare Society,
Transactions, 316. 1875.

in various separate treatises. It is true, indeed, that occasionally his interpretations may seem strained and far-fetched, but even then they are interesting as proofs of his ingenuity and research.

The present work is based on a folio MS. of Mr. Simpson's of some 200 pages, which was composed under the following circumstances. In 1858 Mr. Simpson published three articles in the *Rambler*, in which he defended the probability of Shakespeare being a Catholic. In 1864 there appeared a work on the subject from the pen of M. Rio, the author of *L'Art Chrétien*. Taken with Simpson's argument, Rio allowed his imagination free rein, and described the poet as an ardent and avowed champion of the Catholic faith, a conclusion far beyond that of Simpson's. The two writers, notwithstanding the totally different character of their works, were however made the object of a common attack in an article in the *Edinburgh Review*, January 1866, which was publicly attributed to Lord Mahon. It was primarily as a reply to this article that the folio above mentioned was written, but it developed into a comprehensive treatise on the subject of Shakespeare's philosophy and religion as manifested in his writings.

But Mr. Simpson's treatise has needed both remodelling and additions. In Simpson's day Shakespeare was regarded, at least by such writers as Knight and Bishop Wordsworth, as an orthodox Protestant, a faithful follower of the established religion. He is now represented as a pioneer of "modern thought." Thus Professor Dowden, Professor Caird, Mr. Tyler, and in Germany Kreysig and Dr. Vehse, amongst others regard him as a positivist, a pantheist, a fatalist, in short, a typical agnostic.

By both these classes of critics Shakespeare, however, is claimed as the product of the Reformation. And it is against this claim that the first chapter is directed, where an endeavour is made to show that Shakespeare, so far from being the product of his times, or the voice of his times, was in direct antagonism to his time. And this point is further developed in Chapter III., in which the marked contrast between Shakespeare and his contemporary dramatists is set forth. That Shakespeare's principles are as little in accord with the prevalent solution of ethical questions as with the principles intellectual, social, and moral of the Reformation, from which those solutions are professedly derived, Chapter IX. purposes to establish.

These three chapters have then been added to Mr. Simpson's work by the present writer, who, however, has derived valuable assistance from Mr. Simpson's MS.

The other six chapters are mainly Mr. Simpson's. Chapter II., "External Evidence," is drawn chiefly from the *Rambler's* article (1858), save the additions called for by Mr. Carter's recent book, "Shakespeare, Puritan and Protestant." Chapter IV., "The English Historical Plays," is recast from the papers read before the New Shakespeare Society, 1875. Chapter V., "The Sonnets," is a summary of Mr. Simpson's "Philosophy of the Sonnets" (1868), a book undeservedly long since out of print. Chapter VI., "The Love Plays"; Chapter VII., "The

Tragedies"; Chapter VIII., "The Didactic Plays,"
are now published for the first time, with such
additions or modifications as seemed necessary.

To preserve the unity of the whole, the parts
contributed by the present writer to the work are
incorporated with Mr. Simpson's; but with the
above indication, their respective portions may be
sufficiently recognised. Any salient point of difference in their opinions is duly noted when it occurs.

The evidence adduced from Shakespeare's writings
in the following pages, which might be indefinitely
strengthened, brings out, we think, two points
clearly. First, that Shakespeare was not on the
winning side in his day in politics or religion;
that he carefully avoided all those appeals to
popular prejudice about monks and nuns, popes
and cardinals, which form the farcical element of so
many plays of his time; nay, more, that in adapting
old plays he carefully expunged every satire of the
ancient faith. Secondly, that he not only habitually
extols the old order of things, but that he
studiously depreciates the new. He surveyed his
own times with an anguish, he says, that made
him "cry for death" (Sonnet 66). He speaks
to his contemporaries in language like that of
John Nichols—language couched on the lines,
we are told, of the Catholic sermons of the day.
"They told them how their forefathers lived,
how that in coming to churches they were very
diligent, in worshipping of images they were devout,
how painful in visiting holy places, how liberal with
the poor, how merciful with the afflicted, and how
careful to keep God's commandments. Where now

are these good works (say they)?   What is become
of them ?   Now one man seeketh to beguile another,
one man speaketh evil of another, their devotion to
the Church is waxen cold, charity towards the poor
is more than frozen."[1]   This judgment of Nichols
on his times is, we believe, also that of Shakespeare.
The evidence in support of that opinion is now
submitted to the judgment of our readers.

Grateful thanks are due to the Very Rev. F.
Gasquet, D.D., O.S.B., the present possessor of Mr.
Simpson's papers, for the kind permission to make
free use of these documents; to Rev. W. Gildea,
D.D., for his careful correction and revision of the
following work; and to Brother Vincent Hayles, of
the Oratory, London, for many details obtained by
his varied research.

[1] " John Nichols, A Declaration of the Recantation of." London :
Barker, February 19, 1591.   Sig. L.iiii.

CONTENTS

CHAPTER III.

Contemporary Dramatists.

THE

RELIGION OF SHAKESPEARE.

CHAPTER I.

SHAKESPEARE AND THE REFORMATION.

DRAMATIC representation had with Shakespeare a
threefold end. Artistically its aim was, he says, to
reflect the image of creation, to "hold the mirror up
to nature." Hence it was essentially objective. His
creations were not arbitrarily drawn from his own
phantasy, but from existing types. Morally his intention was to exhibit the great characteristics of
virtue and vice, to show virtue "her own image,
scorn her own feature," to portray what was essentially
and necessarily good or evil in its nature, origin,
development, and result. Historically, or politically,
its purpose was to set forth the "very form or
pressure of the age and body of the time." And
this meant, not the pedantic reading in of lessons
from parallel passages of history, nor a caricature
of passing events, drawn by the pen of a partisan,

A

but the presentation of the great questions of the age, with what he conceived to be the best method of their solution.

A Drama, then, according to Shakespeare, was a moral discourse, and an historical and philosophical essay, as well as a great poem. Hence, the question arises, what system of morals or philosophy is apparent in Shakespeare's plays? And since philosophy and religion alike profess to teach the knowledge of things by their higher causes, and the laws and principles of human conduct, we are brought at once to the question of his creed, the subject discussed in the following pages.

We are indeed sometimes told that such a discussion is useless, that the poet's writings furnish no trustworthy data on this matter, that the scenes and actions of his drama are strictly mundane, that the characters work out their development from purely natural causes and motives. Yet, in spite of all this, the question is ever proposed and answered anew. And this is so, because the very nature of the poet's writings forbids the exclusion of such an inquiry. He puts before us types of good and evil; what is his attitude towards them? He treats of human nature; does he make man a free and responsible agent, or the mechanical slave of destiny? He constantly speaks of God; does he mean a personal and intelligent, omniscient, omnipotent, and all-perfect Creator, or a mere *anima mundi*, coincident with the phenomena of the universe, and bound by its laws? He is the poet of love; is his theme sensual passion or the celestial fire? Lastly, every play is a comment on human life; where, with Shakespeare, is its final purpose found, in this world, or the next?

These questions then arise, and according to some writers, English and German, Shakespeare in setting forth their solution proves himself the representative of the positive practical view of life inaugurated by the Reformation. In the past, Catholicism with its mysticism, dogmatism, and asceticism, taught man that he was a stranger in this world, and that his true home and *patria* were in heaven. According to Protestantism, on the other hand, the spirit of England in the time of Elizabeth, " to be great, to do great things [here] seemed better than to enter the celestial city, and forget the city of destruction; better than to receive in ecstasy the vision of a divine mystery, or to be fed with miraculous food." [1] " A vigorous mundane vitality thus constitutes the basis of the Elizabethan drama," [2] and as Shakespeare was the product of this time, he was necessarily the exponent of its spirit. [3]

[1] Dowden, "Mind and Art of Shakespeare," 18 (1892).
[2] Ibid., p. 23.
[3] The following passage, quoted from Professor Dowden with approval from Dr. Edward Vehse, is in substance his own view of Shakespeare's philosophy : "Shakespeare der ungelehrte, unstudirte Dichter ist der erste in welchem sich der moderne Geist, der von der Welt weiss, der die gesammte Wirklichkeit zu begreifen sucht, energisch zusammenfasst. Dieser moderne Geist ist der gerade Gegensatz des mittelalterlichen Geistes ; er erfasst die Welt und

Now we admit that the poet usually is, in a sense, the product of his age, and speaks with its voice, and where an age has been stamped by one dominant idea, the poet has often been its exponent and panegyrist. Thus Homer represents the Hellenic world of his day; he adopts its crude notions of heaven and earth, its human gods, its simple customs; while its unceasing combats and its heroes' valiant deeds, as sung by him, tend to glorify the Greek nation. Virgil discovers in the mythological descent of the Latin race a prophecy of its future triumph, culminating in the empire of Augustus and in the inauguration of a reign of peace. Dante, again, gives us in the *Commedia* the whole culture of his time. Its philosophy, astronomy, arts, politics, history, together with pagan myths and mediæval legends, all serve to illustrate his theme and are brought into unity and order by the theology of the Church. He calls his work

> "The sacred poem that hath made
> Both heaven and earth copartners in the toil."[1]

The sixteenth century was, however, a transitional period, and embraced three very diverse systems of thought. First came Catholicism. This included the whole Christian tradition of the past fifteen centuries, the learning of East and West, the philo-

namentlich die innere Welt als ein Stück des Himmels, und das Leben als einen Theil der Ewigkeit."—*Shakespeare als Protestant, Politiker, Pyscholog und Dichter*, i. 62; "Mind and Art," 13.

[1] Par. xxv. 1.

sophy of Greece, as found in the writings of St. Augustine and the Fathers, of St. Thomas and the Scholastics, and also the Christian Renaissance with its classic scholarship, its critical examination of texts and codices, and its revival in the arts and architecture as guided and sanctioned by the Church.   Next came the heathenising Renaissance.   Its aim, whether in the arts, learning, or philosophy, was the revival of Paganism, to the exclusion of Christianity, and its ultimate end was solely man's temporal pleasure and satisfaction.   Thirdly came the religious revolt of Luther, Calvin, and Cranmer, which was slightly differentiated in each country by the special influences determining its development.   The latter two systems, though united in their rejection of the Papal authority, and in a common materialistic tendency, were by no means in complete agreement; for the dominant party in the reform was alike opposed to learning or art of any kind, and it is strange that the Reformation and the Renaissance should ever be spoken of as one and the same movement.[1]

When, then, and where do we find the true Renaissance in England ?   The sixty years following on the wars of the Roses, and immediately preceding the Reformation ;   i.e. from about 1470 to the fall of Wolsey, witnessed the new birth in learning and architecture.   The chief leaders of the new learning were William Sellyng, the Benedictine monk

---

[1] *Cf.* Professor Dowden, "Mind and Art of Shakespeare," 11 (1892).   Professor Caird, *Contemporary Review,* lxx. 820.

of Canterbury, the pioneer of Greek scholarship
in this country, Grocyn, Linacre, Dean Colet, Sir
Thomas More, Archbishop Warham, and Abbot Bere
of Canterbury, to whom Erasmus sent his Greek
Testament for revision.[1]

The ecclesiastical revival was manifested in the
quantity and magnificence of the work done in
church-building, restoration, and decoration. Among
the more notable examples may be mentioned
King's College, Cambridge, 1472–1515; Eton Col-
lege, founded 1441, completed about 1482–3; St.
George's Chapel, Windsor, 1475–1521; Henry VII.'s
Chapel, Westminster, 1502–1515, both the work of
Sir Reginald Braye; Bath Abbey, rebuilt by Bishop
King, 1495–1503, and Prior Birde, and finished
under Prior Holloway only six years before the
surrender of the Abbey to Henry VIII. in 1533;
Corpus Christi College, Oxford, built by Bishop
Fox of Winchester, 1501–1528, in conjunction with
Prior Silkstede; also Fox's beautiful chantry at Win-
chester, and the carved wooden pulpit of Silkstede;
Jesus College, Cambridge; the Collegiate Church at
Westbury, founded by John Alcock, Bishop of Ely,
1486–1500; the chantries in Ely of Bishop Red-
man, 1501–1506, and of Bishop West, 1515–1534;
Brazenose College, Oxford, founded by William
Smith, Bishop of Lincoln, 1496, and Sir Richard
Sutton; St. John's College, Cambridge, founded at
the advice of Bishop Fisher, by Margaret Beaufort,

---

[1] Gasquet, " The Old English Bible and other Essays, " 317 (1897).

Countess of Richmond, who also built a school and chantry and other works at Wimborne Minster; Christ Church, Oxford, and Ipswich College, founded by Cardinal Wolsey; St. Asaph's Cathedral, rebuilt by Bishop Redman, 1471–1475; Bangor Cathedral, rebuilt by Bishops Dene and Skevington, 1496–1533.

Such, then, is a brief and imperfect outline of the work effected and the spirit shown by the true Renaissance in England. That it was Catholic and Roman is seen both from the character of its promoters and the nature of their works. Now what was the action of the Reformation? Did it give a fresh stimulus to learning, or found a new era in religious art? The colleges and schools founded under Elizabeth and Edward VI. are sometimes quoted as marking the dawn of education in the country. As a fact, they represent a miserably inadequate attempt to repair the losses effected by the new barbarism.

The Reformation was inaugurated by the dissolution of the monasteries, the dispersion of their libraries with their unique treasures of codices and manuscripts, and completed with the spoliation of the churches and the destruction of the highest works of art in the kingdom. The mural decorations of cathedral, church, and shrine, some of which, as the retable of Westminster Abbey, were of very high excellence, and only just completed, were all obliterated by whitewash or distemper. The woodcarving, the rood-screen with its "goodly images," the carved stalls, canopies, and magnificent embossed roofs, perished under the hands of the reforming iconoclasts. The metal-work, the silver and gilt shrines, images, reliquaries, lamps, crucifixes, candlesticks, chalices, patens, monstrances, pyxes, processional and pastoral staves, spoons, cruets, ewers, basins, the jewelled clasps for missals, antiphonaries, and copes, all these works of an art which, in Italy, was stimulating the genius of a Cellini, in England passed into the royal melting-pot, to the value of some £850,000 of present money, or nearly a million sterling.[1] The painting of the needle shared a similar fate. The richly embroidered chasubles, copes, dalmatics, maniples, stoles, were consumed in huge bonfires, or became furniture in the palaces of the king and the new nobles, and the art of embroidery, as of metal-work, for religious purposes ceased to be.

That this account is not exaggerated may be seen in Spenser. As a courtier he extolled Elizabeth and all her works, and vilified grossly the ancient faith. But as a poet and philosopher he was wholly opposed to the new order of things. In the "Tears of the Muses," while paying, of course, the usual compliment to the "divine Eliza," he deplores the degradation of the public taste, the contempt for learning, the universal sway of "ugly barbarism" and brutish

[1] Gasquet, "Henry VIII. and the Monasteries," vol. ii. 3rd ed., 417.

ignorance, of "scoffing scurrility and scornful folly."
Spenser was in truth very far from being the Puritan
that Mr. Carter would make him.[1]   His whole
theory of sacrificial love is, as we shall see, directly
opposed to the school of Geneva.   In the "Faërie
Queene" itself the Red-Cross Knight is purified on
the lines of Catholic asceticism, and under the
character of the "Blatant Beast," Puritanism with
its destroying hand and railing bitter tongue, is thus
described :—

> "From thence into the sacred church he broke
>   And robbed the chancel, and the desks downthrew
>   And altar fouled and blasphemy spoke,
>   And the images for all their godly hue
>   Did cast to ground, whilst none there was to rue
>   So all confounded and disordered there."
>
> —*Book* vi.

Was, then, a movement so levelling and destructive
likely to produce the dramatic and poetic outburst
of the Shakespearian age?   That movement, with
its brief duration of some fifty years, came indeed
in spite of the Reformation, not because of it.   No
doubt the circumstances of the time, the wealth and
ease of the court and its supporters, called for such
entertainment as the drama supplied.   But the plots
as well as the style and art of the great English poets
and dramatists came, not from Germany or Switzer-
land, but from Italy.   Dante, Ariosto, Petrarch, not
Luther or Calvin, were the masters of Wyatt and

---

[1] "Shakespeare, Puritan and Recusant," 79.

Surrey and of their disciples.   An impartial examination of Shakespeare's writings will, we believe,
make clear that Shakespeare was no "product of
the Reformation."[1]

First, consider one of his chief poetic characteristics,
his imagery.   It is only by symbols that the poet's
theme, the spiritual, the ideal, the supersensuous,
finds expression; and of all poets, Shakespeare is
perhaps the richest in his creative power.   He has
a figure, a metaphor for every thought; his images
seem to come spontaneously and to express exactly
their maker's idea.   He speaks himself as if these
operations of his phantasy were produced in a kind
of ecstasy.

> " The poet's eye, in a fine phrenzy rolling,
>   Doth glance from heaven to earth, from earth to heaven ;
>   And as imagination bodies forth
>   The form of things unknown, the poet's pen
>   Turns them to shape, and gives to airy nothings
>   A local habitation and a name."
>   —*Midsummer-Night's Dream*, v. i.

Now, much of his imagery is drawn from religious
subjects; of what kind, then, is it ?   He was perfectly free to choose either the new creed or the
old, for he never allowed himself to be hampered
by dramatic conventionalities, and he frequently
commits glaring anachronisms.   We find, then, that

[1] "And remark here as rather curious, that Middle Age Catholicism was abolished as far as Acts of Parliament could abolish it,
before Shakespeare, the noblest product of it, made his appearance."—Carlyle, *Heroes and Hero Worship*.

the object of his predilection is the ancient faith, and he introduces the Church of Rome, her ministers and doctrines and rites, not, after the manner of Spenser, as a type of falsehood and corruption, nor like Marlowe and Greene, as the symbol of exploded superstition, but as the natural representative of things high, pure, and true, and therefore to be treated with reverence and respect. Take, for example, his illustration, drawn from vestments, of how royalty enhances its dignity by habitual seclusion; and remember that, when he wrote, vestments were being publicly burnt, as has been said, for popish, massing, idolatrous stuff.

> "Thus did I keep my person fresh and new,
>   My presence like a robe pontifical,
>   Ne'er seen but wondered at; and so my state,
>   Seldom but sumptuous, showed like a feast,
>   And won by rareness such solemnity."
>   —1 *Henry IV.*, iii. 2.

The same idea is expressed in the Sonnets, where he compares, and in the same religious tone, the visits of his beloved in their rareness and worth to great feasts, precious pearls, and costly robes:—

> "Therefore are Feasts so solemn and so rare
>   Since seldom coming in the long year set,
>   Like stones of worth they thinly placèd are,
>   Or captain-jewels in the carcanet.
>   So is the time that keeps you as my chest,
>   Or as the wardrobe which the robe does hide,
>   To make some special instant special blest
>   By new unfolding his imprisoned pride."
>   —*Sonnet* cii.

The readiness and aptitude with which he avails himself of Catholic imagery are manifested again and again. He puts before us temples, altars, priests, friars, nuns, the mass, sacrifices, patens of gold, chalices, incense, relics, holy crosses, the invocation of saints and angels, the sign of the cross, the sacraments of baptism, penance, holy eucharist, extreme unction, details of the ritual, as for instance the *Benedictio Thalami*. All these and many other Catholic rites and usages are introduced with a delicacy and fitness possible only for a mind habituated to the Church's tone of thought. Nay more, when he is recasting an anti-Catholic play, as in the case of " King John," he is careful to expunge the ribald stories against Nuns and Friars, notwithstanding the popularity of such tales with the audiences of the time. He drew indeed from the new creed his Falstaff, Malvolio, and Holofernes, types of the hypocrite, the canting knave, the pedant, but turned to the ancient faith for his images of what was noble and sacred.

The other chief source of Shakespeare's imagery was Nature itself. There are, broadly speaking two views of Nature—the Catholic, the Protestant. What may be the Protestant view at the present day is perhaps difficult to determine, for Protestantism is fluctuating and manifold. But the Protestantism of Shakespeare's day was clearly defined. Nature was a synonym for discord. Man through his fall was in essential discord with God; the lower world was in discord with man. The Redemption had brought no true healing of this rupture; for salvation was wrought, not by internal restoration, but by mere outward acceptance. Saint and sinner were intrinsically alike. In saint as in sinner there was, to use the words of a reformed confession of faith, " an intimate, profound, inscrutable, and irreparable corruption of the entire *nature*, and of all the powers, especially of the superior and principal powers of the soul." [1] The saint, a sinner in his nature and his powers, is a sinner also in all his works, for the products of corruption must be themselves corrupt. His corruption is subjective and intrinsic; his justification is objective and extrinsic. He has apprehended by faith the merits of Christ, and God no longer imputes the sin that is truly there. Nor will God impute to him - the sinfulness of his works, so long as by faith he continues to apprehend the saving merits of Christ. But the essential corruption of his nature always remains. The lower world is as divorced from man as man has become divorced from God. The destiny of inferior creatures had been a higher one than that of ministering to the earthly needs of man. Their office had been to speak to him of God, to inspire him with the love of God, to be as the steps of a ladder which leads the soul to

[1] *Solida Declaratio*, i. 31. The *Solida Declaratio* drawn up (1577) after Luther's death was the authorised Lutheran Confession of Faith.

God. But their power of appeal has vanished. The mind of man has grown darkened; he cannot see in creatures the beauty of Him that made them. The will of man has grown hardened; he can no longer see in creatures the bounty and goodness of the Lord. Creatures can teach man no moral lesson, for man is no longer a moral being. His freedom of will has left him; his instincts are all towards vice. Nature can only find food for his passions and minister to the vices of his fallen estate.

Catholicism, on the other hand, presents a picture the reverse of this. Man has indeed forfeited his supernatural estate by sin; but his nature though fallen remains unchanged; and every creature by nature is good, and by grace man can and does recover his supernatural condition. From God all things proceed, and to Him they return by obedience to His law and by the mutual offices they respectively discharge. No creature is a separate or independent unit, but each is in a necessary relation and correspondence with its fellows. From the lowest to the highest, all things in their genera, classes, kingdoms are in an ascending scale, in which the lower order ministers to the higher, and is ennobled thereby.

From which point of view does Shakespeare regard nature? He dwells at times on its fairness. He can speak of the glorious morn—

"Kissing with golden face the meadow green,
Bathing the pale stream with heavenly alchemy."

To him nature is no accursed thing.   It is a scene
of wondrous beauty.   But he valued nature chiefly
as a storehouse whence he drew moral lessons.   To
Shakespeare nature was the mirror of the human
soul with its joys and sorrows, and its virtues and
vices.   "Each drama," says Heine,[1] "has its own
special elements, its definite season, with all its
characteristics.   Heaven and earth bear as marked
a physiognomy as the personages of the play."
"Romeo and Juliet," with its theme of passionate
love, speaks of summer heat and beauty and fra-
grance.   Lear's wreck, political and physical, is
attested by the thunder and drenching storm.
Macbeth's crime is conceived on the blasted heath
and in the witches' cave.   Flowers and plants, again,
each have their significance.   The rose, above all,
as with the classics and with Dante, is the chief
symbol of innocence, purity, and love.   Of the
murdered princes Forrest says—

> "Their lips were four red roses on a stalk,
>   Which in their summer beauty kissed each other."
> —*Richard III.*, iv. 3.

Percy compares Richard II. as the sweet rose to
the thorn Buckingham.   Hamlet says his mother's
second marriage was such an act

> "That blurs the grace and blush of modesty,
>   Calls virtue hypocrite, takes off the rose
>   From the fair forehead of innocent love,
>   And sets a blister there."—*Hamlet*, iii. 4.

---

[1] Works, iii. 312, ed. Rotterdam (1895).

The whole story of Viola's secret attachment is thus related :—

> " She never told her love,
> But let concealment, like a worm i' the bud,
> Feed on her damask cheek."—*Twelfth Night*, ii. 4.

Lilies, again, are the emblems of chastity, but

> " Lilies that fester smell far worse than weeds."
> —*Sonnet* xciv.

Ophelia in "Hamlet" and Perdita in "Winter's Tale" teach many a lesson on the symbolism of flowers; and the gardener in " Richard II." finds in the neglected garden the image of the king's misrule :—

> " The whole land
> Is full of weeds, her fairest flowers choked up,
> Her fruit trees all unpruned, her hedges mixed,
> Her knots disordered, and her wholesome herbs
> Swarming with caterpillars."—*Richard II.*, iii. 4.

The animal world supplies images mostly of the evil passions of man. Shylock has a " tiger's heart," Goneril, " boarish fangs." Edgar describes himself as a " hog in sloth, a fox in stealth, a wolf in greediness, a dog in madness, a lion in prey." Richard III. is a bloody and usurping boar, a foul swine. On the other hand, the lark in its rising typifies prayer; the swallow in its swiftness, hope piercing every obstacle; the eagle, strength, majesty, loyalty.

Nature, then, with Shakespeare furnishes a theme, not for mere pastoral melodies or idyllic strains, though of these we have some exquisite examples, but for deep moral lessons; and this parable teaching of the visible world is rendered more forcible and more graphic by being frequently presented through the medium of classic myths and deities. For with Shakespeare, as with Dante, the pagan fable is made the preacher of Christian truth. One of his most Christian and Catholic dramas in its moral teaching is perhaps "The Tempest"; and its lessons are inculcated by the aid of witches and fairies; of Isis, Ceres, and Juno; of nymphs and spirits, the demi-puppets evoked by Prospero's staff; nor without them would the tale or moral ever have had the same dramatic force.[1] The same may be said of "Cymbeline," of "Midsummer-Night's Dream," and many others, where the Christian idea is conveyed through a heathen rite or myth. To take what was true in Paganism, while rejecting what was false, had been the work of the Christian poets and philosophers from the first. But what we wish to draw special attention to is that such a philosophy of nature, which finds

> "Tongues in trees, books in the running brooks,
> Sermons in stones, and good in everything"
> —*As You Like It*, ii. 1,

is in its very essence opposed to the fundamental doctrine of the Reformation, as we have already shown.

---

[1] Ariel imprisoned in the cloven pine and Caliban immersed in the foul lake are distinctly Dantesque images. Cf. *Inferno*, cantos vii. and viii.

B

But more. In the doctrine of the Catholic Church not only does Nature in its individual and several parts inculcate and illustrate moral lessons, but Nature in its entirety is like a magnificent symphony proclaiming the praises of God. Thus creation becomes a many-tongued choir, and the elements, plants, animals, man himself, intone together, in union with the angels, the praises of their Creator. In perhaps the oldest inspired poem we read of the music of the spheres, " The stars praising me together, the sons of God making glad melody " (Job xxviii. 7). The same theme repeats itself in the Psalms, and is the keynote of the *Paradiso*—

> " When as the wheel which thou dost ever guide,
>   Desired Spirit ! with its harmony
>   Tempered of thee and measured, charmed mine ear,
>   Then seemed to me so much of heaven to blaze
>   With the sun's flame, that rain or flood ne'er made
>   A lake so broad. The newness of the sound,
>   And that great light, inflamed me with desire,
>   Keener than e'er was felt, to know their cause."
>   —*Paradiso*, i. 74–81.

Here, then, it is light, as the instrument of God's power and the witness of His presence, which both produces the motion and evokes the harmony of the spheres, and this light and motion are love— *Luce intellettual pien d'amore*. And so in Shakespeare. In the sweetness of the moonlight and the effulgence of the stars the music of the heavens becomes audible, and the smallest orb joins in alternate choirs with the angels, and each immortal soul gives forth its own harmony, inspired and moved by love.

> " How sweet the moonlight sleeps upon this bank !
> Here will we sit, and let the sounds of music
> Creep in our ears : soft stillness and the night
> Become the touches of sweet harmony.
> Sit, Jessica.   Look how the floor of heaven
> Is thick inlaid with patines of bright gold !
> There's not the smallest orb which thou behold'st
> But in his motion like an angel sings,
> Stil quiring to the young-eyed cherubims :
> Such harmony is in immortal souls ;
> But whilst this muddy vesture of decay
> Doth grossly close it in, we cannot hear it."
>
> —*Merchant of Venice*, v. 1.

Now it might have been thought that such a conception of creation and of men and their relation to God shows clearly the Catholic character of Shakespeare's cosmology.   But no.   Though the poet's idea is found in the revealed Word, in the works of Dionysius the Areopagite, in St. Augustine, in St. Thomas, and Dante, it is derived from none of these sources, but, according to Professor Elze,[1] from Montaigne.   Now Montaigne nowhere teaches the existence of unity, order, or harmony in creation.   On the contrary, he held that all knowledge, whether acquired by sense or reason, was necessarily uncertain ; and of the music of the spheres he incidentally observes, that it is inaudible to us, because our hearing is so dulled by the ceaseless clamour of

[1] I. 22 ; Hense, " Shakespeare," 361.

created things.[1] Here, then, the unbroken and universal tradition of some fifteen centuries is to be ignored in favour of the shallow casual remark of this French sceptical essayist. But Shakespeare's teaching finds too commonly a spurious origin. Does Hamlet say that there is nothing good or evil (in the physical order), but thinking makes it so?[2] This idea of his is borrowed from the pantheist, Giordano Bruno, who was in London from 1583 to 1586, just after Shakespeare's arrival there, and who denied the existence (in the moral order) of either absolute good or evil.[3] Again, Hamlet's

---

[1] "We need not go seek what our neighbours report of the cataracts of the Nile, and what Philosophers deem of the Celestial music, which is that the bodies of its circles being solid, smooth, and in their roving motion touching and rubbing against one another, must of necessity produce a wonderful harmony; by the changes and entercaprings of which, the revolutions, motions, cadences, and carols of the asters and planets are caused and transported. But that universally the hearing and senses of these old worlds' creatures, dizzied and lulled asleep, as those of the Egyptians are, by the continuation of that sound, how loud and great soever it be, cannot sensibly perceive or distinguish the same."—*Montaigne's Essays* (Florio's trans.), i. 22, ed. 1892, modernised spelling.

It is only fair to Montaigne to state, that though philosophically a sceptic in matters of belief, he professed entire and loyal allegiance to the Church of Rome. His position was that of an extreme Traditionalist, and with the strange want of logic that is characteristic of the Traditionalist position he held that Faith is best honoured by divorcing it from reason. In his essay "On Prayer" he submits "his rhapsodies," as he calls his writings, to the judgment of the Church, and he died, having received the last sacraments.

[2] B. Thomas More expresses the same thought in "Dialogues of Comfort."

[3] Tschifschwiz, *Shakespeare-Forschungen* (1568), i. 65.

praise of Horatio's equanimity, which "takes buffets and reward with equal thanks," proves Shakespeare a Stoic. The poet's desire for the immortality of his verse in praise of his beloved, indicates his disbelief in the immortality of the soul. His phrase, "the prophetic soul of the world," proves his pantheism; and the duty of meeting necessities as necessities clearly shows his determinism.

With these various points in his philosophy we shall deal later as occasion arises. We now proceed to take the one essential point of his philosophy, namely, his teaching on love. It will mark for us the distinction between the true and false Renaissance already spoken of; for the Renaissance poets were pagan or Christian according to their teaching on this theme. The object of the pagan love was the satisfaction of the senses, the pleasure that could be derived here and now at any cost. Lorenzo Valla, the leader of the heathen Renaissance, in his "Gospel of Pleasure," made sensuality a virtue, because it was natural.[1] Beccadelli in his Epigrams,[2] which are of singular poetic grace, is even more materialistic, and the majority of Shakespeare's contemporaries followed this teaching. "If I may have my desire while I live, I am satisfied; let me shift after death as I may," writes Greene in his "Groatsworth of Wit." And though he confessed his vices with tears, his life and his poetry were based on these lines.

---

[1] *De Voluptate et Vero bono*, Libri iii.
[2] Hermaphroditus, v.; Pastor, "History of the Popes," vol. i. 13.

The triumph of sensualism, the glorification of beauty, the gratification of the passions, with the consequent profligacy, crime, treachery, cruelty, poisoning, and murder — these form the basis of Marlowe's "Jew of Malta," Webster's "Duchess of Malfi," of his "White Devil," of Ford's "'Tis Pity," among many others. A picture of this school is seen in Jonson's "Every Man out of His Humour"; and it reads like a chapter from Symond's "Renaissance in Italy." But there was another school of English dramatists, including Surrey, Sidney, Spenser, whose theme indeed was love, but the object of love with them was not the outward fairness of form or face, but the inward beauty of truth and holiness, as sung by Catholic poets in all time. Thus Sidney writes :—

> " Leave me, O love, which reacheth but to dust,
> And thou, my mind, aspire to higher things ;
> Grow rich in that which never taketh rust ;
> Whatever fades but fading pleasure brings.
> Oh, take fast hold, let that light be thy guide
> In this small course which birth draws out of death."
> —*Last Sonnet.*

Thus Spenser :—

> " For love is Lord of truth and loyalty,
> Lifting himself out of the lowly dust
> On golden plumes up to the purest sky,
> Above the reach of loathly sinful lust,
> Whose base affect, through cowardly distrust
> Of his weak wings, dare not to heaven fly,
> But like a moldwark in the earth doth lie."
> —*Hymn in Honour of Love*, 176-182.

If we find vestiges of Catholic teaching on this subject in Sidney and Spenser, we find the doctrine fully worked out in Shakespeare. We do not include the poems " Venus and Adonis " and " Lucrece." It is true that the poet deals with the subject as a spectator, not as an actor, and teaches incidentally some deep moral truths; yet his theme in these poems and his descriptions are of " loathly sinful lust," not of pure Christian love. Like Chaucer, like Spenser, Shakespeare had reason for bewailing these, the compositions of his youth. It is far otherwise with the work of his life, the sonnets and the plays.

In the sonnets which, according to Simpson, embody the poet's philosophy of love cast in allegorical form, the battle of life, as experienced in his own soul, is fought between true and intellectual and false and sensual love, or the " loves of comfort and despair." The object of true love is described now as a youth of exceeding beauty, now as an angel; of false love, " a woman coloured ill." In the first series of sonnets (1–125) the youth leads the poet, much as Beatrice did Dante, not without severe conflict, much failure, and many tears, above the pleasure of sense, above the creation of phantasy, to the stage of ideal love ; and with each succeeding step a higher conception is formed of the purity and devotion his love requires, and of the falsehood and nothingness of the world in which he lives. At last, by a supreme act of oblation and consecration, the poet dedicates himself, in words taken from the Church's Liturgy, to the one, eternal, and only, fair.

The second series (123–146) show the misery of false, sensual love, and of the soul vanquished and wrecked by the siren's charms. The delusion consequent upon such a state, the degradation and blindness of the soul enslaved, its vain attempts at freedom, the fickleness and tyranny of the destroyer are clearly portrayed, and mark the essential opposition in the poet's mind between sensual and spiritual love.

And if it be said that this conclusion is only obtained by a strained, allegorical interpretation of the sonnets, at least of the first series, if we turn to the comedies and tragedies we find the same truth. The action of the play, the development of the characters for good or evil, the final issue for happiness or woe, are determined as the dominating principle is true, pure love or disordered passion. Nor does Shakespeare ever allow this issue to be confused. The principle of degree, order, priority, which he considers a fundamental law in the physical universe and also, as we shall see, in the body politic, applies with equal strictness to the moral sphere, the government of the appetites in the human soul. The lower appetite must yield to the higher, sense to reason, and this at any cost. All love, true or false, demands the surrender of all else for the one object: but in the one case the sacrifice ennobles and perfects the victim, in the

other, it degrades and destroys. " Omnis disor-
dinatio poena sua "—Every disordered act brings
its own punishment. Isabella, in " Measure for
Measure," is the most perfect type of true love.
Votarist or Postulant of St. Clare, she is " dedicate
to nothing temporal." " By her renouncement " she
had become, even in the eyes of the licentious and
scurrilous Lucio, a " thing enskied and sainted," an
immortal spirit. Yet hers is no spectral figure,
devoid of human feeling. She is not a spirit, but
a woman, and her natural affections are intensified,
because purified by her supernatural love ; and she
undertakes the advocacy of Claudio, " though his
is the vice she most abhors." The nature of true
love is seen in the choice made between her honour
and her brother's life. In both Cinthio's " Epitia "
and Whetstone's " Cassandra," the sources of Shakespeare's plot, the heroines yield their chastity for
their brother's sake ; and, were domestic love the
highest, their conduct would be worthy of praise.
Isabella has no doubt ; and her decision is inflexibly
rooted, not from any principle of independent
morality, but because her love of the All pure was
her life, her life eternal, and

> " Better it were, a brother died at once,
>   Than that a sister, by redeeming him,
>   Should die for ever."
>   —*Measure for Measure*, ii. 4.

She had rather be scourged and flayed than yield

her body "to such abhorred pollution." She casts off her brother and his sophistries as a foul tempter, defies him, and bids him perish. No wonder that her conduct has been so generally criticised for its gloom and asceticism. Hazlitt "has not much confidence in the virtue that is sublimely good at other people's expense." Knight finds the play full of revolting scenes. Coleridge thinks it the most painful of Shakespeare's plays. To the Catholic, Isabella represents the noblest ideal, the brightest, most blessed of Shakespeare's heroines, as the type of supernatural charity or of the highest sacrificial love.

In contradiction of what has been said, "Romeo and Juliet" is quoted by rationalist critics to show that Shakespeare knew nothing of this distinction of spiritual and sensual love. Romeo and Juliet are his ideals of perfect love, and the character of their affection was passionate throughout. "Such love," says Kreyzig, "is its own reward : life has nothing further to offer." But, all would admit, we suppose, that the poet never intended to exhibit in each play a type of absolute morality, but such a manner of conduct as essentially befitted the character represented. Thus Cleopatra and Cressida are dramatically perfect characters ; but morally they are a shame to their sex. Now, Romeo and Juliet are types of passionate love, that is, love in which passion, not reason, is the dominant principle. The passions indeed are not evil, they are part of our nature, and are powerful agencies for good, but within their proper sphere, and under the control of reason. Without such control, when the senses or feelings master reason, misery and disorder follow; and this is exactly what we find in "Romeo and Juliet." The whole play portrays the consequences of ill-regulated passion. The scene is laid in an Italian summer, and the emotions of Romeo and Juliet are at fever heat. Impetuosity, vehemence, agitation, disturbance, mark their conduct throughout. The whole action consumes but five days from the Sunday to the following Friday morning. Within this space of time are the first meeting of the lovers, the stolen interview, the secret marriage, the duel, Tybalt's death, Romeo's banishment, and the double suicide of Romeo and Juliet. The whole lesson of the play is taught by Friar Lawrence in explicit terms :—

> " These violent delights have violent ends,
> And in their triumph die ; like fire and powder,
> Which as they kiss, consume : the sweetest honey
> Is loathsome in his own deliciousness,
> And in the taste confounds the appetite :
> Therefore love moderately ; long love doth so ;
> Too swift arrives as tardy as too slow."
> —*Romeo and Juliet*, ii. 6.

Just as the "Midsummer-Night's Dream" shows the folly of love based merely on the imagination, so "Romeo and Juliet" manifests the ruin which follows in love, which, though not coarse or sensual,

is still determined mainly by passion.   Thus Hamlet
repeats Friar Lawrence's teaching :—

> " What to ourselves in passion we propose,
>   The passion ending doth the purpose lose.
>   The violence of either grief or joy
>   Their own enactions with themselves destroy."
>
> *—Hamlet,* iii. 2.

And the reason is that the object of passion is
something here and now, and therefore temporal
and passing, and when it passes leaves a blank, for
" this world is not for aye."   The object of true
love must be, like Silvia, " holy, fair, and wise "; the
love it inspires knows neither doubt nor fear nor
change, and the bond it forms is eternal.

> " Love is not love
> Which alters when it alterations finds
> Or bends with the remover to remove :
> Oh no ! it is an ever-fixèd mark
> That looks on tempests, and is never shaken ;
> It is the star to every wandering bark,
> Whose worth's unknown, although his height be taken ;
> Love's not Time's fool, though rosy lips and cheeks
> Within his bending sickle's compass come ;
> Love alters not with his brief hours and weeks,
> But bears it out, even to the edge of doom."
>
> *—Sonnet* cxvi.

We have now said enough to determine a further
characteristic in Shakespeare's love philosophy, since
the object of true love with him is the eternal
truth, goodness, and beauty, and is only to be won
by the renouncement of all else for its sake, love
and religion with Shakespeare become identified, and

religion like love bears an essentially sacrificial character, as we shall see in detail in our consideration of the love plays. In what religions, then, is the idea of sacrifice found ?

We find it in the old-world religions, and obscured indeed, but still expressed in the Greek tragedies in their doctrine of the nemesis consequent on sin, and the possibility and hope of a Divine atonement. It is seen again, but in its fulness and completeness, in the Catholic Church, and in the miracle and mystery plays of the Middle Ages, which were based in one way or other on the central mystery of the atoning sacrifice of the Redemption. But we may look for it in vain in the teaching of the Reformers. Their theory of salvation by election alone, already noticed, and its correlative doctrine of the worthlessness of works, excluded all idea of any sacrificial action being needed on the part of the believer. Nor does it find a place in the form of Protestantism dictated and enforced by the Crown in England. The surest way to wealth and preferment was the first purpose in the new Erastianism ; and creed and discipline were accommodated to keep the royal favour. Men like Cranmer could boast with the poet in Timon of Athens :—

> " My free drift
> Halts not particularly, but moves itself
> In a wide sea of wax."—*Timon of Athens*, i. 1.

" The Church of England," says Dr. Dollinger, " is content with taking up just so much share in life as commerce, the enjoyment of riches, and the habitudes of a class desirous before all things of comfort, may have left to it."[1] Hence it abolished celibacy, the religious state, with its three vows of poverty, chastity, and obedience, and the ascetic exercises of the ancient faith, and made the celebration of mass, on which they were all based, a capital offence. Such a system, whatever temporal advantages it might offer, was essentially of the earth, earthy, and could never have evoked the veneration of Shakespeare, or kindled, as did the proscribed creed, the fire of his muse.

The Reformed creed was then, we think, from its negative and materialistic tendency, unfitted to give birth to a poet.[2] "Catholicism," says Mr. Matthew Arnold, "from its antiquity, its pretensions to universality, from its really widespread prevalence, from its sensuousness, has something European, august, and imaginative; Protestantism presents, from its inferiority in all these respects, something provincial, mean, and prosaic."[3] Nor are Milton and Keble, the poets respectively, according to Professor

[1] "The Church and Churches," 119, 146 (1862). He quotes Hallam to the effect that the supremacy "is the dog's collar which the State puts on the Church in return for food and shelter."— Hallam, "Constitutional History," iii. 44.

[2] The late Archbishop Trench, in his comparison of Calderon and Shakespeare, takes a precisely opposite view, and speaks of the advantages enjoyed by the latter, because "as the child of the Reformation," "he moved in a sphere of the highest truth."—*Life and Genius of Calderon*, 78 (1880). What that truth was or where it is found in Shakespeare we are not told.

[3] "Essays on Criticism," 133, ed. 1869.

Dowden, of Puritanism and Anglicanism, proofs to the contrary. Milton is great in his theme. He sings "in glorious hymns the equipage of God's almightiness, the victorious agonies of saints and martyrs, the deeds and triumphs of just nations, doing valiantly in faith against the enemies of Christ." As an epic poet he has been ranked above Homer and Dante, yet his vision of the other world is materialistic, prosaic, and dull, and he fails just where the voice of the seer should speak. This is so because his Calvinistic creed forbade mystery.

He was deaf to Dante's constant warning, "State, umana gente alla quia." Everything must be explained—the secrets of the divine counsel; the strife between good and evil; the precise cause of each individual fall—all must be laid bare. Hence God justifies himself, Adam excuses himself, and Satan is defiant. Adam and Eve, at dinner with the angel in Paradise, talk and act, says M. Taine, like Colonel Hutchinson and his wife; and their want of clothing is felt to be wholly incongruous. "What dialogues!" that somewhat caustic critic goes on to say. "Dissertations capped by politeness, mutual sermons concluded by bows. What bows! Philosophical compliments and moral smiles. . . . This Adam entered Paradise *via* England."[1] The "Para-

---

[1] "English Literature," i. 443. Col. Hutchinson sat in the Long Parliament for Nottingham, and in the High Court of Justice, which sentenced Charles I. to death. His memoirs were written by his wife, Lucy Hutchinson, and were printed in 1806.

dise Lost" could never be called divine.   How is
it that Dante, in spite of his detailed, precise, and
realistic treatment of the supernatural, succeeds in
creating an impression so precisely spiritual?   It
is because he works on the lines of dogma and
mystery, the ideal of the supernatural fixed for him
by his faith.   The Puritan poet, on the other hand,
had to draw exclusively on his own human and
utterly inadequate conceptions, and thus instead of
sublime he becomes grotesque.   Milton brings down
heaven to earth and makes spiritual things terres-
trial.   Dante transports earth to heaven, and shows
all transformed in the light of God's anger or of
His love.

So too with Keble.   Professor Dowden calls him
the poet of Anglicanism, but in ritual, liturgy, doctrine, what material did it present for his muse?
"The Catholic Church," says Cardinal Newman, "is
the poet of her children, full of music to soothe the
sad and control the wayward, wonderful in story for
the imagination of the romantic, rich in symbol and
imagery, so that gentle and delicate feelings, which
will not bear words, may in silence intimate their
presence or commune with themselves.   Her very
being is poetry; every psalm, every petition, every
collect, every versicle, the cross, the mitre, the
thurible, is a fulfilment of some dream of childhood
or aspiration of youth."[1]   How much of this divine
element did Keble find in the Anglican system?

[1] "Essays Critical and Historical," vol. ii. 443, 9th edit.

"A ritual dashed to the ground, trodden on and broken piecemeal; prayers clipped, pieced, torn, shuffled about at pleasure, until the meaning of the composition perished, and what had been poetry was no longer even good prose—antiphons, hymns, benedictions, invocations shovelled away; Scripture lessons turned into chapters, heaviness, feebleness, unwieldiness . . . and for orthodoxy a frigid, un-elastic, inconsistent, dull helpless dogmatic, which could give no just account of itself, yet was intole-rant of all teaching which contained a doctrine more or a doctrine less, and resented every attempt to give it a meaning."[1] And then Cardinal New-man goes on to show how Keble's "happy magic made the Anglican Church seem what Catholicism was and is."[2] How the bishops, to their surprise, were told of "their gracious arm outstretched to bless," and the communion table became "the dread altar," and "holy lamps were blazing" and "perfumed embers quivering bright," with "stoled priests ministering at them," while the "floor was by knees of sinners worn."

Two other points call for notice in contrasting Shakespeare's teaching with that of the Reforma-tion. The one system of philosophy attacked, ridi-culed, and vilified by Luther and his followers in every land, was the scholastic. Hence, new theories constantly sprang into existence, even within the

---

[1] "Essays Critical and Historical," vol. ii. 443, 9th edit.
[2] Ibid.

Church, and the doctrines of Pythagoras, Plato, and
Aristotle were interpreted anew, and in an anti-
scholastic sense, with the purpose of harmonising
Catholic doctrine with the new modes of thought.
The attempt was an utter failure, the new systems
perished of themselves, or were obliterated in the
wild doctrines to which they gave birth.   Now
among this multitude of systems and confusion of
ideas, it is remarkable how constantly Shakespeare
adheres in philosophical questions to the scholastic
system.   He is distinctly Thomist on the following
points: his doctrine of the genesis of knowledge
and its strictly objective character;[1] the power of
reflection as distinctive of rational creatures;[2] the
formation of habits,[3] intellectual and moral; the
whole operation of the imaginative faculty.[4]   And
he shows his opposition to the Pantheism of Giordano Bruno and others in insisting on the individual
and permanent subsistence of each human being—
the "I am that I am," and on the law of self-preservation, as flowing therefrom.   This insistence on
the individual is seen again in his teaching of the
eternal consequences of single acts, in his reprobation
of suicide, and in such lines as the following:—

> " The single and peculiar life is bound,
>   With all the strength and ardour of the mind,
>   To keep itself from 'noyance."—*Hamlet*, iii. 3.

---

[1] " Troilus and Cressida," iii. 3.   [2] Ibid.
[3] " Hamlet," iii. 4.   [4] " Midsummer-Night's Dream."

From the same principle was derived, as we believe, Shakespeare's extraordinary and perhaps unequalled power of delineating character. Each individual, with him, is a separate creation of his genius. Each stands by itself in its beginning, growth, and term. The growth may be from evil to good, as with Henry V., or from bad to worse, as with Antony; but with each, the germ of the im· provement or the declension is seen in its beginning and throughout its course, till it bears its legitimate fruit, as the voice of conscience or of self-love has been followed. And these individual creations are so real and lifelike, because the poet believed in the "peculiar and single" reality of each human life.

Shakespeare's adherence to the scholastic philosophy in these and other points, and the predilection which he generally manifests for a system so unpopular, and essentially unprotestant, is a further proof of his antagonism to his times. He may ridicule Pythagoras and his transmigration of souls, the Stoics and their affected indifference as to sufferings they had never experienced, the philosophical persons who account for everything by natural causes. But of Aristotle he speaks with respect. Lucentio, at Padua, is not to be so absorbed in Aristotle as to forget Ovid; but the teaching of that philosopher is for the serious and sincere, not for the shallow and superficial, those "young men whom Aristotle thought unfit to hear moral philosophy."[1]   The ease

---

[1] "Troilus and Cressida," ii. 2.

and accuracy again with which he employs scholasticism as the vehicle for his deepest thoughts show, that with a master mind like his, as with Dante and Calderon, poetic and philosophic truth are one, and that a nomenclature, superficially regarded as crabbed, meaningless, and obsolete, can furnish expression for the richest poetry.

Another distinctive characteristic of Shakespeare is his use of casuistry, or the science which decides the application in particular cases of a general moral law or principle; there being many cases when such a decision is, for unaided reason, extremely difficult. For instance, does a rash oath bind? Must the truth be always told, even to one who has no right to know, and when its disclosure inflicts a grievous injury on an innocent person? The dilemma in both cases is, that if the obligation hold, wrong is done, whichever course is taken. Now, according to the main principles of Protestantism, by which each man is the sole interpreter of the moral law, as of revealed doctrine, and human engagements are supreme, the oath or word must be kept at any cost; and the difficulty of the sinful consequences would be met by the Calvinistic axiom, that "some commandments of God are impossible." Now Shakespeare discusses both these cases, and teaches exactly the contrary doctrine. He shows by the mouth of Pandulph that the sanctity of an oath or vow is based primarily on our reverence to God, whose name has been invoked, and that a rash or sacrilegious oath must not be kept, else art thou

> "Most forsworn to keep what thou didst swear."
> —*King John*, iii. 1.

And a complete exposition of when an unlawful oath may be kept, not *vi juramenti*, but through a notable change of circumstances, is found in the same speech, as will be seen in Chapter III. Similarly, the lawfulness of the use of equivocation, when the truth is unjustly demanded, is laid down by the Duke in " Measure for Measure " in precise terms :—

> " Pay with falsehood false exacting."
> —*Measure for Measure*, iii. 2.

Truth is a coin, and we may pay a thief in false money. Isabella feels the difficulty of following the Duke's advice and "speaking thus indirectly"; but she is advised to do it "to veil full purpose." That is, the truth and fidelity we owe to some may be at times only discharged by veiling truth to others. This is so, of course, as regards the professional secrets of lawyers, physicians, priests; but though recognised and acted on in practice, the theory of equivocation was denounced in Shakespeare's time as Jesuitical and vile, as much as it is now; and it is remarkable that he should be again found defending the unpopular and Catholic side.

Proceeding now from Shakespeare's philosophy to his portraiture of his age and its politics, his antagonism will, we think, be found equally apparent.

It has been remarked that Shakespeare, in spite of the all-embracing character of his verse, makes no allusion to ecclesiastical architecture, "a fact the more remarkable because of the number of grand churches, abbeys, and shrines he must have passed in his annual journey from Stratford to London."[1] The omission is doubtless remarkable, but it becomes intelligible when we remember that church-building practically ceased in England from the accession of Elizabeth till the reign of Charles I., and that the ancient fanes and sanctuaries had been wrecked and gutted. What Shakespeare did see was, not the noble abbeys and religious houses in their sacred grandeur and beauty, but

"Bare ruined choirs, where late the sweet birds sang."
—*Sonnet* lxxiii.

There have been repeated suppressions of religious orders; but nowhere as in England has the work of the spoiler left so indelible a mark. In the French revolution the monastic buildings were quarried or otherwise effaced. In Italy, in our own times, the religious houses when secularised have been converted into hospitals or barracks, or preserved as national monuments. In our own country they fell into the hands of the king or his favourites, who unroofed and gutted them for the lead and valuables they contained, but left the walls as a witness to their work of destruction.

[1] *Guardian*, March 19, 1897.

Now, besides the ruins of the Augustinian monastery at Kenilworth, and of the Benedictine monks at Coventry in his own Warwickshire, there lay in or about his London journey, ruined, dismantled, or secularised, St. Frideswide's priory of Augustinian friars, six Benedictine monasteries and colleges at Oxford, the Benedictine nunneries at Godstone, Abingdon, and Wallingford, the Augustinian Canons at Goring and Dorchester ; the vast remains of Reading Abbey, the last superior of which, Abbot Cook, had been hanged and martyred at the Abbey Gate, November 15, 1539; Medenham Abbey of the Augustinian Canons, and the Benedictine nunnery at Marlow, both on the river-side. Again, on the Thames, at Twickenham, of the Brigettine nuns of Sion, and the Carthusians at Sheen, built by Henry V., as Shakespeare himself tells us, in expiation of his father's dethronement of Richard II., the

> " Two chantries, where the sad and solemn priests
> Sing still for Richard's soul."—*Henry V.*, iv. 1.

The poet knew then the origin of the monastic foundations and some of the purposes they served ; and the two last named had been restored by Mary, and suppressed only on Elizabeth's accession.

And what was the motive of all this wreck and ruin ? The visitation conducted by the king's commissioners had proved the religious houses, great and small, free from scandals, observant, and reli-

gious, as became their state.   One motive alone
destroyed these abodes of hospitality, learning, and
prayer—the greed of gold.   How does Shakespeare
regard this religion of naturalism?   In what language of bitter scathing invective does he denounce
covetousness and its effects?—

> "Gold? yellow, glittering, precious gold?—
> No, gods, I am no idle votarist.[1]
> Roots, you clear heavens!   Thus much of this will make
> Black, white; foul, fair; wrong, right;
> Base, noble; old, young; coward, valiant.
> Ha, you gods! why this? What this, you gods? Why this
> Will lug your priests and servants from your sides;
> Pluck stout men's pillows from below their heads;
> This yellow slave
> Will knit and break religions; bless the accurs'd;
> Make the hoar leprosy ador'd; place thieves,
> And give them title, knee, and approbation,
> With senators on the bench: this is it
> That makes the wappened widow wed again:
> She whom the spital-house and ulcerous sores
> Would cast the gorge at, this embalms and spices
> To the April day again."—*Timon of Athens*, iv. 3.

And if his purpose was to represent "the very
age and pressure of the time," is the picture of it
drawn here favourable or not?   And observe that
the effect of avarice is to "knit and break religions";
and this is precisely what it did.   It unmade the
old faith, and constructed the new.

And when he arrived in London, he would have
seen, besides the religious houses secularised and
ruined, the widespread misery wrought by their

[1] Religious.

destruction. Professor Dowden dwells with complacency on the visible pomp and splendour of life, which burst forth in the Tudor age; on Raleigh's silver armour and his shoes worth 600 gold pieces; and tells with evident pleasure of the charm exercised by the new mundane ritual on Bacon as shown in his Essays on Buildings and Gardens. Shakespeare himself describes in " Cymbeline " the interior of a lady's room with all its artistic beauty, showing the luxury of the age. But the picture had its reverse. This very display was obtained only at the expense of much suffering. What Shakespeare writes of Henry VIII. may equally be applied to Elizabeth's courtiers. Her entertainers might appear in their pageants

> " All clinquant, all in gold, like heathen gods."
> —*Henry VIII.*, i. 1.

each new masque might be " cried incomparable ": but with what result ? The irreparable impoverishment of many a fair estate, and the bankruptcy of many a noble house, without a hope of compensation or gratitude from the royal guest.

> "O, many
> Have broke their backs with laying manors on them
> For this great journey. What did this vanity,
> But minister communication of
> A most poor issue ?"—*Henry VIII.*, i. 1.

Yet one issue it had. The peasantry, once the prosperous tenants of churchman and abbot, now the oppressed vassals of the new spendthrift nobles, were in a starving condition; and their miserable and desperate appearance alarmed the queen in her royal progresses, and with reason. For such suffering

> "Makes bold mouths :
> Tongues spit their duties out, and cold hearts freeze
> Allegiance in them ; their curses now
> Live where their prayers did ; and it's come to pass
> That tractable obedience is a slave
> To each incensèd will.—*Henry VIII.*, i. 2.

Elizabeth felt the truth of this, and in 1595 ordered that all vagabonds near London should be hanged; and along with the religious and priests— peaceable citizens put to death for practising the Faith, which the queen at her coronation had sworn to defend—some 500 criminals or vagrants were executed every year. Hentzner says that he counted above thirty heads on London Bridge.[1] Elizabeth's merciless decree seems indeed to have been carried out in the spirit of Timon's speech :—

> "Put armour on thine ears and on thine eyes ;
> Whose proof, nor yells of mothers, maids, nor babes,
> Nor sight of priests in holy vestments bleeding,
> Shall pierce a jot."—*Timon of Athens*, iv. 3.

And the condition of the new nobility revealed equally the weight of the new despotism now pressing on the country. Mere upstarts and adventurers, like Cecil and Paulet, without name or lineage, with no principle but their own gain, the servile instruments of the Crown, were wholly incapable of

---

[1] "Travels in England" (edited by H. Walpole, 1797), 3.

resisting its encroachments, and were poor substitutes for the Neviles, Percys, Howards, who, whatever their faults, had repeatedly saved the liberties of their country. The Commons also were reduced to a state of vassalage. Elizabeth informed her first Parliament, through Bacon, that she consulted them not from necessity, but from choice, to render her laws more acceptable to the people. Parliaments were in fact summoned only to legalise some act of royal oppression. So too with the executive: the judge ruled and the jury found, not according to law or fact, but as the sovereign willed; and with the army of spies and informers ready to offer any evidence required, no subject's life was safe. The Tudor sovereignty, then, represented a new Cæsarism; all the intermediary checks on absolutism were swept away; the body politic consisted of two factors, the monarch and the multitude.

Now, such a system was in Shakespeare's judgment destructive of the very life of a State. In Ulysses' speech, condemning the factions in the Grecian camp, we have the poet's principle of government. All things in nature, he says, are in a graduated scale, and their strength and stability depend on the due subordination or relation of part to part.

> " The heavens themselves, the planets, and this centre,
>   Observe degree, priority, and place,
>   Insisture, course, proportion, season, form,
>   Office, and custom, in all line of order."
>   —*Troilus and Cressida*, i. 3.

" Degree being vizarded," without this order and the
due nexus of link to link, "the unity and married
calm of states is rent and cracked." By degree
alone or the ordered juncture of successive grades,
merit is recognised, scholarship, civil and commercial
life, are advanced and secured.   Degree gone, when
all men are kept under the mask of a dead level,
there is no distinction between the unworthiest and
the most deserving.   To respect of superiors succeeds
an "envious fever" of those in authority.   Justice
is no more; force alone is right; and force is but
the instrument of appetite or greed, "an universal
wolf," which, after consuming all else, "last eats up
himself."

Such was Shakespeare's view of a levelling
tyranny, and he saw his country the victim to this
scourge.   The England, then, which he loved,

> " This dear, dear land,
> Dear for her reputation throughout the world,"

was not the England of his day.   No, his country
might be great in naval adventure, in industrial
and commercial enterprise; new fields of wealth
might be opened out to certain classes, but its
true greatness and ancient liberty, its former glory,
its true chivalry were gone, and

> "That England which was wont to conquer others,
> Is now made a shameful conquest to itself."

The Elizabethan pageants might dazzle others, to
him they were but pinchbeck splendour and tinsel

pomp, the trappings of oppression and shame. Thus
he delivers his soul :—

> "Tired with all these, for restful death I cry,—
> As, to behold desert a beggar born,
> And needy nothing trimmed in jollity,
> And purest faith unhappily forsworn,
> And gilded honour shamefully misplaced,
> And maiden virtue rudely strumpeted,
> And right perfection wrongfully disgraced,
> And strength by limping sway disabled,
> And art made tongue-tied by authority,
> And folly (doctor-like) controlling skill,
> And simple truth miscalled simplicity,
> And captive good attending captain ill :
> Tired with all these, from these would I be gone,
> Save that to die, I leave my love alone."
> —*Sonnet* lxvi.

Professor Dowden says that Shakespeare must
have been the product of his age, unless he were
in antagonism to it. We think we have already
given considerable proof of the existence of such
antagonism, and the proof will be confirmed if we
consider his historical plays.

In dealing with English history, consider then
the subjects he might have chosen, had he been
the product of the Elizabethan era. The overthrow of the Pope, as treated by Bale in "The
Troublesome Reign of King John," or by Spenser
in "The Faërie Queene"; the Gunpowder Plot denounced by Ben Jonson in his "Catiline"; the
destruction of the Armada, as sung by Dekker;
the glorification of Elizabeth, as added by Fletcher
to "Henry VIII."—all these themes, instinct with

the triumphs of the new order, were before him, yet not one of them finds mention in his song. On the contrary, his Muse is occupied, almost exclusively, with the men and women, the spirit and temper, the speech and customs of feudal times. His ideal prince is Henry V., and his portraiture is drawn in markedly Catholic lines. King John, the accepted representative of a Protestant king, the prototype of Henry VIII. in his triumphant conflict with the Pope, becomes in Shakespeare's hands a mean villain and the vanquished suppliant to the Roman Legate. Henry VIII. himself is depicted as a cruel, selfish, base hypocrite, with an audacity which made Dr. Dollinger remark, as Simpson tells us, that, seeing what Shakespeare might have made of him as the founder of Protestantism, this play furnishes the strongest proof of the poet's Catholic sympathies. Elizabeth herself is passed over in silence; and even at her death, when all the contemporary poets were chiming her glories and virtues, Shakespeare alone was silent; and to mark still further the contrast, the heroine of his choice in Tudor times is the pure, noble, Catholic queen, the divorced and dethroned Katherine.

In opposition to what has been said, Shakespeare's frequent biblical references and quotations are advanced as a convincing argument on behalf of his Protestantism; especially by the late Bishop Wordsworth of St. Andrews, and recently, by the

Rev. T. Carter in his "Shakespeare, a Puritan and Recusant." The use of the Bible was indeed a test question in the poet's time. The Reformers alleged that Rome had withheld the Bible from the laity or obscured its meaning. Luther was the first, they said, to place it within reach of the people by the translation he had prepared. Thus the Homilies exhort all " to diligently search the well of life in the Old and New Testaments, and not run to the stinking puddles of men's traditions," meaning thereby, of course, the Church's authority. The shibboleth, then, "the Bible only," signified both that the Bible was the sole rule of faith, and that each individual was its authorised interpreter, and was free to choose his own text and to put his own interpretation upon it; even though the sense selected was explicitly contradicted by other passages of the sacred volume.

> "I am Sir Oracle,
> And when I speak, let no dog ope his mouth."
> —*Merchant of Venice,* i. 1

fitly expresses the new mode of biblical Hermeneutics, and it is precisely in this manner that Shakespeare's Bible Christians use, or rather abuse, the Holy Scriptures. The characters conspicuous in this respect are Jack Cade and his followers, Costard and Holofernes, Quince and Bottom, Parson Evans, in a very mixed fashion, and above all Falstaff. All these, as will be seen, quote individual texts or apply scriptural references in some strained sense for their own ends, just as the Presbyterians or Covenanters do in the Waverley novels. The method of reasoning, then, used to prove Shakespeare a Protestant from this kind of biblical quotation would equally make Scott a Puritan. So evident is Shakespeare's satire that Bowdler repeatedly omits these biblical quotations because of their profaneness. Wordsworth takes him to task for so doing, and the point of many a speech and the individualisation of the speaker are undoubtedly lost by such omission. But though Shakespeare did not intend to be profane himself, for "Reverence," as he says, "is the angel of the world," he did intend the speaker to be so, and to show by his profanity the abuse which must result from "the Bible only" theory, and that "there is no damnèd error but a sober brow will write a text on," or that "the devil himself can quote Scripture." With this well-known power of irony, could he have chosen a more efficacious method of exposing the abuse of the new "Gospel method," than by making it the favourite weapon of canting fools, knaves, and hypocrites?

With regard to the version employed by Shakespeare, we do not think any trustworthy argument can be drawn for either side; and we willingly concede to the followers of Bishop Wordsworth any consolation they may derive from Shakespeare's employment of the "Amen" sixty times, in proof of his being a member of the Church of England. But could it be proved demonstrably that the poet had used exclusively a Protestant version, it would only be what we should expect. If he meant his Bible Christians to speak as Protestants did, he would naturally make them use the phrases proper to that body; and his doing so would show nothing as to his own religious belief.

The foregoing pages will, we think, have shown that Shakespeare's ideas, whether philosophical or political, moral or religious, were in no way those of the Elizabethan era; and the opposition is enhanced if we consider the poet himself and some of his characteristics. We know how hard it is to speak of a character so silent and reserved as Shakespeare. Unlike Ben Jonson, who loved to talk himself, and to have his conversation reported, Shakespeare, though loving and loved, has left no record of himself or his friends. We can gather from his writings that constancy, fidelity, secrecy, truth, were the qualities he most esteemed. His ideal man is true to himself, true to his friends. He scorns to betray even the devil, and despises "graceless spies" and "suborned informers." He hates "encounterers glib of tongue,"

> "That wide unclasp the tables of their hearts
> To every ticklish reader !"—*Troilus and Cressida*, iv. 5.

The self-revelation made in the sonnets, though most obscure, is yet like personal pain, the "goring

D

his own thought," a sort of sacrilege, selling cheap by the fact of publicity "what was most dear." Others may win respect by truth of words; his thoughts should be dumb, "speak only in effect" (by facts). Nay, he would be dead to all else but to one dear friend, his own secret love.

> "None else to me, nor I to none alive."
> —*Sonnet* cxii.

His was a soul, then, that dwelt apart, evoking out of its own depths his mighty works, but veiling its still greater self. This secrecy is consistent with his philosophical doctrine that the mind is nothing till it has gone out of itself and is "married" to its true object. It is consistent also with the kind of development his character would have taken, were his sympathies wholly with a proscribed religion whose followers knew each other by secret signs and communicated in passwords. But such a disposition, so reserved, sensitive, fastidious, bears no resemblance to certain modern portraitures of him. To our mind, Shakespeare, with his high and hidden ideals, was far more like a veiled prophet than the mere Hooker and Bacon combination of utilitarian common-sense and experimental science described by Professor Dowden. Had he been a "sort of Gradgrind," a man "wanting nothing but facts, who knows that two and two make four and nothing more," he would doubtless have been satisfied with the ecclesiastical compromise, the most concrete fact of his age, and he would not have satirised its originators under such personages as Polonius and Shallow, or its ministers in the figures of Sir Topas and Holofernes.

It is strange, indeed, how prejudice may blind the eyes of otherwise acute critics to evident fact. The one indisputable characteristic of his writings, as manifested in his dramas and poems, is his deep discontent with, and contempt for, the world in which he lived. Reserved as he is about himself, of his age and its evils he speaks openly. The most sacred natural ties dissolved, oppression, falsehood, treachery, ingratitude, faith forsworn, imposture triumphant, truth and goodness held captive—these are the main features of his portrait of his times, and their originals are easily recognised. And this is the poet whom we are told to regard, not as a teacher of dry dogma, or a sayer of hard sayings, but

> " A priest to us all
> Of the wonder and bloom of the world." [1]

Far from extolling the pride and pomp of earthly greatness, no poet more constantly reminds us how soon " mightiness meets with misery," that this world is not for aye, and that we all " owe a death to God." How solemnly he warns us that

> " The great globe itself,
> Yea, all which it inherit, shall dissolve ;
> And, like this insubstantial pageant faded,
> Leave not a rack behind."—*Tempest*, iv. 1.

---

[1] Bagehot in Dowden, " Mind and Art," 40.

And the moral is drawn with the same sternness and power—

> "What win I, if I gain the thing I seek ?
> A dream, a breath, a froth of fleeting joy.
> Who buys a minute's mirth to wail a week,
> Or sells eternity to get a toy ?"—*Lucrece.*

And this *contemptus sæculi* [1] and world-weariness grows with his advancing years. Even Professor Dowden, who paints him as a Positivist, admits that the last period of his writings shows a growing disgust with the base facts of this life. His works in their usually accepted sequence demonstrate this. The comedies and lighter pieces, together with the English historical plays, appear before 1600; while from 1600 to 1611 succeed tragedies of the most solemn cast and dramas of more or less tragic colouring. But while his writings manifest a growing seriousness of thought, and an increased conviction of the utter vanity, which the multitude around him made their sole and final aim, yet he is never a pessimist, nor ever leaves us oppressed with a sense of morbid or sentimental gloom. With him the tragic and comic were so marvellously blended, that the darkest scenes of woe and catastrophe are illumined with rays of light, while the lightest pieces are not

---

[1] Mr. George Wyndham, in his valuable introduction to his edition of the Poems of Shakespeare (1898), calls special attention to the world-weariness manifested in the Sonnets (p. lxxviii), and again in "Lucrece" (p. xcvii), almost Shakespeare's earliest work. But we have tried in vain to agree with Mr. Wyndham that the "Venus and Adonis" "contains nowhere an appeal to lust."

without some solemn warnings. Cordelia relieves the horrors of Lear, and Theseus speaks like a sage in " Midsummer-Night's Dream."

He thus teaches again, in opposition to the reform, that man himself is neither wholly bad nor wholly good, but "that the best men are moulded out of faults," and that " the web of our life is a mingled yarn of good and evil together," which serve in turn for our probation and support.

Shakespeare's use of comedy served yet another purpose. In every age there have been wolves in sheep's clothing, and we do not forget Chaucer's caricatures of the Friars, or Boccaccio's of priests and religious. But the Reformation produced, as its natural child, a special type of sanctimoniousness and cant. Religion was valueless unless it appeared under the mask of sour faces and Geneva cloaks. Since man's soul was destitute of grace, propriety took the place of holiness, and rigid primness and affected solemnity were the marks of the elect.

Now, against the tyranny of a religion of mannerism, texts, and phrases, Shakespeare's irony was a most effective weapon. Far more powerfully than any formal polemic does his treatment of Falstaff, Malvolio, and Holofernes expose the hollowness of a system productive of such types. He taught men to laugh at the solemn pretentiousness, and to despise the wiles and hypocrisy of many a self-canonised saint. But at what was truly high, noble, or pure, no shaft of his sarcasm was ever winged. In this, as in so many other points, he exhibits a close resemblance to the Blessed Thomas More, of whom Shakespeare speaks with deep respect.   Both show the same mixture of humour and sarcasm, of lightest wit and deepest pathos; both lived in antagonism to their times; both employed their marvellous intellectual power to expose its abuses.   But the saintly Chancellor had the courage of his convictions, and sealed them with his blood, while the poet, we admit, kept his concealed.

While, however, we have no wish to ignore the poet's weakness and defects, we do not believe that he was ever himself reconciled to them. At times he may have been inclined " to envy a blessed fellow like Poins, who thought as every one else thought, and whose mind was always in the beaten track"; but he was in reality far more like Hal than Poins.   Like the madcap Hal, he may have given rein to his unruly youth, and lived only for the pleasures of the hour.   But like Hal also he could recognise the call to higher things, and be no longer his former self.   The motley once his garb and its surroundings, " the ready nothing trimmed in jollity," were to him a reproach, and his later years of solitude and seclusion in his Midland home, when " every third thought was to be his grave," mark the contrast with his youth.   That death, on which he so often ponders, was to him with its pangs and horrors a fearful thing, but to die unprepared was vile.   " Ripeness is all "; and he shows us in all his penitents how that ripeness is secured, sin forgiven, and heaven won, only on the lines of Catholic dogma, and by the sacraments of the Church; and there is evidence, as we shall see, that this was so in his own case.

Neither from single texts nor isolated phrases, but from the whole tenor of his writings, from the principles he constantly advocates, from the chosen objects of his praise or scorn, we arrive at the conclusion that the greatest of English poets was not the product of the Tudor age, nor of any past mediæval system, but of that Catholicism revealed and divine which is in all time. And herein we believe lies the secret of his marvellous power and the impenetrable vitality of his work.

CHAPTER II.

WE found our argument in favour of Shakespeare's Catholicism on the internal evidence offered by his writings. Nevertheless, as it has been urged that Shakespeare was a Protestant on the ground that his parents had conformed to the new religion, it will not, we trust, be considered out of place if we investigate the evidence as to the religion of the poet's parents. Of those that maintain the conformity to the new order of Shakespeare's parents, some advance no better proof than the assumption that as under Elizabeth all England had become Protestant by statute law, every Englishman must be presumed to have embraced the new creed unless evidence be produced to the contrary.

Let us consider the value of this assumption. Macaulay quotes Cardinal Bentivoglio's "State of Religion in England" as well deserving attention: "The zealous Catholics Bentivoglio reckoned at one thirtieth part of the nation. The people who would without the least scruple become Catholics if the Catholic religion were established, he estimated at four-fifths of the nation." "We believe," says

Macaulay, "this account to have been very near the truth."[1]   In support of the supposed universal and instantaneous conformity of England to the Reformed religion, the Edinburgh Reviewer uses the old argument of the Visitation-returns. "Out of 9,400 parochial clergy," he says, referring evidently to the Visitation of 1559, "less than 200 refused to give in their allegiance to the supremacy of the Queen."[2]   Now, these records still exist, and were studied and analysed by Mr. Simpson, who reports as follows : Out of 8,911 parishes and 9,400 beneficed clergymen, only 806 clergymen took the oath of supremacy ; 85 absolutely refused. The remaining 8,509 either evaded appearing, or were unsummoned by the Commissioners.

Thus the true inference from these returns is exactly the contrary to that which is commonly drawn. Instead of its being true that only an insignificant fraction of the clergy held aloof from the new order of things, the fact is that eight-tenths of the whole did not take the oath, many of them, indeed, not being called upon to do so. In the province of York, in August and September 1559, to give a single instance of the working of the Commission, out of 89 clergymen summoned to take the oath, 20 appeared and took it, 36 came and refused to take it, 17 were absent, unrepresented by Proctors, while 16 sent Proctors.[3]   Such results proved the

---

[1] "Critical and Historical Essays : Burleigh and his Times," 230, ed. 1877.   [2] Vol. cxxiii. p. 147.   [3] Dom. Eliz., vol. x.

futility of the commission, which in December 1559 was ordered to suspend its proceedings, and only terminate cases already commenced.[1]

The change in religion was indeed effected slowly and gradually, and this was equally the case with the laity and clergy. What proportion remained firm it is very hard to determine. The position of Catholics under the penal laws of Elizabeth was very similar to that of Christians under the persecutions of Nero and Diocletian. At neither period were there professed Christians or Catholics, for the public profession of the Faith meant grave risk of life, if not certain death; and such risk might not be voluntarily incurred. An individual was supposed to be a member of a proscribed creed, rather from his abstaining from any participation in the worship ordained by the State, and from his family antecedents, friends, birthplace, and political party, than from any overt religious act. As the first Christians practised their faith in secret when opportunities occurred, and took part in public life as far as was possible for them without doing violence to their conscience, so did the Elizabethan Catholics. And the temper of the rulers in both periods favoured intervals of comparative truce; for men of tried ability and position were valuable to the State, and were worth winning, if position, honour, or power could win them. It was only when a policy of persecution

---

[1] Dom. Eliz., vol. vii. No. 79.

was deemed expedient, that a formal profession of faith was demanded with the alternative of apostasy or death. Thus a Sebastian could remain unmolested in the bodyguard of Diocletian, and a Howard among the courtiers of Elizabeth, till the summons to the tribunal or the rack-chamber was heard. These facts, showing the condition of Catholics at the period under discussion, must be borne in mind, if we are to estimate rightly the kind of historical evidence available as to Shakespeare's religious belief.

That evidence will be necessarily, as a rule, circumstantial, consisting of indications, inferences, probabilities, as all direct external proof of their religion, whether in documents, goods, words, or acts, was studiously concealed by Catholics during the period treated of. But it should be remembered that while with direct evidence its strength is measured by its weakest link, in circumstantial evidence, facts which taken singly are of no appreciative value, combined together may produce moral certitude.

What then was the religious condition of Stratford and of Warwickshire in the sixteenth century? The most prominent institution of Stratford, and one which tells us most of its religious history, was its Guild of the Holy Cross.[1] " The Guild has lasted,"

[1] The following particulars of the Guild are taken from Halliwell, "Descriptive Calendar of the Records of Stratford-on-Avon, 1863," and from S. Lee, "Stratford-on-Avon in the Time of the Shakespeares."

wrote the chief officer in 1309, "and its beginning was from time whereunto the memory of man reacheth not." The earliest extant documents are from the reign of Henry III., 1216–1272, and include a deed of gift by one William Sude of a tenement to the Guild, and an indulgence granted October 7, 1270, by Giffard, Bishop of Worcester, of forty days to all "sincere penitents who had duly confessed and had conferred benefits on the Guild." By the close of the reign of Edward I. (1307) the Guild was wealthy in houses and lands, and the foundation was laid of its chapel and almhouses, which, with the hall of meeting, the "Rode" or "Reed Hall," stood where the Guildhall is at this day. In 1332 Edward III. granted the Guild a charter confirming its rights. They were again confirmed by Richard II. in 1384, who sent commissioners to report on the ordinances of all the Guilds throughout England. During the fifteenth century the Guild increased in importance and wealth. Gifts in kind are recorded, of silver cups, spoons, chalices, vestments, missals, statues of saints, wax; also of corn, wine, and malt. A schedule of 1434 is remarkable for the numerous and costly offerings registered. In 1481 the Guild acquired the Rectory and Chapelry of Little Wilmcote, the home of the Ardens and of the poet's mother. About the close of the century, the Guild chapel was rebuilt by Hugh Clopton, the head of the great Catholic family of Stratford.

This marks the most flourishing epoch in the history of the Guild. Of purely local origin, its fame had now spread so wide as to attract to its ranks noblemen like George, Duke of Clarence, brother of Edward IV., together with his wife and children; the Earl of Warwick and the Lady Margaret; Sir Thomas Littleton, the eminent judge; and also merchants of towns as distant as Bristol and Peterborough.

We now come to the objects of the Guild as set forth in its ordinances.

The first object was mutual prayer. The Guild maintained (in 1444) five priests or chaplains who were to say five masses daily, hour by hour, from six to ten o'clock. They were to live in one house under strict discipline, and were to walk in procession with the Guild in their copes and surplices, with crosses and banners. Out of the fees of the Guild, one wax candle was to be kept alight every day throughout the year at every mass in the church, before the blessed cross, " so that God and our Blessed Virgin and the Venerated Cross may keep and guard all the Brethren and Sisters of the Guilds from every ill."

A second object was mutual charity and works of mercy. The needs of any brother or sister who had fallen into poverty or been robbed were to be provided for " as long as he bears himself rightly towards the Brethren. When a Brother died, all the Brethren were bound to follow the body to the

church and to pray for his soul at its burial. The
Guild candle and eight smaller ones were to be
kept burning by the body, from the decease till the
burial. When a poor man died in the town, or a
stranger without means, the Brethren and Sisters
were 'for their souls' health' to find four wax
candles, a sheet, and a hearse-cloth for the corpse.
Once a year, in Easter week, a feast was held for
the upholding of peace and true brotherly love.
Offerings of ale were made for the poor, and prayer
was offered by all the Brethren and Sisters," that
"God and our Blessed Virgin and the Venerated
Cross, in whose honour they had come together, will
keep them from all ills and sins." The framers of
this ordinance evidently believed with Corin—

> "To find the way to heaven
> By doing deeds of hospitality."
> —*As You Like It*, ii. 4.

Thirdly, the Guild provided for the education of
the young by establishing, about 1453, a free
grammar-school for the children of the members.
The schoolmaster was forbidden to take anything
from the children. At this school, as reconstituted
under Edward VI., the poet was educated, and he
has given us a picture of his master in the peda-
gogues Holofernes and Sir Hugh Evans.

Lastly, the Guild was a self-governing body
founded and ruled by lay persons only, the clergy
belonging to it acting solely as its chaplains. Its

corporation was in fact the sole guardian of order in the town. This was seen when, on its dissolution in 1547, Stratford found itself in a chaotic state with no security of the life or property of its inhabitants. Hence they petitioned Edward VI. to reconstitute the Guild as a civil corporation, which he did by charter 1553.

The history of this Guild shows Stratford both in its civil and religious life to have been essentially a Catholic stronghold down to the middle of the sixteenth century, and its traditions, customs, ordinances, and observances still remaining or remembered in the poet's time may help to explain his remarkable familiarity with the usages and ways of the ancient faith.

We now come to the first sign of religious discord. We will begin with an incident which occurred in the year 1537, seven-and-twenty years before the birth of Shakespeare, and some fifteen years before his father had removed from Snitterfield into Stratford, when fierce contests about the doctrine of the Reformation were first disturbing the rural districts of England. On Easter Monday of that year, the sister of a churchwarden of Bishop Hampton was married to a substantial man of Stratford, and the event was celebrated with a church ale. Sir Edward Large, the curate of Hampton, "noted for one of the new learning, as they commonly call those that preach that pure, true, and sincere word of God, and also all that favour them that preach the same," was glad of the opportunity of holding forth to a crowd. In the course of his sermon he said divers strange things—some probably misunderstood by his rustic audience—that " all those that use to say Our Lady's psalter shall be damned;" and that the Ember-days were instituted by " a Bishop of Rome who had a paramour named Imber, who desired that she might have, every quarter, three fasting days; whence the said Bishop for her sake caused the fasting days to be had which are now called Ember-days." A poor man named Robert Cotton interrupted the preacher; for which he was brought before the king's commissioners— William Lucy, John Greville, and John Combe— and sent to gaol. His case was taken up by Master Clapton or Clopton, of Stratford, who defended Cotton so vigorously that he got him out of prison, and brought Lucy into trouble both with the men of Stratford, who were heartily opposed to any innovations in religion, and with Mr. Justice Fitzherbert, the founder of the family that still perpetuates his name and his faith.[1]

Here then is the first glimpse we get of the state of religious feeling in the neighbourhood of Stratford—on the one side, the Lucys, Grevilles, and the Coombes of Stratford all favouring the new learning; on the other, the Cloptons and the men of Strat-

[1] The document from which these facts are gleaned was published in the *Athenæum* of April 8, 1857, from the original in the Rolls-Chapel Record Office.

ford remaining steadfast in the old ways. Of the neighbouring families, the Catesbys, the Middlemores, the Throckmortons, the Ardens, were Catholics; and of the last-named family came Mary Arden, the poet's mother; and this brings us to the question of the religion of his parents.

There were numerous families of Shakespeares in various parts of England, especially in Warwickshire, in the sixteenth and seventeenth centuries; and there were two John Shakespeares, one a glover and the other a shoemaker or corvizer, in Stratford at the same time. Our poet's father, John Shakespeare, the glover, and later a wool merchant, apparently removed from Snitterfield to Stratford in 1551, and in 1557 we find him a Burgess of Stratford, and in 1558–59 one of the four petty constables for the town. This tenure of municipal office by him in 1557–59, when the laws against heretics were rigidly enforced, is our first direct evidence of his Catholicism. Mr. Carter, in fact, says, speaking of Robert Perrot, then High Bailiff of Stratford, that none but "an ardent and pronounced Roman Catholic"[1] could have accepted so high an office in times of bitter persecution under a most bigoted king and queen. He, however, entirely overlooks the fact that the same reasoning must apply proportionately to the other members of the corporation at this date, among whom we find, besides John Shakespeare, John Wheeler, his constant

[1] Ibid., p. 20.

E

associate in his various vicissitudes.   The poet's
mother was, as has been said, Mary Arden of Wilmcote in Snitterfield, of an old and stanch Catholic
stock, and through her he was connected with the
Montagues (Browne), Catesbys, Throckmortons, leading Catholic families, and distantly with Henry, the
Earl of Southampton, the poet's munificent friend
and patron.[1]

Mrs. John Shakespeare, then, was undoubtedly a
Catholic; nor is there any proof that she ever
changed her religion, though Mr. Carter pictures
her as a strict Puritan, teaching her son William
the Holy Scriptures from the Genevan Bible.
But did John Shakespeare, who, if Mr. Carter's
reasoning be valid, must have been a Catholic
under Mary, become a Protestant under Elizabeth?
It is argued that he must have done so, inas-
much as he continued to hold various municipal
offices up to 1571, when the Oath of Supremacy,
passed 1559,[2] was in force.   But, as we have
seen in the case of the clergy, it is one thing to
pass a new enactment, another to carry it out.

---

[1] Mary Arden was descended from Thomas, a brother of Sir John
Arden (*ob.* 1526), esquire of the body to Henry VII.; from whom
came Edward Arden of Parkhall, not far from Snitterfield, who
was married to Mary, daughter of Sir George and sister of Sir
Robert Throckmorton of Coughton, and consequently aunt of Sir
Robert's daughter, the wife of Sir William Catesby of Bushwood
Park in Stratford.   Anne, the daughter of Lady Catesby, was married
to Sir Henry Browne, son of the first Lord Montague; and Sir
Henry Browne's sister Mary was Countess of Southampton and
mother of Henry, Earl of Southampton.

[2] 1 Eliz. c. 1.

At first the lay peers were exempt from taking the oath, which was aimed specially at the bishops and clergy, and it was not till 1579 that it was required of the justices; and in Warwickshire, out of thirty magistrates, Sir John Throckmorton, Simon Arden, and eight others refused to be thus sworn. Up to 1579, then, one third of the magistrates of Warwickshire were Catholics. There is no proof whatever that John Shakespeare ever had the oath of supremacy tendered to him as a qualification for his municipal office. On the contrary, it is in the highest degree improbable that the Sheriff of the County (1568–69), Robert Middlemore, himself a recusant, should have administered to him an oath which he refused to take himself. As regards the oath of supremacy, then, there is no valid argument for John Shakespeare's Protestantism during these years.

Mr. Carter argues that the Protestantism of John Shakespeare is sufficiently proved by the fact that he remained a member of the Corporation, which under Elizabeth became strongly Puritan, as is seen, he says, by the defacement of crosses, images, and the sale of vestments effected under their rule.

Let us consider the value of this argument. In Elizabeth's first parliament Mass was suppressed throughout the kingdom, and by the Queen's injunction (1559), all shrines and altar-candlesticks, pictures, &c., were to be destroyed "so that not a memory of them remains," and inventories of the vestments, plate, and books were to be given to the visitors. These measures were universally carried out. But though shrines and altars were mutilated and desecrated, and the churches had become "barns," Protestantism only slowly made its way. With equal violence Catholicism had been suppressed under Edward VI. to be reintroduced four years later under Mary. Nor did the mass of the people know now what the new creed meant, or whither it would lead. It must further be remembered that for the first years of her reign, before the northern rising (1569) and the excommunication of Elizabeth by Pius V. (1570), Catholics, apart from the open exercise of their religion, were comparatively tolerated. "Until the eleventh year of Queen Elizabeth," writes Sir Robert Cotton, "a recusant's name was scarcely known."[1] So, too, Parsons and Creswell write to the Queen: "In the beginning of thy kingdom thou didst deal something more gently with Catholics. None were then urged by thee, or pressed either to thy sect or to the denial of their Faith. All things did seem indeed to point to a far milder course. No great complaints were heard. Then were seen no extraordinary contentions or repugnancies. Some there were that to please and gratify you went to your churches."[2]

In fact, Elizabeth, as long as she could usurp

[1] "Posthuma," 149 (1651).
[2] Watson's "Important Considerations," 1601.

unquestioned, the Church's authority and appropriate its goods, was content to let things be. And Catholics, it must be said, whether in good or bad faith, offered no opposition. "The majority," writes Father Parsons, "attended the heretical church and services, opinions being divided on the subject."[1] The priests who had conformed and publicly celebrated the "spurious liturgy," said Mass in private for the benefit of the more faithful Catholics, and would even bring consecrated hosts to the public service to communicate those who would not receive the bread prepared according to the heretical rite.[2] "It was indeed a mingle-mangle which every man made at his pleasure, as he thought would be most grateful to the people."[3]

Thus the fact that John Shakespeare was a member of the Corporation of Stratford during this period proves absolutely nothing as to his change of religion. On the contrary there are strong indications that the Corporation of Stratford was far more inclined to Catholicism than to Puritanism at this time. First, John Brethgirdle, the vicar appointed on February 27, 1560, in succession to Roger Dios, the Marian priest, was both unmarried and had no licence to preach; the Bishop of Worcester apparently being unsatisfied as to his orthodoxy. Both these facts point to the probability of his having

[1] "Brief Apologie," 2.
[2] Sander's "Anglican Schism," 269.
[3] Parsons, "Three Conversions of England," ii. 2c6, ed. 1688.

been one of the numerous conforming priests. In any case, as he had no licence to preach, the new doctrines must have made but little progress up to June 1565, when he died from his labours in the plague.[1] From 1565 to 1569 Stratford was apparently without a vicar. In 1569 Henry Heycroft was appointed, but he again had no licence to preach till January 7, 1571, when, as we shall see, a change began. From all, then, that can be gathered from the registers, Stratford never heard a sermon for eleven years; and John Shakespeare's ears were unassailed during this period by the eloquence of any Puritan Boanerges.

But Mr. Carter quotes the sale of church vestments by the Corporation as an additional proof of John Shakespeare's Puritanism. Now, the time and manner in which the Queen's injunctions on this subject were carried out in any place, offer a fair indication of the state of religious feeling then prevalent. In London, for instance, where the Puritan feeling was strong, at St. Bartholomew's Fair, August 24, 1559, or within a few months of the issue of the injunction, there were blazing in St. Paul's Churchyard two great bonfires for three whole days, of church furniture and vestments.[2] Again, at St. Mary's, Woolnote, in the same year

[1] His will, made the day before his death, of which we have seen a copy by the courtesy of Mr. Savage, Librarian of the Shakespeare Memorial Library, Stratford, gives no indication of his religious belief.

[2] "Machyn Diary," 207, 208. Stow, 640.

(1559), the copes, vestments, and ornaments were sold with consent.   Again, at St. Martin's, Leicester, in 1561, the vestments were sold for 42s. 6d.[1]   In contrast with this prompt action, we find that the vestments at Stratford were not sold till September 1571, and their sale then coincides with the concession of a preaching licence to Heycroft, and was probably due to his newly kindled zeal.   Thus, as far as this sale proves anything, its late date points to the predominance of a Catholic rather than of a Puritan element in Stratford up to 1570.   In that year a new penal statute against Catholics, Elizabeth's answer to the excommunication, was passed.   By this act, reconciliation to the Roman faith was made a capital offence; any person harbouring any one holding any Bull or instrument from Rome became guilty of treason, and the possession of crosses, pictures, beads, or an Agnus Dei blessed by the Pope or his authority, incurred forfeiture of all goods and imprisonment.[2]   Such a measure evidently rendered Catholics subject to continuous and harassing persecution, and from the date of its enactment the fortune of John Shakespeare appears to decline.   In 1575 he begins to sell and mortgage his property.   In 1577 he was assessed at a lower rate than the other aldermen.   In 1578 he was not rated for the poor at all.   In 1579 his name occurs among the defaulters for the armour and weapon tax, and in the Spring

---

[1] Churchwarden Accounts ; *Month*, December 1897.
[2] 13 Eliz. c. 2.

of the same year he mortgaged the revenue of his
wife's property to one of her relations for £40, and
sold some of his property at Snitterfield for £4.
These facts may point to real losses in trade or to
a practice common with suspected recusants, by
which, to escape from the grasp of the penal laws,
they conveyed their property to trustworthy persons
by colourable mortgages and sales, while retaining
themselves the income.   The latter supposition
seems to us far the more probable.   First, because
of the small sums received for the large amount of
property parted with ; again, because he was employed as trustee for valuable property during the
time of his alleged poverty ; and lastly and prin-
cipally because a few years later he was presented,
as we shall see, for the second time as a recusant.

His civic life during the last-named period shows
similar symptoms of decline.   From 1570 to 1586
he continued to hold his post as alderman.   But
after 1577 there were long periods of absence till
September 1586, when we read that two others
were chosen "in the places of John Wheeler and
John Shakespeare; for that Mr. Wheeler doth desire
to be put out of the Company, and Mr. Shakespeare
doth not come to the halls when they be warned,
nor hath done of any long time."   Thus closed his
connection with the Corporation, and the reason of
his continued absence and final retirement is furnished for us by the next document we have to
examine—the Recusancy-returns for Warwickshire

of September 25, 1592. The certificate still exists at the Record Office, and we shall discuss it at some length, both because it has now become contentious matter and also because it manifests the state of religion in Warwickshire.

The list of recusants in which John Shakespeare's name appears Mr. Carter classes with remarkable audacity, as we think will be shown, among " Puritan Recusancy-returns," [1] and he founds on it what he considers another convincing argument of John Shakespeare's Puritanism. Mr. Carter argues that this return included Puritan as well as Catholic recusants, because the Commissioners, Sir Thomas Lucy and others, who furnished it were appointed under the Recuscancy Act of 1592 ; [2] and this Act was aimed specially against Puritan Nonconformists.[3] Let us examine both these statements and see against whom the Act was directed, and also its date and that of the Warwickshire Recusancy-return.

First, then, against whom was this Act (35 Eliz. c. 1) directed ? The fanatical outbreak of Hackett and his associates, following on the Marprelate tracts, called for this measure. " The law was chiefly aimed," writes Marsden, " against Brownists and Barrowists. Cartwright and such as he, who still conformed, were not affected by it." [4] Now, Mr. Carter assumes John Shakespeare to have been a devout follower of Cart-

---

[1] p. 179.   [2] pp. 160, 161.   [3] p. 152.
[4] " History of the Early Puritans," 204 (1850).

wright, and imagines him walking over Sunday after Sunday from Stratford to hear him preach in the Leycester Hospital at Warwick.[1] If this were so, the presumption is that in 1592 John Shakespeare would have followed his master's example, and by his conformity have escaped persecution as a recusant. "The moderate Puritans," says Neale, "made a shift, to avoid the force of this law, by coming to church when common prayer was almost over, and by receiving the Sacrament in some church where it was administered with some latitude, but the weight of it fell upon the Separatists. These were called Brownists and Barrowists."[2]

Secondly, although the Act 35 Eliz. c. 1, as first

[1] p. 170. It is difficult indeed to follow Mr. Carter in his historical researches. He explains that Cartwright was thus able to preach at Warwick on his return from exile in Antwerp (1585), because "The Leycester Hospital was exempt from episcopal jurisdiction, and Cartwright could preach there without a bishop's licence and in defiance of all ecclesiastical deprivation."[1] As a fact, so far from this hospital being exempt from episcopal jurisdiction, the Bishop of Worcester was appointed its visitor,[2] and used his power. He summoned him (Cartwright) in the Consistory Court, and charged him with instilling the peculiarities of Genevan churchmanship.[3] Cartwright was, however, allowed to return to Warwick, where he wrote a treatise against the Brownists. In 1590, Leicester his patron died, and Cartwright was shortly after summoned before the Court of High Commission, and eventually committed to the Fleet, where he remained till Burghley obtained him his release about May 1592.

[2] "History of Puritans," i. 362.

[1] Ibid., p. 169.
[2] Art. Cartwright, Dict. Nat. Biography.
[3] Marsden, "Early Puritans," 173.

introduced was, according to its preamble, aimed against "such as are enemies to our State and adherents of the Pope,[1] yet as finally passed it expressly excluded Papists from its operation. The twelfth article of 35 Eliz. c. 1 runs—"Provided also that no Papist recusant or *Femme coverte* shall be compelled to abjure by reason of this act."[2] It is clear then, from the very wording of the Act, not only that it does not intend to include Papists in its operation, but that it expressly and distinctly excludes them.· How then can Mr. Carter ascribe to the operation of this Act "the Warwickshire Recusancy-returns, in which no denomination but those of Papists is named."

Thirdly, as regards its date, the Act in question, entitled, "An Act to retain the Queen's (Majesty) subjects to their due obedience," was the first act of the *thirty-fifth* year of Elizabeth. The Parliament which passed it only sat three months, from February 19, 1592, till April 10, 1593.[3] On the other hand, the return of the Commissioners for Warwickshire is dated in the heading "25 September, *in the thirtyfourth* year of her Majesty's most happy reign," or 1592. We must therefore leave Mr. Carter to explain how the Warwickshire Commissioners were appointed by an Act of Parliament passed five months *after* they

---

[1] D. Ewes, "Journal of Parliament," 500 (1682).

[2] The statutes at large from Edward IV. to end of Elizabeth, ii. 671, ed. 1770.

[3] Ibid., p. 671.

had sent in their return. He has failed to realise that as, according to the old style, the year 1592 began on 25th March, September 1592 was four months earlier than February of the same year, which ended March 24.[1]

What then was in reality the origin and purpose of the Warwickshire Commission ?

In October 1591 Elizabeth, in reality alarmed at the conversions effected by the missionaries from abroad, but avowedly to frustrate another apprehended attack by Spain, issued a proclamation stating the traitorous intrigues on hand, and directing the appointment of Commissioners for each shire. These Commissioners were charged to inquire of all persons as to their attendance at church, their receiving of seminarists, priests, and Jesuits, their devotion to the Pope or King of Spain, and to give information as to suspicious change of residence.[2]

In accordance with this proclamation Commissioners were appointed, and we find notices of their appointment and documents relating to the Commission for the following counties: Durham,[3] Oxford,[4] Hampshire,[5] Surrey and Dorsetshire,[6] Kent, Middlesex, Surrey, Bucks, and Durham, "for adding to Commission,"[7] Notts, Salop, Norfolk, Cambridge,

---

[1] The old style prevailed in English history up to September 2, 1752 (De Morgan, "Book of Almanacks," Introd., ix.).

[2] Dom. Eliz., ccxl. 42, October 18, 1591.

[3] Ibid., 66, November 1591.   [4] Ibid., 70, November 1591.

[5] Ibid., 82, December 1591.   [6] Ibid., 84, December 1591.

[7] Dom. Eliz., ccxli. 17, January 1592.

Herts, and the Isle of Ely,[1] East, West, and North
Ridings of Yorkshire, Northumberland—renewed,[2]
Cheshire, Lancashire.[3]

The State Papers, Dom. Eliz. ccxl., ccxli., ccxliii.,
and the Hist. MS. Com. Salisbury, P. IV., show clearly
that during the year November 1591–November
1592, the country was sifted and searched for the
discovery of Papists.   One list of names in nineteen
counties[4] contains 570 names, entirely of laymen,
and includes nearly all the old Catholic families of
those counties.   In some counties more than one
Commission was held.   This was the case in Warwickshire.   The return before us is entitled "The
second certificate of the Commissioners, &c."   Of the
first certificate no trace is as yet apparent.   At the
head of the second Commission are Sir Thomas
Lucy and Sir Fulke Greville, both active persecutors
of the Papists, and the lineal descendants of those
very men whom we have seen in 1557 imprisoning
Robert Cotton for defending the ancient faith.

The document, in modernised spelling, runs as
follows:—"The second certificate of the Commissioners for the county of Warwickshire touching
all persons . . . as either have been presented to
them, or have been otherwise found out by the
endeavour of the said Commissioners to be Jesuits,

---

[1] Dom. Eliz., ccxli. 40, February 1592.
[2] Ibid., 89, March 1592.
[3] Hist. MSS. Com. Salisbury, Part IV. p. 240, October 1592 ; Dom.
Eliz., ccxliii. 52, November 1592.
[4] Hist. MSS. Com. Salisbury, Part IV. p. 263-275, October 1592.

seminary priests, fugitives, or recusants, within the said County of Warwick, or vehemently suspected to be such, together with a true note of so many of them as are already indicted for their obstinate and wilful persisting in their recusancy. Set down at Warwick the 25th day of September in the 34th year of her Majesty's most happy reign, and sent up to the lordships of her Majesty's most honourable Privy Council."

It is divided into five lists. The first list contains the names of those who have been indicted for persisting in their recusancy. Among these obstinate recusants are Dinmock, a relation of the Catesbys, and champion of England, the whole family of Middlemore of Edgbaston (here we have the father, mother, two sons, and two daughters all indicted); Mountfort of Coleshall, the place frequented by the Martyr Monford Scott; Bolt and Gower of Tamworth; Thomas Bates, steward to Sir William Catesby of Bushwood Park in Stratford parish, who with his son John was afterwards compromised with Robert Catesby in the Gunpowder Plot; Richard Dibdale of Stratford, who had been formerly presented for a wilful recusant, and "continues still obstinate in his recusancy"—probably a relation of Richard Dibdale, the martyr, hanged for his priesthood in 1586. Other obstinate Papists of Stratford were Mrs. Jeffreys and Richard Jones. There is a long catalogue from Rowington. At Coughton, Mrs. Mary

Arden, the widow of the martyred squire of Parkhall, with her servants "continues obstinate." At Exhall we meet with one William Page, who had not been to church for three months past at least. A whole batch of Huddesfords and others from Solyhill are dismissed on submitting to the articles of the Commission and their declaration that they neither had been moved to give aid to the King of Spain or the Pope. In this list several persons are noted as having become recusants since the last presentment, a fact which shows the revival of the Faith in Warwickshire during the months immediately preceding this second Commission.

The second list contains the names " of such dangerous and seditious Papists and recusants as have been presented to us, or found out by our endeavour to have been at any time of, or in the county of Warwickshire, and are now either beyond the seas or vagrants within the realm." This list contains chiefly the names of priests: " William Brooks, thought to be a seditious seminary priest, sometime servant to Campion in the Tower. His friends give him out to be dead, but it is thought that he is lurking in England." " Barlow, an old priest and great persuader, who uses to travel in a blue coat with the eagle and child on his sleeve," as retainer to the Stanleys; another, "suspected to be a lewd seditious Papist, wanders about under colour of tricking out arms in churches." At Stratford there was George Cook, suspected to be a seminary priest, who could not be found. At Henley-in-Arden, Sir Robert Whateley, and at Rowington, Sir John Appletree, both old "massing priests." The same list contains the names of Dr. William Bishop, afterwards Bishop of Chalcedon, and his father and brother, and of Dr. Barrett, who were also Warwickshire men.

The third list contains "the names of recusants heretofore presented in the county, but now dwelling elsewhere, or gone away on just occasion, or lurking unknown in other counties." Here we have a short history of long hardships. "Mrs. Francis Willoughby, presented first at Kingsbury, afterwards at Stratford-on-Avon, then, indicted at Warwick, now fled to Leicestershire; the Middlemores, fled from Packwood to Worcestershire; John Buswell, fled from Stratford; the wife of Philip Moore, physician of Stratford, gone away to Evesham;" and "one Bates, a virginal player, a most wilful recusant, now, as is said, in Staffordshire."

The fourth list contains "the names of recusants heretofore presented," who are thought to forbear the Church for "debt and fear of process or for some worse faults, or for age, sickness, or impotency of body." In this list we have nine persons bracketed together as not coming to Church for fear of debt, "Mr. John Wheeler, John Wheeler his son, Mr. John Shakespeare, Mr. Nicholas Barneshurst, Thomas James, *alias* Giles, William Bainton, Richard Harrington, William Fluellen, and George

Bardolph—all supposed to abstain from Church for fear of process for debt; Mrs. Jeffreys, widow, Mrs. Barber, Julian Court, Griffin ap Roberts, Joan Welch, and Mrs. Wheeler, who all continue recusants except the last, but who are too infirm to come to Church." This list Mr. Carter seriously asserts to be composed of Puritan not Papist recusants; for " Papists," he says, " were persecuted for being Papists, not for forbearing attendance at the Parish Church." [1]

Now we have seen that the first act of parliament above recited, which Lucy's Commission was charged to carry out, was framed solely to enforce the attendance of Papists at church, under the fine of £20 a month for nonconformity, and the plea of sickness or poverty was the stereotyped excuse with nonconforming Papists to escape the fine. Thus Bishop Cheney (or Cheyney) of Gloucester, in a return of recusants furnished by him to the Council, October 24, 1577, divides the recusants of his diocese into three classes. First, those who refused to come to church, or open, obstinate recusants; secondly, some supposed to savour of Papistry alleged sickness, some others debt, and therefore refused, fearing process; the third sort, commonly called Puritans, refuse, as not liking the surplice.[2] Here then it is Papists, not Puritans, who allege the excuse of debt, for the latter were only too willing to express their repugnance to anything in their eyes

---

[1] Hist. MSS. Com. Salisbury, Part IV. p. 164.
[2] Dom. Eliz., vol. cxvii., October 24, 1577, No. 12.

F

savouring of Papistry. Now in this fourth list we know, that of the nine persons bracketed together, John Shakespeare and John Wheeler were Catholics, for they held office under Mary; and the very first entry in this fourth list shows that it is still Papists, not Puritans, who are aimed at. It runs thus— "Thomas Bartlett of Middleton, presented here for a recusant, is thought to forbear coming to church for debt or for some other causes, rather than of any popish devotion."

The fifth list gives the names of those who have already conformed or promised conformity. At Solyhull, forty-eight persons had either conformed or had faithfully promised to do so; at Edgbaston, one of the Middlemores and John Burbage were among those who had made the same promise; at Packwood, Christopher Shakespeare and his wife are in the same category; at Warwick there is William Cook, *alias* Cawdry, probably a Stratford man; at Stratford there are seventeen names of similar persons—the first is " Mrs. Clapton, wife of William Clapton, Esq., now dead, was mistaken, and goes now to church"; another of the number was Joan Cook, *alias* Cawdry, a member of a family which figures in Halliwell's biography of Shakespeare; another was Edward Green, perhaps a relation of Shakespeare's friend the actor;[1] and another of

---

[1] Green calls Shakespeare his cousin. One Thomas Green, *alias* Shakespeare, was buried at Stratford, March 6, 1589-90—*Halliwell*, 269.

these conformists is Thomas Reynolds, gentleman, whom we find elsewhere selling property in Stratford to Sir William Catesby.

Such then is the Recusancy-return, and its impartial perusal can leave no doubt, we think, that it includes none but Catholics, and that John Shakespeare was at that time a Popish recusant, sheltering himself under the excuse of debt. From 1592 there is no evidence of his having conformed nor again of his being presented for nonconformity, so that it may fairly be inferred that the same protest was allowed to hold till his death in 1601, and there is further reason for believing that he persevered in his faith to the end.

Before leaving the Recusancy-return we would, however, make two remarks it suggests. First, according to Aubrey, the names of the poet's dramatic personages were often taken from the circle of his acquaintance, for he and Jonson gathered humours of men wherever they came. Thus the original of Dogberry was a constable he met one midsummer night at Crendon in Bucks; and part of Falstaff's character, as Bowman the player relates, was drawn from a townsman at Stratford, who either faithlessly broke a contract or spitefully refused to part with some land adjoining Shakespeare's house. Now in this one return we find seven of his characters among the Warwickshire recusants—Page, Fluellen, Gower, Bates, Court, Bardolph, and Bolt—a fair indication at least that he was tolerably familiar with the adherents of the proscribed creed in his own county.

Secondly, it must not be supposed that the large list of conformists really represented the march of Protestant conviction. It was always the interest of the Commissioners to make their task appear a success, and so to be easily satisfied with the promises of conformity. Their certificates are not much more credible than the reports of an Indian missionary to his paymasters at Exeter Hall. As a matter of fact the certificate shows on its face the futile character of these sham conversions, extorted by fear and violence. Thus we have one Michael Commander, at Tachbrook Episcopi, who "made show of conformity, and went to church, but hath since used so bad speeches as have made the Commissioners to fear that he will start back like a broken bow." Of John Arrowsmith, of the same place, they say, "He makes some show of conformity and goes to church; but when the preacher goeth up to the pulpit to preach he goeth presently out of the church, and saith he must needs go out of the church when a knave beginneth to preach." Again, Joan Jennings "promised conformity, but did not perform it." So John Wise, Esq., of Coleshall, did "humbly and faithfully promise conformity, and not long after came once to his parish church; but never came since." The fact is that in 1592 the persecution had reached such a pitch in England that the Catholics were reduced to the last extremity, and many a man, to rescue the poor remnants of his patrimony for his starving wife and family, was persuaded to do violence to his conscience once or twice, and to appear at the hated services which his tyrants prescribed for him.

The next point we have to consider regarding John Shakespeare is that of his spiritual will. The document opens thus: " (1). In the name of God, the Blessed Virgin, the Archangels, Angels, Patriarchs, Prophets, Evangelists, Apostles, Saints, Martyrs, and all the Celestial Court and Company of Heaven, I, John Shakespeare, an unworthy member of the Holy Catholic religion, do, of my own accord, freely make this spiritual testament." (2 and 3). He then confesses that he has been an abominable sinner, begs pardon for all his offences, and begs his guardian angel to be with him at his last passage. He declares that he hopes to die fortified with the sacrament of Extreme Unction : if he be hindered, then, he does now, for that time, demand and crave the same. (5 and 6). He affirms his hope of salvation solely in the merits of Christ, and renounces beforehand any temptation to despair. - (7). He protests that he will bear his sickness and death patiently, and if any temptation leads him to impatience, blasphemy, or murmuring against God or the Catholic faith, he does henceforth and for the present repent, and renounces all the evil he might have then done or said. (8). He pardons all the injuries done to him. (9).

He thanks God for his creation, preservation, and vocation to the true Catholic faith (speaking as if he had never left it), and, above all, for His forbearance in not cutting him off in the midst of his sins. (10). He makes the Blessed Virgin and St. Winefride executrixes of his will, and invokes them to be present at his death, as also and again, his guardian angel. (12). He beseeches his "dear friends, parents, and kinsfolk," whom he assumes to be all Catholics, to assist him in Purgatory with their holy prayers and satisfactory works, especially with the holy sacrifice of the Mass, as being the most effectual means to deliver souls from their torments and pains. (13). He prays that his soul at death may find its repose in the sweet coffin of the side of Jesus Christ. (14). He concludes by confirming his testament anew, in presence of the Blessed Virgin and his angel guardian, and begs that it may be buried with him.

Such then are the contents of the will, and it must be remembered that the practice of making these spiritual testaments was common with Catholics. Forms for the *Testamentum animæ* are to be found in English Primers of the sixteenth century, and the document in question corresponds in matter and style with this form.[1] Yet the will is generally rejected as spurious ; and why ?

On internal grounds the Edinburgh Reviewer

[1] F. Loarte's "Exercise of the Christian Life," 155 and 218, translated and printed in English in 1579, is quoted by F. Thurston

thinks it evidently supposititious. Knight[1] will not believe it to be the work of a Roman Catholic at all, both because of its uncontroversial character, and because its doctrinal expressions are both raving and offensive. As examples, he quotes in proof " direful iron of the lance," which is, in truth, derived from the line " quae vulnerata lanceæ mucrone diro " of the ancient hymn, " Vexilla Regis," and " Life giving Sepulchre of the Lord's Side," an expression not only common in Catholic devotions, but imitated by Shakespeare in his thirty-first sonnet, where he says to his friend—

"Thou art the grave where buried love does live."

The objections to the genuineness of the will on doctrinal grounds arise only from ignorance of Catholic practices and devotion. The phrases and manner pronounced absurd and offensive are precisely those usually employed in testaments of this kind.

But the will is rejected on external grounds as a forgery. It was " composed," Halliwell Phillipps says, as is most likely, by Jordan,[2] while Mr. Sidney Lee calls " the forgery of the will of Shakespeare's father, Jordan's most important achievement." [3] Let

(cf. *Month*, May 1882) as containing a similar protestation abridged. Maskell, *Monument. Ritual. Eccles. Anglic.*, 262, 263, 1846, contains two other brief forms of spiritual wills englished from the *Sarum Horæ* of 1508.

[1] " Biography of Shakespeare," 30.
[2] " Outlines," ii. 403. 1890.
[3] " Life of Shakespeare," 366. 1898.

us see how far the history of the document, as far as
it can be gathered from Halliwell's extracts from the
evidence of Malone, Jordan, and Davenport,[1] warrants
the statement.

(1). In 1757[2] a small paper book consisting of six
leaves, purporting to be the spiritual testament of
John Shakespeare, was found by Thomas Moseley
between the rafters and the roof when retiling the
house of Mr. Thomas Hart, a lineal descendant of the
poet's sister.   Moseley was a master bricklayer who
sometimes worked with his men.   He was sufficiently
educated to transcribe a portion of the document.

(2). Moseley lent the discovered will to Mr.
Alderman Payton sometime prior to 1785, who
read and returned it, saying that he wished the
name had been William instead of John.   In 1785
Jordan made a copy of the manuscript which he
sent to the *Gentleman's Magazine*, but that journal
rejected it as spurious, as did also the Rev. T.
Green, the rector of Wilford, near Stratford, an
antiquary of some repute.   In 1788 Moseley died,
leaving the original manuscript in the hands again
of Payton, who sent it in 1789, through the Rev.
T. Davenport, the vicar of Stratford, to Malone.

(3). Malone took pains to investigate the matter
thoroughly.   He ascertained through Davenport
that Moseley was a thoroughly honest, sober, indus-

---

[1] "Outlines," ii. 400–404.

[2] Jordan says 1757, Malone 1770, but the difference is immaterial,
as the supposed forgery was in 1785.

trious man, and had neither asked for nor received any payment for the document in his possession, and that his daughter, who was still living, and Mr. Thomas Hart, in whose house it was found, both perfectly remembered the fact of its discovery by Moseley. Malone also obtained from Jordan his account of his connection with the document, and with this evidence before him, and with the knowledge that Jordan's copy had been rejected by the *Gentleman's Magazine* and by Green, he published in 1790 the history of the manuscript in his possession, declared himself perfectly satisfied as to its genuineness, adding "that its contents are such as no one could have thought of inventing with a view to literary imposition."

Such is the history of the will to 1790. On what grounds rests the supposed forgery? Malone, it is said, in 1796 recanted his verdict. He declares indeed that he was mistaken as to the writer of the document, for from documents since obtained " he is convinced that the will could never have been written by any of the poet's family." These words of Malone need mean nothing more than that he had satisfied himself that the will was neither in the autograph of John Shakespeare nor in the writing of a member of his family. But a will may be authentic without being an autograph, and the authenticity of the will Malone never calls in question. To suppose, as some have done, that Jordan, instead of making an exact copy of the will, when the document was lent to him by Moseley, fabricated a will and returned his fabrication to Moseley instead of the original document, is to suppose what is absurd.   The original document was *already* known to Moseley and Payton, and was subsequently again in their possession, and transmitted by them as genuine through Davenport to Malone.   They must therefore have perceived at once any discrepancy between Jordan's copy and the original, and it is simply incredible that had such existed, neither Moseley, Payton, Davenport, nor Malone should ever have exposed Jordan's forgery, nor entered a word of protest against its circulation.

Further, we may ask, what motive was there for such a forgery ?   There was no controversy then as to John Shakespeare's religion, nor did the Ireland forgeries, prompted according to Malone by this very will, appear till eleven years later.   The history of the forged will of William Shakespeare offers an instructive contrast indeed to that of the will of John Shakespeare.   Ireland produced a will professedly made by William Shakespeare, having found it, he said, in the house of a gentleman whose name he could not give.   The contents of this document are of a colourless, stilted character, and Ireland's son Samuel Henry admitted, within twelve months of the publication, that he had himself fabricated the document, though without his father's knowledge. The will of John Shakespeare was found in Mr. Hart's house by Moseley, a man of unimpeachable integrity, and his statement as to its discovery is confirmed by independent testimony.   The genuineness of the will is guaranteed by a chain of witnesses during some thirty or forty years, and its contents are in complete agreement, as has been shown, with the spiritual testaments drawn up by Catholics at that period.   Against the evidence, internal and external, in favour of the will, the unsupported assumption of its forgery is not, we think, tenable. The will has therefore a right in our judgment to be regarded as genuine till further evidence to the contrary be adduced, and thus we leave it as forming the last witness to John Shakespeare's religious belief.

There is good reason, then, for believing that the poet's parents were Catholics.   But it is objected the fact remains that the poet himself, whatever was the religion of his parents, was baptized, married, and buried in the Protestant Church.

First, then, as regards the baptism.   Catholic parents knew that if the matter and form were duly applied, that sacrament was valid, by whomsoever administered, lay or cleric, heretic or Catholic.   The law enforced the baptism of all children by the minister in the Parish Church, and we shall see in the Recusancy-return how carefully evidence was taken on this head.   There was a great difficulty in finding a priest, and Catholics, even the parents of the child, were subjected to severe penalties for conferring that sacrament.   Lord Montague, for baptizing his own son, was visited by a pursuivant, forced to dismiss all his servants, and incurred much persecution. So, too, as regards marriage; the non-performance of the ceremony at the Parish Church always aroused suspicions that the services of a priest had been secretly employed. Thus Arden, we find, was examined concerning his daughter's marriage to Somerville. " Where was he married? in what church? and by what minister? Did not Hall the priest marry Somerville and your daughter at a Mass, at which you were present?"[1] Shakespeare, then, like his connection Somerville, may have been secretly married by some priest, and when the persecution waxed hot in 1581–82, obtained a licence from the Bishop of Worcester, both to screen his secret espousals and to obtain a legal certificate of his union. His burial in the Protestant Church proves nothing as to his religion, for it was the only official place of interment, for priests as well as laity, when there were no Catholic cemeteries. F. Thurston mentions three priests, besides Dr. Petre, Vicar of the Western District in the last century, all of whom were buried in Protestant Churches.[2]

The performance of these three rites according to the new creed prove, then, nothing conclusively as to the poet's religion. We believe, however, that surer evidence as to his religion is to be found by considering the creed and politics of his friends,

[1] Dom. Eliz., vol. clxvii. No. 59.
[2] *Month*, May 1882, 12.

associates, and patrons. The Protestant and Catholic parties in Warwickshire, as well as in every part of the kingdom, were in a position of bitter antagonism, and in this strife the poet soon became involved. The leader of the Protestant party in Shakespeare's county was the new upstart favourite Dudley, Earl of Leicester. Absolutely devoid of principle, religious or other, and at times indeed favourable to Catholics, as for instance in his relations with Campion, he found it to his interests in Warwickshire to play the part of a zealous Puritan; and he thus secured the support of the Grenvilles, Lucys, the Combes, the Porters and others, all zealous adherents of the new religion. Leicester's iniquities, his criminal relations with the Lady Sheffield and Lady Essex, his murder of both their husbands and of his own wife at Cumnor, were condoned or ignored by his partisans, in return for his Puritan zeal.[1] Not so, however, with the Catholics, and conspicuous among them in his sturdy independence was Edward Arden, the Squire of Parkhall, and the cousin of Shakespeare's mother. He refused to wear the Earl's livery, and openly expressed his disgust at his infamies. Arden was supported in his contest by the prayers and good wishes of all that was respectable in the county, but the Earl had the machinery of Cecil's statecraft at his command, and knew how to use it. In 1583, Somerville, Arden's son-in-law, a youth of naturally weak mind, which had become still further

[1] Parsons, " Leicester's Commonwealth."

unbalanced by his brooding over the wrongs of Catholics, went up to London with the avowed purpose of shooting the Queen. This was Leicester's opportunity. Somerville was arrested, as were also the Ardens and Hall, their chaplain. They were indicted for treason at Warwick, but fearing Arden's popularity there, Leicester got the venue changed to London. They were all condemned. Somerville was found strangled in Newgate, Arden suffered a traitor's death at Smithfield, his wife, his daughter, Mrs. Somerville, and Hall the chaplain endured a long imprisonment at the Tower. One of Leicester's henchmen, meanwhile, was in possession of Arden's and Somerville's estates, till he was finally ejected by Arden's son.

But what has this to do with Shakespeare? Mr. Simpson hazarded the supposition that he had served Arden in the capacity first of a page, and then in that of a legal secretary or agent, under the assumed name of William Thacker. The Edinburgh Reviewer has, however, since shown that William Thacker was a real personage. But, even though Shakespeare had not been a member of the Arden household, the poet's blood connection with the Ardens could have scarcely suffered him to remain indifferent to the bitter persecutions they endured. He was, at this time, an ardent youth of nineteen; was there any one on whom he could in any way avenge the wrong done to his own kith and kin? Within a few miles of Stratford lay the property of Sir Thomas Lucy, the

Puritan tool of Leicester, and the persecutor of the Warwickshire Papists. He had twice summoned Shakespeare's father for recusancy, and was a leading member of the commission on Somerville and Arden. In those days deer-killing was not a mere poaching venture for gain's sake, but was employed by both sides as an act of retributive justice or revenge. Thus in 1556 divers "ill-disposed" showed their hostility to Heath, the Archbishop of York and Queen Mary's Chancellor, by destroying his deer, and in 1600 the "evil affected" slew the cattle of William Brettergle, High Constable of the county, doubtless in revenge for his persecuting tactics.[1] And it is just about the date of the Arden and Somerville trials, *i.e.* 1583, that, as all the poet's biographers agree, Shakespeare was forced to leave Stratford, because of the unduly severe punishment that he received from Sir T. Lucy, for killing his deer. Halliwell, indeed, thinks that nothing short of persecution could have provoked an attack from one usually so moderate and gentle as the poet. That the persecution in question arose from the poet's indignation at Lucy's treatment of his relations, there is, we think, good reason, from what has been said, for believing. Later on he revenged himself again on his persecutor by holding him up to ridicule in the person of Mr. Justice Shallow, whose identity is determined by the "luces" in the Shallow Coat-of-Arms, explained by Parson Evans

---

[1] Dom. Eliz., vol. cclxxv. No. 115.

in his equivocal speech; "the dozen white louses do become an old coat well."

In 1584–85, Shakespeare, then "having"—according to the Rev. T. Davis, a Protestant clergyman, writing eighty years after the poet's death—"been oft whipt and sometimes imprisoned" by Lucy, found himself obliged to fly to London.   For a young man in trouble the stage presented perhaps the only opportunity of a livelihood, and to Catholics it offered special attractions.   They were trained by their religion to delight in the dramatic representations employed by the Church in her services. The Corpus Christi and other processions were duly held during Mary's reign, and had been only of late prohibited.   The stage again offered peculiar protection for suspected persons against domiciliary visits, tests, and oaths—for actors were classed as vagabonds, or persons having no fixed address. The theatre thus became held in favour by Papists, as the following petition from a Puritan soldier will show :—

"The dailie abuse of Stage Playes is such an offence to the godly, and so great a hindrance to the gospell, as the papists do exceedingly rejoice at the bleamysh thereof, and not without cause; for every day in the weeke the players' bills are sett up in sundry places of the cittie, some in the name of her Majestie's menne, some the Earl of Leicester, some the Earl of Oxford, the Lord Admyralles, and divers others; so that when the belles tole to the

Lectorer, the trumpetts sound to the Stages, whereat the wicked faction of Rome laugheth for joy, while the godly weepe for sorrowe. Woe is me! The play houses are pestered, when churches are naked: at the one it is not possible to gett a place, at the other voyde seats are plentie."[1]

Of Shakespeare's early years in London little is known; but as Lord Southampton, his supporter and friend, was the patron of the Blackfriars Theatre, it is naturally supposed that he there began his career as an actor. Henry Wriothesley, Earl of Southampton, was cradled in Catholic surroundings. His father also, Henry, second Earl, was a well-known papist, and a devoted adherent of Mary, Queen of Scots, and for his action in her behalf was sent to the Tower in 1572. He died in 1581, aged thirty-five, leaving £200 to be distributed amongst the poor of his estates to pray for his soul and the souls of his ancestors. His wife, Mary Brown, Southampton's mother, was the daughter of Lord Montague, who suffered much for the Faith. The poet's patron himself was trained, indeed, in the opposite camp. He was brought up under the guardianship of Burleigh, and took his degree at St. John's College, Cambridge. Nevertheless his friendship with Essex, together with the traditional associations connected with his name, led to his being regarded, as we shall see, as champion of the Catholic party. Through

[1] "Dramatic Poetry," by J. Payne Collier, F.S.A., i. 263-264; Harleian MSS., 286.

Southampton, therefore, the poet would have found himself among many papist associates.

The first certain allusion to him as an author is in 1592, in Greene's "Groatsworth of Wit," when the dying dramatist, jealous of Shakespeare's success, writes to warn his fellow-playwrights against putting any trust in actors, "for there is an upstart crow beautified with our feathers, that with his *tyger's heart wrapt in a player's hide*, supposes he is well able to bombast out a blanke verse with the best of you; and being an absolute *Johannes factotemi*, is in his owne conceit the onely Shake-scene in a country."[1] The words "tiger's heart, etc.," are a parody on the line in the third part of "Henry VI.":—

"Oh tyger's heart, wrapt in a woman's hide."

In 1594 he appears in the accounts of the Treasurer of the Chamber as having twice played before Elizabeth with Richard Burbage,[2] at Christmas time at Greenwich Palace. In 1596 he had attained such success, both as an author and actor, that he was able to become proprietor of the Blackfriars Theatre, and in 1597 to buy "New Place," his subsequent place of residence at Stratford. But during these years — 1593–97 — fresh political

[1] For this envious attack Chettle, Greene's editor, made Shakespeare a handsome apology.—*Outlines*, i. 100.

[2] Mr. Halliwell Phillipps considers there is no evidence for the opinion held by Simpson and others that Richard and James Burbage were of the Warwickshire Catholic family of that name (i. 344).

troubles were gathering, and Shakespeare's part in them shows us where his sympathies lay. The English people had become disgusted with Elizabeth and Cecil's tyranny, and the Queen was detested by Papists and Puritans alike. Of both these parties the Earl of Essex was the hope and the champion, for he was known, on the one hand, to be in correspondence with the Pope,[1] and on the other he openly advocated religious toleration. The supporters of Essex, to avoid suspicion, held their deliberations at Drury House, the residence of Lord Southampton, Shakespeare's patron. Some means were, however, needed to stir the popular discontent and to familiarise the public mind with the idea, if not of deposing Elizabeth, at least of making Essex practically supreme. At that time political movements were not begotten by theories, arguments on the rights of the people, or abstract principles, but by precedents, privileges, and charters. An example was then required of how a tyrannical, usurping sovereign might be coerced, and this was furnished by Shakespeare's play of " Richard II."

Dr. Hayward had already composed, with the same end, a history of the deposition of that monarch, and had dedicated it to Essex, but it was altogether too dry and prosaic for the stage. Shakespeare's play presents the same theme

---

[1] His chaplain, Alabaster, had already become a Catholic in Spain (Dom. Eliz., vol. cclxxv. nn. 32, 33, 35, July 1600).

and moral, cast in dramatic form. The play of
" Richard II." was pronounced treasonable on the
following heads : the selection of a story 200 years
old, in order to demonstrate the misgovernment of
the Crown, the corruption and covetousness of the
Council, the promotion of unworthy favourites, oppression of the nobles, and the excessive taxation
of the people, enacted professedly to prosecute the
suppression of the Irish rebellion, but in fact to line
the pockets of the king.[1]   The following extracts
will show how exactly these objections apply to
Shakespeare's play :—

> " Now for the rebels which stand out in Ireland,
>   Expedient manage must be made. . . .
>   We will ourselves in person to this war ;
>   And, for our coffers—with too great a court
>   And liberal largess—are grown somewhat light,
>   We are enforced to farm our royal realm.
>   . . . If that come short,
>   Our substitutes at home shall have blank charters,
>   Whereto, when they shall know what men are rich,
>   They shall subscribe them with large sums of gold,
>   And send them after to supply our wants."

Richard wishes his uncle, John of Gaunt, a speedy
death, when

> " The lining of his coffers shall make coats
>   To deck our soldiers for these Irish wars."

And he carried out his threat, too, by seizing all his

---

[1] Dom. Eliz., vol. cclxxv. No. 25, i.

" plate, coin, revenue, and moveables." The old duke
had told him that

> "A thousand flatterers sit within thy crown,
> Whose compass is no bigger than thy head ;
> And yet encagèd in so small a verge
> The waste is no whit lesser than thy land."

We may easily fancy with what excitement the
conversation of Northumberland, Ross, and Willoughby would be listened to by the favourers of
Essex :

> " *North.* Now, afore heaven, 'tis shame such wrongs are
>   borne.
> The king is not himself, but basely led
> By flatterers ; and what they will inform,
> Merely in hate, 'gainst any of us all,
> That will the king severely prosecute
> 'Gainst us, our lives, our children, and our heirs.
>   *Ross.* The commons hath he filled with grievous taxes,
> And lost their hearts ; the nobles hath he fined
> For ancient quarrels, and quite lost their hearts.
>   *Willo.* And daily new exactions are devised ;
> As blanks, benevolences, and I wot not what.
> But what, o' God's name, doth become of this ? "

Cecil felt the lines applied to his own policy, and
the Queen exclaimed to Lambarde, " Know ye not
I am Richard II. ? " The conspiracy, however, failed.
Essex himself was beheaded in the year 1600.
Southampton was sent to the Tower. The Earls of
Rutland, Monteagle ; Sirs John Davies, C. Danvers,
C. Blount ; Robert Catesby and William Green, both
Warwickshire men ; John Arden, the poet's con-
nection ; John Wheeler, John Shakespeare's friend

and fellow-recusant, all Catholics, were among those involved in the consequences of the conspiracy.[1] The poet, although his play was condemned, himself escaped. Hayward instead was chosen as the victim of the royal vengeance, and was imprisoned and racked. But here again, as in the Lucy whippings and imprisonment, so now in the Essex conspiracy we find the poet connected apparently with the Catholic party.

In 1603 Elizabeth died, and Shakespeare alone of his contemporary poets and dramatists refused to compose one line in honour of her memory. Chettle, indeed, thus complains, that though she favoured him in life, he neglected her when dead.

> " Nor doth the silver-tonguèd melicent
>   Drop from his honeyed muse one subtle tear
>   To mourn her death, that granted his desert ;
>   And to his lays opened her royal ear.
>   Shepherd, remember our *Elizabeth*
>   And sing her rape, done by that *Tarquin*, Death."
>   — *England's Mourning Garment*, 1603.

That he knew and appreciated her falseness and infamy, we shall see later.

With the accession of James, the hopes of Catholics rose ; he promised toleration, and was hailed as a deliverer. But though he spared the lives of Catholics, he adopted a mode of persecution, by fines and penalties, which reduced them

---

[1] Dom. Eliz., vol. cclxxvii., February 1601, MSS. 38, 39, 40, 41 ; Rutland MSS., vol. i. 367 ; Townsend MSS., p. 10, where the name of Thomas Wheeler is given as well as that of John.

to beggary, and filled his treasury by some
£360,000 a year. Their rage in consequence was
intense; they had already grievously suffered for
their allegiance to his mother, and their hearts were
hardened by the ingratitude and baseness of her
son. The prospect of any constitutional redress
seemed hopeless; their policy was one of despair.
Instigated by the tools of Cecil, a number of Catholics, many of whom had been in the Essex plot,
combined in the hope of destroying, at one blow,
King, Lords, and Commons. When the conspirators were sufficiently implicated, their apprehension
followed, according to the correct State method.
Among the chief actors in the so-called Gunpowder
Plot were Catesby, the two Bates', John Grant of
Norbrook near Stratford, Thomas Winter, Grant's
brother-in-law, all Shakespeare's friends and bene-
factors. Now it is remarkable that in the two
plays of this period, " Julius Cæsar " and " Hamlet,"
which alike turn on tyrannicide, all the sympathy
is evoked in favour of the conspirators.

The concluding eight or ten years of his life, till
his death in 1616, Shakespeare spent in comparative
obscurity at his native place. His retirement is
commonly attributed to the desire to live as a
country gentleman at Stratford. Why he was thus·
relegated to the background may be gathered from
the history of his contemporaries, Ben Jonson and
Donne, both at one time Catholics, who procured
for themselves places at court, the laureateship, and

other preferments. The history of Jonson's conversion shows how easily a man, in those troubled times, might become a Catholic without the world at large having any suspicion of the change.

Jonson, having slain Gabriel Spencer, the actor, in a duel in 1593, found himself in the Marshalsea under sentence of death. Among the prisoners were many priests, also awaiting trial; and these were, in fact, far more at liberty to pursue the functions of the ministry in their confinement, than when at large. They said Mass, as a rule, daily, though they were forced to substitute tin for silver chalices, as the latter were so constantly appropriated by Sir George Carey, the Governor. They preached at times, and instructed their fellow-prisoners, whenever opportunity offered. Jonson, then, having eternity before him and a priest at his side, thought of setting his soul in order, and embraced the faith. Having found means to obtain his release, he married a wife, a Catholic like himself. By her he had two children, a girl who died, aged six months, and a boy to whom Shakespeare was godfather. The epitaph written by Jonson on the former shows that both parents were at that time Catholics, and would, therefore, probably have chosen a Catholic godfather for their son. The verses run as follows :—

> " At six months' end she parted hence
> With safety of her innocence ;
> Whose soul Heaven's Queen, whose name she bears,
> In comfort of her mother's tears
> Hath placed among her virgin train."—*Epigram* 22.

At Christmas 1598, Shakespeare brought out Jonson's play "Every Man in his Humour" at the Blackfriars Theatre, an act of special kindness, seeing that Jonson up to August of that year had been in the pay of a rival company. They seem to have drawn apart after the exposure of the Gunpowder Plot in 1605. The country was now in a state of violent agitation, and a sifting-time for Catholics followed. Shakespeare retired, as we have seen, from the company of king's actors, immured himself at Stratford, and his plays seem to have been no longer performed at Court. But timid and time-serving Catholics like Ben Jonson took another line. Jonson hastened to conform, and offered his services to the Government. He took the oath of supremacy, went to church, received the Sacrament, drank the whole cup at a draught, and secured his place at Court. He further proved his loyalty by commemorating the plot in his tragedy of "Catiline," in which he talks of the bloody and black Sacrament taken by the conspirators, the "fire and balls, swords, torches, sulphur, and brands" prepared by their hands, while the conspirators themselves were described as the foulest murderers and villains.

Or consider, again, the case of the metaphysical poet Donne. Handsome and accomplished, of a singular personal attractiveness, he found preferment by abusing the faith he had professed, and vilifying the noble stock from which he sprang. "The Pseudo-Martyr," published in 1610, was

written to prove that his own ancestral relative,
the Blessed Thomas More, had suffered, not for the
Faith but for his own obstinacy; and that the
thousands of Catholics persecuted and beggared by
James were no deserving objects of sympathy.   He
could speak with experience; his two maternal uncles,
Jasper and Elias Heywood, of the Society of Jesus,
died abroad after much suffering, Confessors for the
Faith.   His own younger brother, Henry Dŏnne, died
of gaol fever in the Clink, where he was incarcerated
for harbouring in his barrister's chambers Father
Harrington, the martyr.   But Donne's servile slander
and flattery served his turn ; he became Royal Chaplain, and finally Dean of St. Paul's.   With the conduct of these contemporaries of his, Jonson and
Donne, Shakespeare's voluntary retirement, when he
was in his prime and at the height of his success
and power, is in marked contrast; and his self-
imposed seclusion seems only explicable by the fact
that the new order of things was thoroughly dis-
tasteful to him.

An argument in favour of his Protestantism
has been drawn from an entry in the Chamberlain's accounts at Stratford, showing that one quart
of sack was given to a preacher at " New Place " in
1614.   But, as a fact, ministers were often quartered on Catholics, who were not sorry to secure
their goodwill in return for the hospitality offered
them.   Thus we read of one " Henry Stamford, a
minister, tutor to Lord Paget's son, who sups at Lord

Montague's (a notorious recusant) at Courdray."[1]
Again, in 1608, we hear of Lord William Howard,
a known recusant, who, being elected a Christmas
Lord, with his tenants and servants at Bampton,
Westmoreland, "most grossly disturbed the minister
in time of Divine Service; the *minister himself grant-
ing toleration*, because he ordinarily dines and sups
at Lord William's table, but never prays with him.
These Christmas misrule men, some of them drank
to the minister when he was at prayers; others
stepped into the pulpit and invited the parishioners
to offer for the maintenance of their sport; others
came into the church disguised; others fired guns
and brought in flags and banners; others sported
themselves with pies and puddings in the church,
using them as bowls in the church aisles; others
played with dogs, using them as they used to
frighten sheep; and all this was done in church and
in time of Divine Service, and the said Lord doth
bring the ministers about him into contempt, scorn,
and derision."[2]

Whether Shakespeare also contributed to bring
the ministers into scorn, contempt, and derision, Mr.
Thornbury, a very strong Protestant, shall tell us.
In his work, "Shakespeare's England," he says:
"The Elizabethan chaplain held an anomalous posi-
tion; he was respected in the parlour for his mission

[1] Dom. Eliz., vol. cxciii. No. 6.
[2] Dom. James I., vol. xl. No. 11.

and despised in the servants' hall for his slovenliness; he was often drunken and frequently quarrelsome; now the butler broke his head in a drinking bout, and now the abigail pinned cards and coneytails to his cassock. To judge from Sir Oliver Martext and Sir Hugh Evans, the parish priests of Shakespeare's day were no very shining lights, and the poet seems to fall back, as in 'Romeo and Juliet' and 'The Two Gentlemen of Verona,' on the ideal priest of an earlier age. It is indeed true that he always mentions the Old Faith with a certain yearning fondness."[1]

Though the poet expresses thus plainly in his writings his predilection for the ancient faith, and though his parents with many of his closest friends and associates were Catholics, and his political sympathies are on the Catholic side, the fact that he allowed both his daughters to be brought up Protestants is a strong argument for his practical indifference in the matter of religion. If he retained the faith of his birth, and there is no proof that he ever abjured it,[2] he must have lived, like so many Catholics of his age, concealing his religious convictions. And his external biography, as far

---

[1] Vol. i., 211.

[2] "Though the names of his fellow-actors are found in the tokenbooks, proving that they received Communion according to law in the parish of St. Saviour's, Southwark, to which the Blackfriars company belonged, Shakespeare's name is not among them."— Collier's "Memoirs of the Principal Actors in Shakespeare's Plays," Introd., 12.

as its meagre outlines extend, would have left us in doubt as to the nature of his creed. We have, however, one further fact positively attested, the only direct evidence, indeed, given us as to his religion, but which shows that, however time-serving and unworthy he may have been as regards his faith in life, it was not so in death. A Gloucester-shire clergyman, Rev. Richard Davies (*ob.* 1708), in his additions to the biographical collection of the Rev. William Fulman, a learned writer and pro-nounced Protestant (*ob.* 1688), expressly states that Shakespeare has a monument at Stratford, " in which he lays a heavy curse on any one who shall remove his bones. He died a Papist." This entry of Davies is often rejected as too remote and un-supported to offer any valid testimony. But we must remember that in the very year of his death, 1616, four priests and one layman suffered for the Faith; so that the ministrations of a priest in Shakespeare's case would have been carefully con-cealed at the time, and even later would have been divulged only with caution, for similar executions continued to take place till 1681. In any case Davies' statement represents, as Mr. Halliwell Phillipps points out, the local tradition of the later half of the seventeenth century; nor does it emanate, as he says, from a man like Prynne, anxious to en-kindle hatred against a stage player by proving him a Romanist; but it is " the testimony of a sober clergyman, who could have had no conceivable motive for deception in what is evidently the casual note of a provincial hearsay.[1]

Lastly, it is objected that if Shakespeare died a Catholic, how could he have been buried in the chancel, the place of honour in the Parish Church? Shakespeare, in virtue of his tenure of half the tithes, was, so to say, lay Rector of Stratford. The chancel belonged to the Corporation, not to the Vicar, and to them, not to him, the fees for burial there were paid. Moreover, just about this time the Corporation was at war with the Vicar. On December 4, 1615, we find the entry: "At this Hall it is agreed that the Chamberlains shall discharge Mr. Rodgers, the Vicar, from receiving any more benefit by burials in the chancel, and that the Chamberlains shall receive it from henceforth towards the repairs of the chancel of the Parish Church, and also to demand of Mr. Rodgers so much as he hath received within the last year."[2] This strife seems to have lasted till May 1617, when Wilson was appointed Vicar. In such a state of things there would have been nothing unlikely in the master of the great house of the town being buried in the place of honour, notwithstanding suspicions of Popery attached to his name. The tombs of Catholic equally with those of Protestant squires are to be found in the chancels of their Parish

---

[1] "Outlines," i. 265.

[2] Halliwell's "Stratford Records," 107.

Churches.   The objection to Shakespeare's Catholicism founded on the site of his grave, sometimes
emphasised as most important, is absolutely incon-
clusive, and leaves untouched the wholly independent evidence in its favour already given.

CHAPTER III.

WHILE Shakespeare's predilection for the old order of things is generally admitted, yet this is said to prove little or nothing as to his religious belief. The traditional mode of thought and speech current in his time forbade, we are told, any scurrilous treatment of the ancient faith, and Catholic modes of expression are to be found in the other dramatists of the period. "The whole English stage at that period," says Gervinus, "never ventured to my knowledge to portray a character even slightly tinged with religious bigotry"; and again, Macaulay writes, "The greatest and most popular dramatists of the Elizabethan age treat religious subjects in a very remarkable manner . . . We remember nothing in their plays resembling the coarse ridicule with which the Catholic religion and its monastics were assailed two generations later by dramatists who wished to please the multitude."[1] Now if the Elizabethan drama was thus conspicuous for its tolerance, the absence of bigotry in Shake-

---

[1] "Burleigh and his Times," Essays, 232, ed. 1877.

speare would of course prove nothing. But the reverse is the case. The stage as a fact was not only a forum for the political strife of the period, as we have seen in the case of the play of " Richard II. ; " it was also the arena for theatrical quarrels, and above all for religious controversy.

In 1588, soon after Shakespeare's arrival in London, Job Throckmorton on behalf of the Puritans attacked the Protestant Episcopacy in a series of pamphlets entitled " Master Marprelate," in which the Bishops were termed " petty Antichrists and swinish rabble." In return, Archbishop Whitgift through Bancroft engaged Nash, Lily, Marlowe, and Greene to satirise the Puritans. A series of scurrilous comedies followed, of so pungent a character [1] that the plays were inhibited and the theatres in the city were closed by order of the Lord Mayor (Harte), 1589. One form of religion, however, might be safely vilified and ridiculed with no danger of any official interference, and that was Catholicism, as we shall proceed to show.

" A Looking Glass for London," written by Thomas Lodge and Robert Greene, and produced in 1591, is an instance of how the stage was used as a Protestant pulpit. The play is an exhortation to London, under the image of Nineveh, to repent of

---

[1] " A Whip for an Ape," Nash's " Countercuffe to Martin Junior," " Pasquil's Return," Lily's " Pap with a Hatchet."

H

its sins.   The last act closes with these words, spoken in the character of the prophet Jonas:—

> "Repent, O London, lest for thine offence
> Thy Shepherd fail, whom mighty God preserve
> That she may bide the pillar of His Church
> Against the stones of Romish anti-Christ,
> The hand of mercy overshade her head,
> And let all the faithful subjects say, Amen!"

Robert Greene again (1593), in his ideal religion which he attributes to Sir Christopher Hatton, writes thus:—

> "Ne was his faith in man's traditions,
> He hated anti-Christ and all his trash;
> He was not led away by superstitions."[1]

George Peele (1589) invites Norris and Drake to lead their armies

> "To lofty Rome,
> There to deface the pride of anti-Christ,
> And pull his paper walls and popery down,
> A famous enterprise for England's strength
> To steel your swords in Avarice's triple crown,
> And cleanse Augean stables in Italy."[2]

John Marston (1598) in his "Scourge of Villany" talks of peevish Papists crouching and kneeling to dumb idols (Pygmalion), and of the monstrous filth of Douay Seminary.   Christopher Marlowe (1593) in his "Faustus" exhibits at length the

[1] "A Maiden's Dream," dedicated to Lady Elizabeth Hatton. 1591.

[2] A farewell entitled, "To the Famous and Fortunate Generals of our English Forces."   1589.

superstition, luxury, and mummery of the Pope and " bald-pate Friars whose *summum bonum* is in ' belly cheer.' "   Faustus, invisible, snatches away at a banquet the Pope's favourite dish and gives him a box on the ear ; and the Friars set to work cursing the ghostly thief " with good devotion."

> " Bell, book, and candle—candle, book, and bell
> Forward and backward to curse Faustus to Hell."

And the whole crazed, cursing pantomime is introduced in what the poet calls a " Dirge for the Dead."

Now Marlowe, though his maxims on religion and morals are wholly unfit for publication, was by no means an ultra-bigot in theory.   On the contrary he thought, according to Barne's information to the king,[1] that if there was any God or good religion it was among the Papists [on account of their ceremonies], and that all " Protestants were hypocritical asses."   Yet he felt that he was much more likely to insure the success of even such a solemn and powerful play as " Faust," by introducing this piece of anti-papal burlesque.

So again in his " Massacre of Paris," published in January 1593, only six months before his death, the poet's object evidently was, says Ulrici, to expose the ambition and the blind, bloodthirsty fanaticism of the Roman Catholic party of the day,

---

[1] A note containing the opinion of one Christofer Marlye concerning his damnable opinions and judgements on Relygion and scorne of God's word. (In 5 Harl. 6858, fol. 320.)

and to exhibit in contrast Protestantism in its glory and future prowess.[1] In this play the Pope promises to ratify aught done in murder, mischief, and tyranny, and the Duke of Guise declares that he has a "Papal dispensation" and pension for the murder of all the Protestants, which is to be effected by 30,000 Friars and Monks from the Monasteries, Priories, Abbeys, and Halls.

Thomas Dekker (1600), who wrote in Shakespeare's later years, presents the same characteristics. The very name of one of his plays, "The Whore of Babylon," sufficiently tells its tale, without need of the introduction to inform us that the general scope of the dramatical poem is "to set forth in tropical and shadowed colours the greatness of our late Queen . . . and on the contrary part, the inveterate malice, treasons, machinations, underminings, and continual bloody stratagems of the purple whore of Rhome."

The above list of quotations might be much augmented, by extracts, for instance, from Webster's "White Devil" and Brookes' "Romeo and Juliet," but enough has, we think, been said to prove that in the works of Shakespeare's contemporaries the bitterness of Protestant bigotry is apparent. In the writings of Shakespeare, on the other hand, as will appear, there is not a disrespectful word of the ancient Church.

We can, however, carry the comparison much

[1] "Shakespeare's Dramatic Art," i. 161. 1876.

further. It was Shakespeare's well-known custom to alter and adapt existing plays ; and by comparing his alterations with the original matter, we discover the strength and direction of his own opinions. One play thus altered and adapted by Shakespeare is that of " King John," a piece commonly instanced as proving beyond question Shakespeare's Protestantism, especially in the two speeches of King John and Pandulph. The latter, the Legate of Innocent III., was sent to call the king to account for refusing Stephen Langton, Archbishop of Canterbury, admission to his See, and for appropriating its revenues. King John replies thus :—

> "*K. John.* What earthly name to interrogatories
> Can task the free breath of a sacred King?
> Thou canst not, Cardinal, devise a name
> So slight, unworthy, and ridiculous,
> To charge me to an answer, as the Pope.
> Tell him this tale ; and from the mouth of England
> Add thus much more,—that no Italian priest
> Shall tithe or toll in our dominions :
> But as we under Heaven are supreme head
> So, under Him, that Great Supremacy,
> Where we do reign, we will alone uphold,
> Without the assistance of a mortal hand :
> So tell the Pope, all reverence set apart
> To him and his usurp'd authority " (iii. 1).

We fully admit the bitterness of this speech. " No good Protestant," as Gervinus says, " denouncing the Papal aggression could have represented more agreeably to his audience the English hatred of Papal intrigue, of Italian indulgences and extortion."

These lines have indeed furnished quotation for anti-Catholic declamations of Prime Ministers, Lord Chancellors, and Archbishops in our own time. Their value as representing Shakespeare's opinions, however, assume a different complexion if we apply one of Aristotle's canons of criticism, and inquire not what the speech is in itself, but who spoke it, and with what end it was spoken. The language and action of a hero may be supposed to represent the poet's type of what is good and noble, and therefore of what he would wish his own language and action to be. The sentiments of a scoundrel, on the other hand, are intentionally drawn as false, base, and treacherous, and therefore presumably not those of the poet's ideal self. Now we are quite content that Shakespeare should be judged by this rule throughout his plays, but this rule must be uniformly applied. According to some critics, if Henry V. speaks as a Catholic, this is only from dramatic necessity, or because the poet is following "Hollinshed's Chronicles," and such speeches therefore give us no clue as to his own judgment. Does John, however, rant in true Exeter Hall fashion, or Duke Humphrey malign Cardinal Beaufort, or an added scene by Fletcher in "Henry VIII." extol Elizabeth, there we have the poet himself. With such a method of argument Shakespeare can be proved as rabid a bigot as these writers desire. But if the canon be impartially applied, an opposite result is, we believe, attained.

In this particular instance is John a hero or a villain? "He begins," says Kreysig, "as an ordinary and respectable man of the world, and he ends as an ordinary criminal; he is not only a villain, but a mean villain. The satanic grandeur of an Edmund or Macbeth is wholly beyond him. His criminal designs are pursued with the instinct common to selfish natures, but without any clear, far-reaching intelligence." [1] His bold defiance proves mere bombast; he ends by eating his words. He humbles himself to the dust before the Legate, and as a penitent receives the crown again at his hands, and his kingdom in fief from the Pope. John's anti-Catholic speeches, then, no more prove Shakespeare a Protestant than the fool's saying in his heart "There is no God," makes David a sceptic.

We now come to the composition of the original play and its alterations by Shakespeare. We must premise that the "Troublesome Reign of King John" which Shakespeare adapted must not be confounded with the earlier "King John" of "Bilious" Bale (1495–1563), a quondam friar who took a wife, became Protestant Bishop of Ossory, and wrote, besides various acrid controversial works, several plays [2] alike doggerel and indecent.

---

[1] "Vorlesungen," i. 462, 559.

[2] One of these is entitled "New Comedy, or Interlude concerning the Three Laws of Nature. Moses and Christ corrupted by the Sodomites, Pharysees, and Papists (1538). London, 1562"; and offers further evidence of the bigotry exhibited by dramatists in Shakespeare's time.

"The Troublesome Reign of King John," the
original of Shakespeare's play, was composed, like
that of Bale, to glorify Protestantism and vilify the
ancient faith.   Shakespeare, in adapting it, had only
to leave untouched its virulent bigotry and its ribald
stories of friars and nuns to secure its popularity,
yet as a fact he carefully excludes the anti-Catholic
passages and allusions, and acts throughout as a
rigid censor on behalf of the Church.   This we
proceed to show.

First, then, in the defiant speeches above quoted
he omits the Tudor claim of spiritual and temporal
supremacy, and the gruesome threat of chopping
heads off after the manner of Henry VIII.   "As I
am king so will I reign next under God.   Supreme
head both over Spiritual and Temporal, and he that
contradicts me in them I will make him hop head-
less."   Again, he suppresses John's contemptuous
reply to the excommunication.   "So, Sir, the more
the fox is curst the better it fares; if God bless
me and my land, let the Pope and his shavelings
curse and spare not;" and also his declared purpose of despoiling the Monasteries, "rousing the
lazy lubbers [the monks] from their cells," and
sending them as prisoners to the Pope.   In Shakespeare's play King John makes no reply to the
prelate after the excommunication is pronounced,
and is singularly silent till he threatens Philip at
the close of the scene.   The excommunication itself,
however, is taken by Hunter and others as con-

clusive proof of Shakespeare's Protestantism.   It
runs thus :—

> " And blessèd shall he be that doth revolt
> From his allegiance to an heretic ;
> And meritorious shall that hand be called,
> Canonisèd and worshipped as a saint,
> That takes away by any secret course
> Thy hateful life " (iii. 1).

These words, we admit, at first sight seem difficult
to reconcile with the theory of Shakespeare's religious opinions which we are defending.   For here
it is Pandulph, the Legate himself, who is giving
utterance to the very doctrines attributed to the
Church by its enemies.   Nor is it any answer to
say that the speech was in substance in the old
play, for our point has been that Shakespeare, in so
far as he follows the original piece, uniformly expur-
gates it of any anti-Catholic virus.   Why then,
while rejecting so much which, as Gervinus says,
was particularly agreeable to the Protestant audiences
of the time, did he allow this one passage to
remain ?

First, then, it might, we think, be urged that a
regard to his personal safety prompted the inclusion
of the speech in question.   His play of " Richard II."
had already, as we have seen, been condemned as
treasonable, and though Hayward was in that
instance the victim, might not Shakespeare himself
be the next victim, if he left no Protestant sentiment to satisfy the royal sensitiveness ?   Such a

motive is indeed unworthy of a bold and fearless
champion of the Faith ; but we have neither regarded
nor represented Shakespeare in such a light, but
rather as one who, whatever his convictions, was
desirous, as far as possible, of avoiding any suspicion
of recusancy.   That he did flatter Elizabeth at
times there seems no doubt.   The imperial votaress
who eludes Cupid's arrow and

> " Passes on
> In maiden meditation, fancy free,"

is universally understood of her, though, if the
comma be omitted, the line might bear, as Simpson
suggests, the very different sense of a mind free
alike from maiden meditation or thoughts of honourable marriage.   In any case, that Shakespeare's
conscience reproached him at times with being
guilty of flattery and falsehood appears from his
confession—

> " I have sworn thee fair, and thought thee bright,
> Who art as black as Hell, as dark as night."
> —*Sonnet* cxlvii.

But yet another motive for the insertion of Pandulph's speech suggests itself.   Might not his words
represent Shakespeare's own feeling with regard to
Elizabeth ?   The lawfulness of tyrannicide was advocated in the sixteenth century by individuals of every
creed, and, though on entirely different grounds, by
Protestants of every shade, as well as by some Catholics.   Melanchthon, the German Reformer, advocated

it in the case of Henry VIII.; Goodman, the Puritan
Divine, in the case of Mary Tudor; and John Kanus,
the Calvinist apostle, in that of that "Jezebel"
Mary Stuart.[1] Some Catholics, as Catesby, Gresham,
Digby, Fawkes, the perpetrator of the Gunpowder
Plot, were of a similar opinion in the case of James.
What then was Elizabeth in Shakespeare's judgment? In the eyes of his kinsfolk, friends, and
associates she was illegitimate, excommunicate, an
usurping, cruel tyrant. Nor would his reiterated
condemnation of rebellion in theory, as fatal to its
perpetrators and disastrous in its results, hinder his
having the warmest sympathy with those who pursued such a line of action. Before the poet's mind, at
the thought of Elizabeth, would have arisen a vision
of victims more numerous than the spectres which
haunted the last moments of Richard III. Arden
and Somerville, his connections; Francis Throckmorton, so cruelly tortured; Babington and Tichborne,
his friends and associates; Mary Stuart, whose shame-

---

[1] Hergenröther, "Church and State," ii. 255-259. The following
extract gives Mr. Andrew Lang's opinion on this subject: "We
cannot be sure that our George Wishart was the man who carried
Brunston's offer (to assassinate Cardinal Beaton for a sum of
money) to Henry; but, if he disapproved of such offers, he was
probably the only public man of the day on either side who looked
on assassination as anything worse than a legitimate political
expedient. Knox regarded it as a thing highly laudable when
performed, of course, by his own party; and it was Knox who
carried the two-handled sword before Wishart in his preaching
progresses. . . . We can only conclude that if Wishart was really
the agent of the conspirators, he was only acting in accordance
with the murderous tenets then held and put in practice by all
parties."—*St. Andrews*, 140-141.

ful death is, according to Simpson, represented in that of Arthur in this very play; Essex, his leader; all these and many others would arise and cry for vengeance. Did he hear their voice? We know not. But it is significant that it is a "blessed spirit" from the other world who lays upon Hamlet the command to put to death the incestuous, usurping king, as a solemn judicial act of retributive justice; and Brutus, the slayer of Cæsar, is admittedly the noblest character in that play. May not Richmond's description of Richard III. be really Shakespeare's judgment on the "virgin queen"?

> "A bloody tyrant and a homicide;
> One rais'd in blood, and one in blood establish'd;
> One that made means to come by what he hath,
> And slaughter'd those that were the means to help him;
> A base foul stone, made precious by the foil
> Of England's chair, where he is falsely set;
> One that hath ever been God's enemy:
> Then if you fight against God's enemy,
> God will, in justice, ward you as His soldiers;
> If you do sweat to put a tyrant down,
> You sleep in peace, the tyrant being slain."
> —*Richard III.*, v. 3.

If these were the poet's own feelings with respect to Elizabeth, they would gain weight by being spoken by a prelate whom Shakespeare portrays as a man of dignity and worth. In any case, the two interpretations suggested do not exclude each other, and Pandulph's speech may have had the double purpose of securing the poet's personal safety, and of expressing to those who knew him his own personal condemnation of the Tudor queen.

In the same scene Pandulph calls on King Philip to break with John, and declares the alliance sworn with him void, but not, as in the old play, because "the oath was made with a heretic." This popular calumny against Catholic doctrine Shakespeare utterly repudiates, and instead he substitutes a careful, accurate, and detailed disquisition on the obligations of an oath, drawn out according to the Church's teaching. An oath is invalid, Pandulph says, when it is contrary to a former oath, or to a prior moral obligation. On both heads Philip's oath to John was invalid. It forswore his previous oath of allegiance to the Church—

> "Therefore thy latter vow, against thy first,
> Is in thyself rebellion to thyself."

And again the calling God to witness that he would attack the Church was by its nature null and void as an oath.

> "It is religion that doth make vows kept,
> But thou hast sworn against religion."

This is not sophistry, as Elze says, but sound morality. So too is the Cardinal's teaching that an oath, though unlawful when sworn to, may by a notable change of circumstance become lawful, and be rightly carried out, not *vi juramenti*, but because of the altered nature of the act; while when the matter of the oath remains unlawful, it is best kept by non-performance.[1]

> "For that, which thou hast sworn to do amiss,
>   Is not amiss when it is truly done ;
>   And being not done, where doing tends to ill,
>   The truth is then most done not doing it" (ii. 1).

Shakespeare depicts Arthur, not as in the old play, a determined claimant to the throne, resisting John to the face with set formal arguments, but as an innocent, timid child devoted to his mother. "Oh, this will make my mother die with grief," is his first thought on being made captive. He yearns for a quiet, sheltered life—

> "So were I out of prison, and kept sheep,
>   I should be merry as the day is long ;
>   .   .   .   .   .
>   Is it my fault that I was Geffrey's son ?"

He pines for some measure of human affection. "I would to Heaven I were your son, so you would love me, Hubert." This conception of Arthur increases the horror of John's crime, and paints his villany in yet blacker colours.

After his victory over the French, John in the old play pours a flood of jeers and invectives over the "mischievous Priest in Italy who calls himself Christ's Vicar," and is now hard at work with Dirges, Masses, Octaves, and Requiems, to assuage the flames

---

[1] On the contrary doctrine that an oath always binds, whatever its nature may be, Herod would have been bound, in deference to his oath, to slay St. John Baptist.

of Purgatory for those who have fallen in battle.
To this succeeds a round of abuse of those princes
who "formerly bore the yoke of the servile priest,"
and in foolish piety submitted to the See of Rome.
Shakespeare simply cuts out all this.   Again he
turns with disgust from the filthy cloister scenes,
and the finding of the nun Alice in the Abbot's
treasure-chest, though all this was, as Gervinus says,
"certainly very amusing to the fresh Protestant feelings of the time."[1]   The old play makes Pandulph
a hypocrite and a Machiavellian simply because he
is a Catholic prelate.   In Shakespeare he appears as
an experienced, far-sighted statesman, but also as a
ghostly Father, full of sympathy for the afflicted.
He grieves for Arthur's capture and pities Constance,
whose maternal beautiful and pathetic appeal proves
that she saw in him a spiritual consoler, and not a
mere cold-hearted, calculating politician—

> "And, Father Cardinal, I have heard you say
> That we shall see and know our friends in Heaven :
> If that be true, I shall see my boy again ;
> For, since the birth of Cain, the first male child,
> To him that did but yesterday suspire,
> There was not such a gracious creature born.
> But now will canker-sorrow eat my bud,
> And chase the native beauty from his cheek,
> And he will look as hollow as a ghost ;
> As dim and meagre as an ague's fit ;
> And so he'll die ; and, rising so again,
> When I shall meet him in the court of Heaven,
> I shall not know him : therefore, never, never
> Must I behold my pretty Arthur more ! " (iii. 4).

---

[1] i. 494 (Burnett's trans.).

Again, Louis, though he changes his tone afterwards, fully recognises the Legate's spiritual character—

> " And even there, methinks, an angel spake :
> Look, where the holy Legate comes apace,
> To give us warrant from the hand of Heaven ;
> And on our actions set the name of right,
> With holy breath " (v. 2).

In his speech to the Dauphin the Cardinal shows his political foresight, and his knowledge of the ways of Providence in the conduct of human affairs. The lost battle and Arthur's imprisonment do not deceive him.[1] He knows " that whiles warm life plays in that infant's veins " John cannot enjoy a peaceful moment—

> " That John may stand, then, Arthur needs must fall ;
> So be it, for it cannot but be so."

He foresees that the King's treatment of Arthur will estrange all hearts from him, and beget a rebellion against the usurper ; and the event fully justifies his prophecy. Arthur is scarcely in the King's power before the latter has engaged his executioner, and from that moment John himself becomes the victim of a vengeful nemesis. According to Kreysig and other critics, John's fall was in no way due " to the excommunication, or the word of the priest, but merely to the natural revulsion of popular feeling consequent on the murder of Arthur. The Pope's

---

[1] We have borrowed largely from Raich, König Johann, *Shakespeare's Stellung zur Katholischen Religion*, 1884, in our interpretation of " King John."

failure is in fact a point in the play." Yet the Church's curse was believed in the Middle Ages to be no idle threat. The Divine vengeance might be delayed, and when it came it might be accomplished, not by any direct supernatural intervention, but by what seemed merely natural means; still its fulfilment was none the less certain. Shakespeare knew this—

> " It is not so with Him that all things knows,
>   As 'tis with us that square our guess by shows :
>   But most it is presumption in us, when
>   The help of Heaven we count the act of men."
>   —*All's Well that Ends Well*, ii. 1.

He develops his plot on these lines ; John wins the first battle. In the eyes of the Cardinal this victory presaged future defeat.

> "No, no ; when Fortune means to men most good,
>   She looks upon them with a threatening eye."

No sooner has the seat of war been shifted to England than Fortune changes. The king is forsaken by the nobles, on account both of the excommunication and of Arthur's murder, and finds himself vanquished. Shakespeare again cuts out the following significant compliment to Henry VIII.'s piety and performing zeal, addressed by John to himself :—

> " Thy sinnes are farre too great to be the man
>   T' abolish Pope and Poperie from thy Realme,
>   But in thy seate, if I may guess at all,
>   A King shall reigne that shall supptesse them all."

I

The prophecy of the Five Moons is stripped of its anti-Papal interpretation, and again, when John seeks reconciliation with the Pope, he addresses the Legate in variance with the old play, without prejudice to his kingly dignity.

> "Thus have I yielded up into your hand
> The circle of my glory."

Whereupon Pandulph gives him back the crown with these words :—

> "From this my hand, as holding of the Pope,
> Your sovereign greatness and authority."

It is no less instructive to remark the poet's representation of Faulconbridge. In the older play he rails at the Pope and the Legate, he discovers the scandals and ludicrous scenes in the monasteries, and is never wearied of declaiming against the arrogance and greed of Rome. In Shakespeare he is represented indeed as ready to levy contributions on the monasteries.

> "Bell, book, and candle shall not drive me back
> When gold and silver beck me to come on."

He is a reckless, careless soldier, but he is not a Protestant bigot. On the contrary, instead of expressing indignant contempt—as he does in the old play— at John's submission to the Legate, by which "friars are made kings, and kings friars," Faulconbridge looks upon Pandulph as the friend of England and

an honourable peace-maker. The anger of the
Bastard is reserved exclusively for France and the
Dauphin—

> "O inglorious league !
> Shall we, upon the footing of our land,
> Send fair-play orders, and make compromise,
> Insinuation, parley, and base truce,
> To arms invasive ?   Shall a beardless boy,
> A cockered silken wanton, brave our fields ?" (v. 1).

And the action of the Cardinal with the Dauphin
justifies the Bastard's view of him. Instead of
mutually cursing each other to their " bellyful" as
in the old plays, in Shakespeare the Cardinal tells
the Dauphin that he looks at but " the outside of
the work," and persuades him though victorious to
offer England terms of honourable peace. The
death of John marks the final contrast between the
two plays. In the older piece the Monk obtains
the Abbot's blessing and the promise of heaven as
the reward for murdering the King. John dies
ascribing all his miseries to his submission to the
Pope, and the Bastard stabs the Abbot. In Shakespeare's play the murderer, " the resolved villain," is
alluded to in one line; and the Bastard, instead of
expressing indignation at the crime, seems rather to
see in it the punishment of a just God, and prays—

> " Withhold thine indignation, mighty Heaven,
> And tempt us not to bear above our power !"

Finally, John dies, not a defiant prophet cursing

Rome, but desolate and despairing, his torments intensified by the impotent sympathy of his friends.

> "There is so hot a summer in my bosom
> That all my bowels crumble up to dust :
>
> .   .   .   .   .   .
>
> And none of you will bid the winter come,
> To thrust his icy fingers in my maw ;
> Nor let my kingdom's rivers take their course
> Through my burned bosom ; nor entreat the north
> To make his bleak winds kiss my parchèd lips
>
> .   .   .   .   .   .
>
> Within me is a hell ; and there the poison
> Is as a friend confined to tyrannise
> On unreprievable-condemnèd blood."

In the Epilogue Shakespeare suppresses a final hit at the Pope, which concludes the old play, and terminates with the stirring words of the true patriot Faulconbridge—

> "Naught shall make us rue
> If England to itself do rest but true ! "

Having now compared the two plays, we can judge of their respective application. The moral of the old play was, that as David was the forerunner of Solomon, so John began the noble work which was to be fully accomplished by the more worthy hands of his descendant Henry VIII.,

> " Whose arms shall reach unto the Gates of Rome
> And with his feet tread down the strumpet's pride,
> That sits upon the Chair of Babylon."

And the play was intended to keep alive the burning hatred of Popery, as was the account of the same transactions in the "Homilies."[1] With Shakespeare all this disappears; in his hands the play becomes a moral and political essay on the events and questions of his time. The slaying of Arthur is closely parallel to that of Mary, Queen of Scots; John, like Elizabeth, first suggests, then commands the deed, afterwards feigns horror at its accomplishment and repudiates the perpetrators. John disowned Hubert, as Elizabeth did Davison,[2] though in both cases the order for the murder was given under the royal hand and seal. In fact Sir Amyas Paulett, the governor of Fotheringay, knowing his mistress's way, refused to carry out Mary's execution till he had Elizabeth's warrant for the same, which angered her much and she complained of him as a "dainty precise fellow" for his insistence. Again, Philip's disinclination after the loss of Angers, to prosecute the war till the prospect of Arthur's death opens his son's claim to the English crown, resembles the delay of Philip II. of Spain to make any serious attack on England till Mary Stuart's death made the Infanta or Duke of Parma possible claimants for the English throne. Louis' intended slaughter of his allies, the English rebel nobles, finds a parallel in the reported intention of the Duke of Medina Sidonia, Commander of the Armada, who declared that, once landed in England, all Catholics and heretics should be one to him, his

[1] Sixth part of the Sermon against Wilful Rebellion.
[2] And as Bolingbroke disowned Exton, the murderer of Richard II.

sword would not discern them! so that he might
make way for his master.[1]

But Shakespeare's "King John" extends beyond
historical parallels and discusses principles.   In the
case of an unsurping ruler, who is to decide between
him and the nation what power has commission,

> "From that supernal Judge, that stirs good thoughts
> In any breast of strong authority
> To look into the blots and stains of right"? (ii. 1).

And the answer is found not in the alliance of
princes which dissolve when

> "That smooth-faced gentleman, tickling Commodity,
> Commodity, the bias of the world,"

insinuates the prospect of gain to any of the contracting parties—but as we think with Raich,[2] in the
action of the Legate.   Here we disagree with Mr.
Simpson, who thinks the play teaches, among other
lessons, the futility of Papal interference in national
disputes.   We know that Pandulph is regarded
generally as being also a slave to commodity, and of
changing sides merely as suited the interests of the
Church.   No doubt those interests were first with
him, but with them were bound up the claims of
justice and right and the liberties of the people.
He is allied with France to enforce John to submit,
but on John's submission he orders, as he was

---

[1] Watson's "Important Considerations," 73.
[2] *Shakespeare's Stellung zur Katholischen Religion*, 167.   Maintz,
1884.

bound, the Dauphin to withdraw his invading force. His mission is completely successful. England is reconciled to the Church, France and England are friends again, the rebel nobles are pardoned, the rightful heir ascends the English throne, and all this is effected by the offices. of the Legate and the action of Faulconbridge, the typical Englishman, of whom the poet is so fond. Shakespeare, then, on our view, appears to have thought that the appeal to an international tribunal in the person of the Pope was not without its advantages ; that the disputes between people and rulers, or between rival sovereigns, found safer, speedier, and more equitable adjustment when settled by a recognised arbitrator, himself the common-head of Christendom, than when decided between the contending parties themselves by rebellion or war.

Shakespeare's Falstaff affords another striking proof of the difference between the attitude of Shakespeare and that of his Protestant contemporaries towards religious questions.

Moreover the stage history of Falstaff furnishes evidence as to the judgment passed by the contemporary public on Shakespeare's religious sympathies.

The identity of Falstaff is disputed, but undoubtedly in " 1 Henry IV." he was originally named Sir John Oldcastle, for Henry calls him " My old lad of the Castle," and the play at first bore that title. Now Sir John Oldcastle, Lord Cobham, who assumed that title through marrying an heiress of the Cobham family, was a notorious Lollard leader, and in the reign of Henry V. twice raised an insurrection of that party. The risings failed, Oldcastle was apprehended, while Henry was in France, found guilty by Parliament of heresy and treason, and put to death at the stake. The character of his religion was sufficiently shown by the blasphemous and indecent writings found in his hiding-place after his capture, yet he was canonised by Bale and Fox as a Puritan or Protestant martyr. Did Shakespeare then intend to reproduce the Lollard champion in Falstaff? The Epilogue of " 2 Henry IV." is quoted as proving the contrary, where it says, " Falstaff may appear again and die of a sweat, unless he be already killed by your hard opinions, for Oldcastle died a martyr, and this is not the man!" But these words are not conclusive. It is quite possible that Shakespeare's caricature of a Protestant hero gave offence, and that he felt constrained to expressly deny the identity of Falstaff and Oldcastle, while the proof which he advanced in support of his denial—viz. that Oldcastle died a martyr, was nothing more than irony. In any case, the popular mind was so strongly convinced, in spite of the changed title of the play, that Falstaff was Oldcastle, that in November 1599, Anthony Munday, Michael Drayton, R. Wilson, and R. Hathwaye brought out their play of " The History of Sir John Oldcastle, the good Lord Cobham," to rehabilitate

Sir John in public estimation, and in 1600 they published it with Shakespeare's name on the title-page, a forgery which they were obliged almost immediately to suppress. Their Prologue expressly warns the audience of what they were *not* to expect—

> "The doubtful title, gentlemen, prefixed
> Upon the argument we have in hand,
> May breed surprise, and wrongfully disturb
> The peaceful quiet of your settled thoughts.
> To stop which scruple let this brief suffice ;
> It is no pampered glutton we present,
> Nor aged counsellor to youthful sin !
> But one whose virtue shone above the rest,
> A valiant martyr. . . .
> . . . Let fair truth be graced
> Since forged invention former time defaced." [1]

The fair fame of the martyr had been disgraced by a calumnious description of him as a pampered glutton, and an aged counsellor to youthful sin ! This is an evident allusion to the words, "That villanous, abominable misleader of youth, Falstaff, that old white-bearded Satan." In the play, mention is made of Falstaff, but only with the view to separating his personality more completely from the hero Oldcastle, who is made a model of a fine old English gentleman—charitable, chivalrous, and slightly given to preaching. The ruffian of the play is a priest, Sir John of Wrotham, who combines with his sacerdotal character the part of a highway-

---

[1] In the original quartos Falstaff is more profane than in the modern editions copied from the folio of 1623.

man on Blackheath, in company with a disreputable woman.[1]   The priest is in fact a grosser compound of iniquity than Falstaff, but without the latter's wit. The villain is the Bishop of Rochester, an impersonation of the stage Jesuit of the day.   The drama is quite vixenish in its Protestantism.   It would be difficult to say why the rehabilitation of Oldcastle should have been made in this spirit of tit-for-tat, if, as is asserted, there had been no intention manifested in Shakespeare's play of slandering his memory. Whether the Falstaff of " Henry IV." had ever been called Oldcastle or not, it is perfectly certain that as late as 1599 theatrical audiences still understood that Falstaff stood for Oldcastle.

Shakespeare's portrait of Falstaff as a Puritan and sanctimonious hypocrite is in keeping with his ordinary treatment of that sect, and explains why the public so readily identified Falstaff in that character.   The pharisaical Lord Angelo is outwardly a "sainted deputy, within foul as hell." Justice Shallow, the Puritan—a portrait drawn from Justice Lucy—is austere-looking, mere flesh and bone, " a forked radish "—yet Falstaff says of him, " This same starved justice hath done nothing but prate to me of the wildness of his youth and the feats he hath done, yet every third word a lie." So in " Twelfth Night," Malvolio is outwardly morose, secretly amatory.   Now Falstaff is drawn on these lines and is essentially Shakespeare's own creation.

[1] The Doll Tearsheet of Shakespeare's play.

In the " Famous Victories," from which Shakespeare borrowed incidents for his two parts of "Henry IV.," Oldcastle appears as one of the boon companions of the wild Prince, but his part is quite insignificant. He opens his mouth on two occasions only. He goes to visit the Prince, who is, as he supposes, in prison, for boxing the Chief-Justice's ears ; he meets Hal by the way and says, " I am glad to see your Grace at liberty; I was come, I, to visit you in prison." Hal makes an answer which concludes with the statement "that if the old king were dead, all should be kings." To which Oldcastle, " He is a good old man: God take him to His mercy sooner." From these bare hints Shakespeare seems to have derived the idea of painting a hoary hypocrite, leading his companions to sin, yet descanting the while on virtue ; and such at least is Falstaff in the first part of " Henry IV." His speeches and repartees teem with scriptural allusions—the special characteristic of the Lollards, who made the Bible the weapon of their attack against Church, Priests, and property — and his arguments abound with that peculiar amplification and affectation of Hebrew parallelism distinctive of Puritan pulpit oratory. We will quote some of them.

He poses as the defender of Hal's character, and the victim of his evil ways.

Act i. *sc.* 2.—" An old Lord of the Council rated me the other day in the street about you, Sir ; but I regarded him not: and yet he talked very wisely; but I regarded him not; and yet he talked wisely, and in the street too (Prov. i. 20). . . . Thou art able to corrupt a saint. Thou hast done much harm upon me, Hal—God forgive thee for it! Before I knew thee, Hal, I knew nothing; and now am I, if a man should speak truly, little better than one of the wicked. . . . I'll be damned for never a king's son in Christendom."

Then comes a gibe at free-will and good works in the person of Poins—

"If men were to be saved by merit, what hole in hell were hot enough for Poins? (who calls himself Monsieur Remorse)."

Again to Poins, on his undertaking to enlist the Prince in the Gad's Hill robbery, is addressed a travesty of St. Paul's words to the Romans—

"May'st thou have the spirit of persuasion, and he the ears of profiting, that what thou speakest may move, and what he hears may be believed," &c. (Rom. x. 14, 17).

His marvellous expostulation with Hal teems with texts.

Act ii. *sc.* 4.—"I would I were a weaver! I could sing psalms (James v. 13) or anything. . . . Clap to the doors: watch to-night, pray to-morrow (Mark xiv. 38), a plague of sighing and grief! it blows a man up like a bladder. . . . There is a thing, Harry, which thou hast often heard of, and it is known to many in our land by the name of pitch: this pitch, as ancient writers do report, doth defile (Eccles. xiii. 1, 7), so doth the company thou keepest —for Harry, now I do not speak unto thee in drink, but

in tears; not in pleasure, but in passion; not in words
only, but in woes also (Rom. xiii. 13).   I see virtue in
his looks.   If then the tree may be known by the fruit,
as the fruit by the tree (Matt. xii. 33), then, peremptorily
I speak it, there is virtue in that Falstaff. . . . If to be
old and merry be a sin, then many an old host that I
know is damned: but if to be fat is to be hated, then
Pharaoh's lean kine are to be loved " (Gen. xli. 19).

Of Bardolph's red nose and face he says—

Act iii. *sc.* 3.—" I never see thy face but I think upon hell-
fire, and Dives that lived in purple (Luke xvi. 19).   Thou
knowest in the state of innocency, Adam fell; and what would
poor Jack Falstaff do in the days of villany?   Thou seest
I have more flesh than another man; and therefore more
frailty."

Act iv. *sc.* 2.—"Slaves as ragged as Lazarus in the
painted cloth, where the glutton's dogs licked his sores
. . . tattered prodigals, lately come from swine-keeping,
from eating draff and husks " (Luke xv. 19).

What then, it may be asked, was the secret
of his influence and the fascination he exercised over Prince Hal.   Falstaff was not merely
a sanctimonious hypocrite like Angelo or Malvolio,
nor a common sensualist or coward or braggart
like Pistol, Nym, or Bardolph; but he was an
extraordinary compound of opposites,[1] and he
could exhibit either side at once in perfection and
with the most complete propriety, much as we may
suppose Leicester did.   An arrant coward, yet he

---

[1] *Cf.* Maurice Morgann, "Essay on the Character of Sir John
Falstaff." 1787.

could draw his rapier and clear Dame Quickly's parlour; a consummate liar, yet a great stickler for truth. A wild braggart, he could draw distinctions and deny the major of a syllogism with the accuracy of a logician. Old in years, and fat, yet he could always pose as a leader of youth. Constantly duped, he was ever outwitting others. His versatility and powers of subterfuge and excuse were simply inexhaustible. To the Chief-Justice's reproach for his scandalous life, seeing his grey hairs and that every part of him was blasted with antiquity, he replied that he was born at three o'clock in the afternoon, with white hair and a round belly, and had cracked his voice with singing anthems; that he was old only in judgment and understanding (1 Cor. xiv. 20), and could caper any man for a thousand marks. He excused his flight at Gad's Hill by saying that he was as valiant as a lion, a Hercules by nature, but a coward by instinct, and that it was instinct which forbade him touching a true Prince. Though he had led Henry into every kind of dissipation, he could personate Henry IV. at a moment's notice and draw tears from his hearers by the pathetic, dignified reproof he administered to the young scapegrace, while he admonishes him to keep one companion if he would persevere in virtue—" a good portly man. I remember his name is Falstaff." And he could act the part of a virtuous man perfectly. Mrs. Ford says of him, "He would not swear;

praised women's modesty, and gave such orderly and well-behaved reproof to all unseemliness, that I would have sworn his disposition would have gone to the truth of his words, but they do no more adhere and keep place together than the 100th Psalm to the tune of 'Green Sleeves.'" Falstaff is impudently shameless only with those who know him well, and whom he knows have seen through him. With strangers he is modest, cajoling, adroit, even edifying and devout. "He is," as he says, "Jack with his familiars, John with his brothers, and Sir John with all the world."

Such was the man who exercised such a baneful spell over Prince Henry in his youth, but the hour of grace struck and Henry obeyed. It was a call to his duty as a king, and his manhood awoke to its true dignity. The change in him was to be no half measure but complete, and when Falstaff approached, befooling, he was met with that word from Henry.

> "I know thee not, old man : fall to thy prayers ;
> How ill white hairs become a fool, and jester !
> I have long dreamed of such a kind of man,
> So surfeit, swell'd, so old, and so profane ;
> But being awake, I do despise my dream.
> Make less thy body, hence, and more thy grace ;
> Leave gormandising ; know the grave doth gape
> For thee thrice wider than for other men.
> Reply not to me with a fool-born jest ;
> Presume not that I am the thing I was :
> For God doth know, so shall the world perceive,
> That I have turned away my former self ;
> So will I those that kept me company."

And he forbids him to approach within ten miles of his person, but makes him a suitable allowance, and promises him advancement if he tries to reform.

Falstaff never reappears, but we read of his death.[1] The classic scene in Dame Quickly's house—his nose sharp as a pen, and a babbling of green fields, fumbling with the sheets and smiling at his fingers' ends; and he cried out, "God! God! God!" three or four times, and "I to comfort him bade him not think of God." . . . "So a bade me lay more clothes on his feet. And I put my hand into his bed and felt them, and they were cold as any stone." And he said, "the devil would have him about women." And he talked about the "Whore of Babylon," the common Puritan term for Rome. The old vice, the old cant, and the grip of death silencing both. The Lollard martyr preaches indeed to the very end.

With Falstaff we will conclude our comparison of Shakespeare and his contemporaries. We have as we think sufficiently shown that the poet defends the doctrines and ministers of the Church, while his fellow - dramatists reviled them, and that his satire of one at least of the Protestant heroes of

---

[1] Falstaff's death is related in "Henry V.," scene 3. The Falstaff resuscitated in the subsequent play of the "Merry Wives of Windsor" is merely an amorous old fool, the butt and dupe of his intended victims. The character was created at Elizabeth's bidding, to show the fat knight in love, the one part she would have known, had she understood him, he could not possibly perform. *Cf.* Braun's "Shakespeare," i., 244.

the day, in the person of the fat knight, was so keen and well directed that the supporters of the new creed felt themselves bound to undertake their champion's defence. Thus in attack as in defence Shakespeare stands alone to manifest his sympathies with the ancient faith.

CHAPTER IV.

THE English historical plays extend with broken intervals from the reign of King John to that of Henry VIII. They may be regarded, therefore, as embracing a period marked by the rise, establishment, and fall of the feudal system in England. Shakespeare's chief, if not sole, authority is "Hollinshed's Chronicles"; but the pre-existing matter is fused in the crucible of the poet's genius, and recast according to the requirements of the historic drama. In a composition of this kind the events themselves, their chronological sequence, their mutual relation and development, the historical reality of the characters as adapted to the personages named, are of comparative unimportance. The aim of the dramatist is not to narrate in order transient and contingent facts, but to portray what is permanent and necessary, the true principles of life and conduct, the spirit working within, which is manifested only partially in outward effects.

The historic plays are not then intended to represent an accurate chronicle of the past. Indeed, in some instances, the poet notably departs from the region of fact. As elsewhere he imparts Christian thought to Pagan times, so here, as in King John, Protestant ideas are found in a Catholic age. He misrepresents individual characters and commits many anachronisms, but all the while he perfectly delineates the constituent elements of the ideas or institutions his personages are intended to portray. Thus the prerogatives of royalty, their source, nature, and extent, the conditions of its lawful tenure; the position and duties of the nobles; the relations of the Church to the State; the reasons which justify rebellion; the shibboleths of the popular demagogue, the causes of a nation's decay, these and other important elements of statecraft appear in the historic plays.

The poet's teaching on the source, prerogative, and restrictions of royalty is very explicit. The king is the deputy, anointed by Heaven, and rules only in God's name. He is the steward or minister of the divine law, and cannot be deposed by his subjects as if he were merely their delegate or executor. Thus the Bishop of Carlisle asks, regarding the proposed deposition of Richard II. :—

> " And shall the figure of God's Majesty,
> His Captain, Steward, Deputy, elect,
> Anointed, crownèd, planted many years,
> Be judg'd by subject and inferior breath ?"
> —*Richard II.*, iv. 1.

The anointing of the sovereign, in the ceremony of consecration, was not in the poet's mind a mere form, but a sacred function, conferring real power from God, and ensuring the divine protection. Thus Richard exclaims :—

> "Not all the water in the rough, rude sea
> Can wash the balm from an anointed king :
> The breath of worldly men cannot depose
> The deputy elected by the Lord :
> For every man that Bolingbroke hath press'd
> To lift shrewd steel against our golden crown,
> God for His Richard hath in heavenly pay
> A glorious angel : then, if angels fight,
> Weak men must fall : for heaven still guards the right."
> —*Ibid.*, iii. 2.

It was indeed the common Catholic doctrine that while the King obtained the *jus ad rem*, the right to reign or his title to the crown, by inheritance or election, his possession of the crown or his actual reign, *jus in re*, began with the sacred unction, which was administered only after the coronation oath had been taken.[1] Elizabeth and her advisers recognised the necessity of conforming, at least outwardly, to this function, as establishing beyond question her right to the crown. She took the usual oath of Christian sovereigns to defend the Catholic faith and to guard the rights and immunities of the Church, and was duly anointed. But when she withdrew to be vested in the royal robes, she is reported to have said to her ladies-in-waiting, " Away with you, this oil is stinking."[2]

[1] Hergenröther, " Church and State," Engl. trans., i. 261.
[2] Sanders, "Anglican Schism," 243. 1877.

In keeping with the sanctity which the poet attaches to the consecration of a king, is the testimony he gives to the miraculous power attributed to sovereigns of healing by their touch the disease known as "king's evil." In "Macbeth" he introduces the following scene, in no way required by the dramatic development of the play, to relate the miraculous and prophetic gifts of St. Edward, and he brings in a physician to testify to the supernatural character of the cures effected :—

> "*Malcolm.* Comes the king forth, I pray you?
> *Doctor.* Ay, Sir : there are a crew of wretched souls,
> That stay his cure : their malady convinces
> The great assay of art ; but at his touch,
> Such sanctity hath Heaven given in his hand,
> They presently amend.
> *Malcolm.*   I thank you, Doctor.
> *Macduff.* What's the disease he means?
> *Malcolm.*   'Tis called the ' evil' :
> A most miraculous work in this good king :
> Which often, since my here-remain in England,
> I have seen him do.   How he solicits Heaven,
> Himself best knows : but strangely-visited people,
> All swoln and ulcerous, pitiful to the eye,
> The mere despair of surgery, he cures ;
> Hanging a golden stamp about their necks,
> Put on with holy prayers : and 'tis spoken,
> To the succeeding royalty he leaves
> The healing benediction.   With this strange virtue,
> He hath a heavenly gift of prophecy ;
> And sundry blessings hang about his throne,
> That speak him full of grace."—*Macbeth*, iv. 3.

James I. is said by Davenant to have written Shakespeare an autograph letter of thanks for this passage. It is no argument, however, against the reality of the gift that non-Catholic kings should have claimed to possess it. Healing, as well as prophecy, belongs to that class of gifts termed *gratiæ gratis datæ*, or gifts given for the benefit of others, which are conferred independently of the sanctity of their recipient.[1] Balaam prophesied, so did Caiaphas, as the Gospel expressly tells us.[2] The "golden stamp" of the passage just quoted refers to the gold medals which, according to the records of the Tower, Edward I. in 1272 gave to the sick persons he had touched. Dr. Johnson, when an infant three years old, was himself touched for "the evil" by Queen Anne, of whom he had a solemn recollection "as of a lady in diamonds and a long black hood." The experiment was made on the advice of Sir John Floyer, a celebrated physician of Lichfield.[3] Dean Swift is also said to have believed in the virtue of the regal touch.[4] The Protestant sovereigns from Queen Elizabeth omitted the sign of the Cross in the ceremony.

Although the sovereign's right to rule is from God, that right is conditioned, like that of any other human authority, by his exercising his power according to the divine law, whose administrator he is. Even Richard II. recognises this clearly.

[1] Matt. vii. 22, 23.
[2] John xi. 51.
[3] Boswell's "Life of Johnson," i. 13.
[4] Wilkes' "Shakespeare," 329.

> " Show us the hand of God,
> That hath dismiss'd us from our stewardship ;
> For well we know, no hand of blood and bone
> Can gripe the sacred handle of our sceptre,
> Unless he do profane, steal, or usurp."
>
> —*Richard II.*, iii. 3.

How far, in the eyes of the poet's friends and associates, Henry VIII. or Elizabeth had been guilty of these three offences—profaning, stealing, usurping—has been already shown. As a rule, the poet seems to regard the deposition of a tyrannical or corrupt ruler, not as a right for courts to enforce, but as a fatal and natural consequence of his misdeeds. This is so in the case of King John ; and the same apparently natural nemesis is seen in the close of the reigns of Richard II., Henry VI., and Richard III. The nobles and people are alienated by misgovernment and crime : the crowning delinquency is often the murder of the heir to the throne, as in the case of both King John and Richard III. Henry VI., by disinheriting his son, really decrees his own downfall. The murder of Richard II. brands the conscience not only of Henry IV. but also of Henry V. What Shakespeare's judgment was, as we suppose, of Elizabeth's judicial murder of Mary, Queen of Scots, has been already stated.

After the murder or disinheriting of the rightful heir, the prince's abuses of his power are ordinarily the causes of his fall. Disregard of the rights of land tenure, " farming his realm," as if he were "landlord, not King of England," and "binding the whole land with rotten parchment bonds"; injustice to the nobles, fining them for old quarrels; the encouragment of flatterers and favourites, "caterpillars who waste the State"; employment of suborned informers; unjust and oppressive taxation of the Commons, with new exactions such as "blanks and benevolences"; inaccurate budgets with prospective bankruptcy; the favouritism of evil-doers, only because of their growing power; the waste of time and opportunities, to the grievous injury of the realm—these, and such like causes, produce the downfall of the king. The royal power, even when undefined by strict constitutional limits, carries with it obligations, for which the ruler is responsible to the nation and to God.

As Richard II., though rightful king, loses his throne by his spendthrift, reckless course; so Henry IV., though an usurper, retains the crown he has seized through skilful statecraft. The "vile politician, Bolingbroke," is incomparably a better ruler than Richard was, or Hotspur would have been, with his proposed division of England into three kingdoms, a retrograde step towards another heptarchy. In Bolingbroke's instructions to his son on the surest way of establishing his throne, little weight is attached to questions of policy, but the personal deportment of the prince is the all-important matter. Prince Henry is emulating Richard in his downward course by frequenting vulgar company, "mingling his royalty with capering fools," "making himself as common as a cuckoo in June, heard but not regarded." Whereas Bolingbroke showed himself but seldom, provoked interest by his retirement, and when he did appear, his presence was "like a robe pontifical, ne'er seen but wondered at." The crown is thus considered, not as a birthright or heirloom, but as the prize of the ablest and most popular competitor. Bolingbroke's intended crusade, announced at the end of "Richard II." "to wash the blood from off his guilty head," is continued in "1 Henry IV.," with the utilitarian purpose of knitting together the unravelled threads of faction and making them "in mutual ranks, march all one way."

In "2 Henry IV." the king's conscience is yet more uneasy, but though repentant, he still looks to securing to himself and his family the crown he had usurped. He comforts his son with the assurance that as he will inherit the crown by peaceable succession, he will not be obliged, like his father, to cut off the friends who had helped him to gain it; and he again urges the policy of keeping the nobles engaged in foreign wars till the memory of his defective title is obliterated.

Shakespeare's teaching on the conditioned rights of the crown, its responsibilities towards its subjects, and the punishment which overtakes an unjust or incompetent ruler, are, it will be observed, wholly opposed to the absolutism claimed by Henry VIII. or

Elizabeth, as also to the Stuarts' pretension to divine, inalienable right. At the same time his treatment of Cade's rising shows him to have been no believer in the sovereignty of the people, a doctrine fully developed in the trial and execution of Charles I. only thirty-three years after the poet's death. As Coleridge says, " he gives utterance neither to the servile flatteries of Beaumont and Fletcher, nor to the Republican sneers of Massinger."[1] To the sovereign he attributes sanctity, majesty, glory, as the source, under God, of the life and power of the State. But he is to use his power not for his personal gain, but for his subjects' good, and when he abuses his trust his power is forfeited.

The religious loyalty which, while indignant at a sovereign's crimes and follies, still remains faithful to its pledged word, is beautifully drawn out in the character of York in "Richard II." So is the deep personal devotion felt by the poor for their sovereign in misfortune and for all belonging to him, a truly Catholic instinct, as we can learn from the pages of history. Coleridge says that it is by the introduction of such incidents as the following scene of Richard II. and his groom, that Shakespeare's plays are dramas, not histories.

> "*Groom.* I was a poor groom of thy stable, king,
> When thou wert king; who, travelling towards York,
> With much ado, at length have gotten leave
> To look upon my sometime master's face.

---

[1] "Literary Remains," ii. 178.

O, how it yearned my heart when I beheld
In London streets that coronation-day,
When Bolingbroke rode on roan Barbary !
That horse, that thou so often hast bestrid ;
That horse, that I so carefully have dressed !
   King Richard. Rode he on Barbary ?"
              —*Richard II.*, v. 5.

Again, with all his reverence for royalty, no preacher has proclaimed the emptiness of earthly greatness more strongly than Shakespeare, or the miseries weighing upon kings by reason of their greatness. Henry IV. complains how the mere cares of royalty drive sleep away. "Perfumed chambers," "canopies of state," "sweetest melodies" cannot obtain for the monarch the rest found by the meanest of his subjects on "uneasy pallets," "loathsome beds," "amidst buzzing night-flies." Henry VI., ever fearful of some traitorous attack, envies the shepherd.

"Gives not the hawthorn bush a sweeter shade
To shepherds, looking on their silly sheep,
Than doth a rich embroider'd canopy
To kings, that fear their subjects' treachery ?"
              —3 *Henry VI.*, ii. 5.

And Richard II. lives expecting the death which mocks his greatness.

"Within the hollow crown,
That rounds the mortal temples of a king,
Death keeps his court ; and there the antic sits,
Scoffing his state and grinning at his pomp ;
Allowing him a breath, a little scene
To monarchise, be fear'd, and kill with looks ;

> Infusing him with self and vain conceit,—
> (As if this flesh, which walls about our life,
> Were brass impregnable) ; and humoured thus,
> Comes at the last, and with a little pin
> Bores through his castle wall, and—farewell, king !"
> —*Richard II.*, iii. 2.

Naturally, then, the same Richard longs to exchange his royal pomp for religious retirement and peace, but in what a Catholic tone he speaks !

> " I'll give my jewels, for a set of beads :
> My gorgeous palace, for a hermitage ;
> My gay apparel, for an alms-man's gown ;
> My figured goblets, for a dish of wood ;
> My sceptre, for a palmer's walking-staff ;
> My subjects, for a pair of carvèd saints ;
> And my large kingdom for a little grave,
> A little little grave, an obscure grave."—*Ibid.*, iii. 3.

We will now consider Shakespeare's view of the nobility. A single thread of history, such as the subject before us, "manifests conspicuously," says Simpson, "the philosophic unity running through the chronicle plays. With the exception of 'Edward III.' and Marlowe's 'Edward II.,' both often attributed in part to Shakespeare, the numerous historical plays by other authors, for instance Heywood's ' Edward IV.' or ' Elizabeth,' would add nothing to the completeness of the picture of the nobility presented in the Shakespearian series." The constitutional origin and status of the nobles, their power and greatness, and the causes of their decay are alike clearly set forth.

In " King John," the nobles appear as deriving

their rights, not from the great Charter, which the
poet ignores, but from common law and immemorial
custom.   The Barons are the King's Peers; his
judges when he breaks the laws of Church or State,
and the executors of their judgments, as far as they
have the power.   Thus they are represented in
"King John" as resisting the encroachments of
the crown, and their rebellion, in alliance with the
French king, is dictated by motives of religion,
duty, and patriotism.   But the poet is careful to
point out in the speech of Salisbury the evils entailed by even justifiable rebellion.   The uncertainty of conscience as to what is lawful or not in
rebellion, the "healing one wound only by making
many," the necessity of fighting with one's own
countrymen and forming alliances with their enemies, these are some of the evils of insurrection.

> "But such is the infection of the time,
>   That, for the health and physic of our right,
>   We cannot deal but with the very hand
>   Of stern injustice and confusèd wrong."
> —*King John*, v. 2.

Hence Salisbury readily profits by the opportunity
afforded by the French king's intended treachery
to rejoin John.

> (We will) "like a bated and retirèd flood,
>   Leaving our rankness and irregular course,
>   Stoop low within those bounds we have o'erlooked
>   And calmly run on in obedience,
>   Even to our ocean, to our great King John."
> —*Ibid.*, v. 4.

The "ocean," though a strong expression, is the natural term of the metaphor of an overflowing river, and John was now reconciled to the Church, and had given the pledges demanded.

Again, the poet represents the suspicion which always attaches to the rebel, or even to those who were regarded as disaffected, however just their cause of complaint may have been. This is why the Dauphin in "King John" had determined to murder all his English allies.

> " Paying the fine of rated treachery
> Even with the treacherous fine of all your lives."
>
> —*Ibid.*, v. 3.

For the same reason the deposed Richard warns Northumberland that Henry IV.

> "Shall think that thou, which know'st the way
> To plant unrightful kings, wilt know again,
> Being ne'er a little urg'd, another way
> To pluck him headlong from the usurped throne.
> The love of wicked men converts to fear ;
> That fear to hate."—*Richard II.*, v. 1.

Worcester speaks in the same strain :—

> " Bear ourselves as even as we can,
> The king will always think him in our debt ;
> And think we think ourselves unsatisfied,
> Till he hath found a time to pay us home."
>
> —1 *Henry IV.*, i. 3.

And afterwards :—

> " Look how we can, or sad, or merrily,
> Interpretation will misquote our looks,
> And we shall feed like oxen at a stall,
> The better cherish'd, still the nearer death."
>
> —*Ibid.*, v. 2.

This makes Mowbray and the Archbishop of York say :—

> " Were our royal faiths martyrs in love,
> We shall be winnow'd with so rough a wind,
> That even our corn shall seem as light as chaff."
> —2 *Henry IV.*, iv. 1.

Henry IV. warns his son to the same effect—

> " I had many living, to upbraid
> My gain of it (the crown) by their assistances ;
> Which daily grew to quarrel. . . ."—*Ibid.*, iv. 5.

Their merits were too great to be rewarded as they deserved. Unrewarded, they would be as faithless to their new master as to their old. Nothing was left than that they should experience the truth of Commines' saying, " Il perd souvent d'avoir trop servi."

The circumstances of Shakespeare's time explain why these warnings should be so often repeated. The English Catholics in exile found that foreign countries offered them no secure asylum against the suspicion which had dogged them at home. According to Camden, the Earl of Westmoreland and the other English resident in the Netherlands were compelled, in 1575, by the Governor Requesens, at the request of Wilson, the British ambassador, to quit the country. Three years later, on March 22, 1578, the seminary of Douay was dissolved, all English capable of bearing arms being forced, by order of the magistrate, to leave the town within two days. The Rector of the University and the Governor alike spoke in favour of the College, alleging the insignificant number of the residents and their peaceful behaviour; but all to no purpose. Elizabeth, through her agents, had inspired the townspeople with the conviction that the English exiles, lay or clerical, were really agents or spies in the French interest, and must be expelled. Such then was the position of English Catholics in exile. When at home they had been represented as traitors corresponding with Spain; abroad, in Spanish territory, they were suspected as agents of the " French." [1]

In England their position was indeed desperate. However loyal they might declare themselves to be, or have proved themselves, as in the case of the Armada, their lives were in constant jeopardy, their property was being ever impoverished by monthly fines, and their homes and family life were rendered almost insupportable, owing to the domiciliary visits to which they were frequently subjected. "The arrival of a stranger, the groundless information of an enemy, a discharged servant, a discontented tenant, the hope of plunder or of reward, the forfeiture of the estate following the apprehension of a priest, were sufficient to procure the intrusion of the pursuivants." [2] Under these intolerable sufferings, where could they look for relief? Constitutional redress was hopeless, the law was their chief torturer. Their only hope seemed to lie in active resistance,

1 " Troubles of our Catholic Forefathers," third series, p. 108.
2 Lingard, viii. 360. 1823.

strengthened by foreign support. The example of "intriguing in foreign politics," as it was called, was set them by the Government. To support her own throne, Elizabeth helped the French rebels after the death of Henri II.; she assisted the Netherlanders against Philip; she interfered in Scotland from the very beginning of her reign, imprisoned the Queen, Mary Stuart, and finally beheaded her. She set up James VI. against his mother, Francis of Valois in Brabant against Philip, Antonio in Portugal also against Philip, and from the first recognised and supported Henry of Navarre as heir and King of France.[1]

It need cause no surprise, then, that Catholic nobles should be disposed to join in alliance with foreign princes to further their cause by procuring a successor to the throne favourable to, or at least tolerant of their own religion. Elizabeth herself had received the addresses of Philip II. of Spain, the Duke of Anjou, and Don John of Austria. There was no reason therefore to suppose that the fact of a prince being a foreigner and a Catholic would be an insuperable objection to his acceptance by the country at large. In fact the English-Spanish party hoped that the Infanta might marry Essex, the most popular Protestant leader of the time. The following lists of the parties to which the nobility belonged in Shakespeare's time is given by Simpson, from documents now preserved in the State Paper office, which had

---

[1] Philopater, 141–143.

been supplied to the Government by their agent abroad, and they show the extent to which the disaffection was spread.

In these lists the nobility and gentry are carefully distinguished as Catholic, Indifferent, or Protestant, not so much for their religious opinions as for the side they took in politics.   Among the Catholics we find the Earls of Northumberland, Shrewsbury, Derby (with his son Lord Strange), Arundel (with his brothers Audley and Lord William Howard), and Westmoreland ; the Lords Vaux, Mountjoy, Paget, Windsor, Mordant, Henry Howard, Dacres of the North, Stourton, Lumley, Wharton, Berkeley, Sheffield, Morley, Kildare (with his son Garrett), and Compton ; the Knights Bapthorpe, Malery, Stapleton, Gerard, Catesby, Tresham, Fitzherbert, Peckham, Godwin, Herbert, Bretherton, Hastings, Browne, Poyntz, Bottley, Arundel, Conway, Petre, Baker, Inglefield, and Winter.

The list of " Indifferents " comprises Lords Rutland, Oxford, Bath, Lincoln, Cumberland, Cobham, Chandos, Delaware, Charles Howard, Cheney, Dacres of the South, Northampton, and Bromley the Chancellor.

That of " Protestants " contains only the names of Leicester, Huntingdon, Warwick, Bedford, Kent, Hunsdon, Burghley, Buckhurst-Grey of Wilton, and Russell, with Sir Francis Walsingham and Sir Francis Knowles.

This list belongs to some year between 1580 and

1588. In 1602 Watson (*Quodlibets*, p. 211) adds up the list of English houses who were all more or less pledged supporters of the Infanta of Spain or of Arabella Stuart, lineal descendant of Henry VII., and looked to the settlement of the succession by foreign arbitration. It includes those of Winchester, Oxford, Arundel, Westmoreland, Northumberland, Lincoln, Cumberland, Shrewsbury, Pembroke, Derby, Hertford, Huntingdon, Leicester, Worcester, Bath, Kent, Sussex, Nottingham, and Montague. Watson's statement must, however, be taken with reserve. He was a violent anti-Spanish partisan, and was anxious to portray in the strongest colours the influence of the Jesuits on behalf of the Spanish party. Watson was put to death for an alleged co-operation in Raleigh's plot against James I. (1603), and is said to have retracted his accusation against the Jesuits and others before he died.[1]

If the country were thus divided and disaffected, and an adherent to the Catholic party might be involved at any moment in an active outbreak, Shakespeare, representing as he did the very "form and pressure of the age," must have had a decided opinion upon the expediency or impolicy of a rising. Now we have seen how strongly he urges the disastrous consequences of such an attempt, yet he makes one exception in its favour, that is when the movement is authorised by religion. Then, and then alone, insurgents act with a good conscience,

---

[1] Dodd's "Church History," ii. 379, ed. 1739.

for they are obeying authority and the movement
succeeds.   Thus the poet makes Morton declare
(" 2 Henry IV.," i. 1), that the first rebellion of the
Percies had failed, because not blessed by religion;
but that the second, under the auspices of the Archbishop, would fare otherwise.

> " For that same word, rebellion, did divide
>   The action of their bodies from their souls ;
>   And they did fight with queasiness, constrain'd,
>   As men drink potions. . . .
>   . . . But now the Bishop
>   Turns insurrection to religion . . .
>   He's followed both with body and with mind . . .
>   Derives from heaven his quarrel and his cause."

In Act iv. 1 the Archbishop speaks of the rising as
a judgment of Heaven on England's sins, a purga-
tion for both parties; his end he declares is peace;
if he makes show of war it is—

> " To diet rank minds, sick of happiness ;
>   And purge the obstructions, which begin to stop
>   Our very veins of life. . . ."

And he fights—

> " Not to break peace, or any branch of it ;
>   But to establish here a peace indeed."

Westmoreland replies—

>   " It is the time
>   And not the king that does you injuries."

Shakespeare's teaching on this point recalls what
Sanders said of the failure of the rebellion of 1569.
The movement turned out otherwise than as they
expected " because all the Catholics had not yet been

authentically informed that Elizabeth was declared
a heretic"; which want of information, adds Burghley, was diligently supplied by sending a multitude
of Seminarists and Jesuits into the kingdom.[1]   It
is noteworthy that Shakespeare condemns rebellion
rather from its political inexpediency than from its
intrinsic immorality under the special conditions of
the age in which he writes.

Henry V. is a very different monarch from his
predecessors.   With the call of duty his wild days
ended, and he appears, as king, the impersonation
of England's greatness.   He is Shakespeare's ideal
Prince, perhaps his ideal self, what in his better
moments he would wish himself to have been ; and
no national hero has such a portrait, says Kreysig,
except perhaps Pelides.   Under Henry the country
is transformed.   Profligates and adventurers like
Falstaff, Bardolph, Pym, Pistol, "the cankers of a
calm world and a long peace," meet with their fitting
deserts.   The conspiracy of Cambridge, Scroop, and
Grey is destroyed in the bud, and the whole nation,
Church and State, King and nobles, with the four
nationalities of Britain—the English, Welsh, Scotch,
Irish—are united in one great patriotic movement,
pointing the moral—

> "O England !—model to thy inward greatness,
>   Like little body with a mighty heart,
>   What might'st thou do, that honour would thee do,
>   Were all thy children kind and natural !"
>   —*Henry V.*, ii. Chorus.

---

[1] "Execution for Treason," 18.   Reprint of 1675.

"The mighty heart" was the king's. His firm sense
of justice redressed wrongs and suppressed disorders
within. His personal grace and bearing; the "cheer-
ful countenance," "sweet ɪ majesty," and personal
interest in every individual soldier, the sound of
his voice, the ring of his words secured victory
abroad. Thus on the eve of Agincourt the confident,
well-fed, and feasting French are boasting of their
horses and their armour, and the morrow's victory
as secure; while the chorus tells us—

> "... ᷄ The poor condemnèd English,
> Like sacrifices, by their watchful fires
> Sit patiently, and inly ruminate
> The morning's danger; and their gesture sad,
> Investing lank-lean cheeks, and war-worn coats,
> Presenteth them unto the gazing moon,
> So many horrid ghosts. O, now, who will behold
> The royal captain of this ruin'd band,
> Walking from watch to watch, from tent to tent,
> Let him cry ' Praise and glory on his head !'
> For forth he goes, ...
> With cheerful semblance, and sweet majesty;
> That every wretch, pining and pale before,
> Beholding him, plucks comfort from his looks."
> —*Ibid.*, iv. Chorus.

It was in making his rounds, disguised, that a
soldier whom he meets questions him on the blood-
guiltiness of war, and the responsibility of the king
in bringing men to be killed unprepared. Henry
replies that the soldier, in going to war, should
"wash every mote from his conscience." If he then
dies, his death is to him a gain; if he escapes, he

is blessed in having prepared his soul, and may believe that his life has been spared, that he may see God's goodness, and teach others how to prepare.

In conformity with this deep, earnest faith and piety, is Henry's prayer before the action commences. His army is spent and worn, and five times out-numbered.

> " O God of battles ! steel my soldiers' hearts !
> Possess them not with fear ; take from them now
> The sense of reckoning, if the opposèd numbers
> Pluck their hearts from them ! . . . ."—*Ibid.*, iv. 1.

One thought, however, disturbs his confidence. His father's non-performance of his vow of a pilgrimage to Jerusalem in expiation of his supposed compli-city in the murder of Richard II. may bring the divine vengeance on his son and procure his defeat. In this fear he prays :—

> " . . . Not to-day, O Lord,
> O not to-day, think not upon the fault
> My father made in compassing the crown !
> I Richard's body have interrèd new,
> And on it have bestow'd more contrite tears,
> Than from it issued forcèd drops of blood.
> Five hundred poor I have in yearly pay,
> Who twice a day their withered hands hold up
> Toward heaven, to pardon blood ; and I have built
> Two chantries, where the sad and solemn priests
> Sing still for Richard's soul. . . ."

These two foundations were situated on the opposite banks of the Thames. That on the Surrey shore at Sheene was given to the Carthusians. The other,

Sion House, facing it on the Middlesex shore, was bestowed on the Bridgettine nuns.

The first cry that burst from Henry's heart on seeing the victory assured, is one of devout thanksgiving :—

> " . . . O God, Thy arm was here,
> And not to us, but to Thy arm alone, ,
> Ascribe we all !   When, without stratagem,
> But in plain shock, and even play of battle,
> Was ever known so great and little loss,
> On one part and on the other ?   Take it, God,
> For it is only Thine ! . . ."

Only with the acknowledgment that God fought for us, does he allow the list of the killed to be proclaimed, and then gives the order of the day,

> " . . . Do we all holy rites,
> Let there be sung ' Non nobis' and 'Te Deum.'"

In the same spirit of humility Henry refused the request of the Lords that he should

> " Have borne (before him)
> His bruisèd helmet and his bended sword."

on his triumphant entry through the streets of London.   As he began his campaign, so he celebrated its victorious issue,

> " Free from vainness and self-glorious pride,
> Giving full glory, signal and ostent
> Quite from himself to God. . . ."

Such, then, is Shakespeare's chosen national hero,

the paragon of kings, "the mirror of Christian knights." In what lines has he drawn him? He is no mere human champion, victor by his own strength, but solely through trust in God. "God before" was his cry, and trust in God means with him trust in his Church. The character of his faith is clearly expressed. He believes in Purgatory, in alms-deeds, prayer, fasting, pious foundations, as satisfactory works for the relief of the souls detained there. All his public acts bear a religious impress, and his portrait as a Catholic hero is complete.

It has been objected that the religious details found in "Henry V." are no argument as to Shakespeare's own opinions, because these details are only copied from Hollinshed. But the poet not only follows the chronicler in attributing acts of Catholic faith and worship to the king, he further gives his hero a character of such practical wisdom, graceful piety, and enlightened religion, that his Popish proceedings appear like the flowers of true devotion, not the weeds of superstition, as they might have been represented under the hands of another dramatist.

In "Henry V." the factions of the nobles disappear, as we have seen, in the complete triumph of the Crown, the new bond of union of all parties and nationalities. Very different, however, is the following reign of Henry VI., of "whose state so many had the managing that they lost France and made his England bleed." These lines in the final chorus

of " Henry V." give the keynote of the trilogy which
is to follow :—

> " . . . No simple man that sees
> This jarring discord of nobility,
> This should'ring of each other in the court,
> This fractious bandying of their favourites,
> But that it doth presage some ill event."
> —1 *Henry VI.*, iv. 1.

> " . . . While the vulture of sedition
> Feeds in the bosom of such great commanders,
> Sleeping neglection doth betray to loss
> The conquest of our scarce-cold conqueror."
> —*Ibid.*, iv. 3.

The subject of the three parts of "Henry VI."
is the factions of the nobles. In the first two
parts the great rivals are Duke Humphrey and the
Bishop of Winchester, representing the two estates
—the Church and the laity; while the Dukes of
Somerset and York represent the dynastic factions
among the nobles. The servants of Duke Humphrey despise the Bishop as an ink-horn mate, just
as Jack Cade and his crew despise all clerks, nobles,
and gentlemen. Duke Humphrey himself detests
the Bishop with all the bitterness which an ambitious political leader entertains for the one rival
who successfully opposes his designs. How the
Beauforts, in fact, supported the throne and the
Lancastrian dynasty, while Gloucester's selfishness
destroyed both, is not shown in Shakespeare or in
the play he adapted.

If the hierarchy appears discredited in Beaufort,

and the clergy in the two conjuring priests, Hume and Southwell, the Catholic religion is respected in Henry, that saintly innocent, of whom his own wife says—

> ". . . All his mind is bent to holiness,
> To number Ave Maries on his beads :
> His champions are—the prophets and apostles ;
> His weapons, holy saws of sacred writ ;
> His study is his tilt-yard, and his loves
> Are brazen images of canonised saints.
> I would the college of cardinals
> Would choose him Pope, and carry him to Rome,
> And set the triple crown upon his head ;
> That were a fit state for his holiness."
>
> —2 *Henry VI.*, i. 3.

Henry, in fact, is the key of the whole trilogy, the design of which is to show that innocence, uprightness, and self-sacrifice are not by themselves sufficient to constitute a powerful ruler. As Richard II. exhibited the divergence between the higher gifts of mind and political sagacity, so Henry VI. exhibits the still greater divergence between statesmanship and personal piety. Henry has the harmlessness of the dove and the wisdom of the recluse, but not the cunning of the king. He would make an excellent Infirmarian brother, to pray by the bedside of the dying, and

> " . . . Beat away the busy, meddling fiend
> That lays strong siege unto the wretch's soul,"

but his scrupulosity is too acute, his simple soul is too much at the mercy of the last plausible speaker to allow of consistent firmness of action. Scrupulous about his title to the throne, yet fearing the suicide of abdication, he compromises the difficulty by keeping the crown during his own life, and only disinheriting his son. Having done so, he is distracted with the injury he has done his own family, and the power he has given to his enemy, now his acknowledged heir. Such is the king who has to grapple with a nobility that cannot understand what conscience is.

In " King John " the nobles revolt for the sake of religion and natural justice. The murder of Arthur and the excommunication are the motives of their conspiracy. In " Richard II." they revolt to preserve their order, and to save the country from ruin ; patriotism is their end. In " Henry IV." their mainspring of action has become their personal safety. They have found that to dethrone one king is to set up another, and however conducive to the progress of the country, is a step downwards for themselves. For a subject unfaithful to one master is suspected by another, and the benefactor of a monarch never thinks himself sufficiently rewarded. In " Henry V." this downward progress makes halt for a few years in a national triumph, the result of the king's personal superiority, but in " Henry VI." we find that the bad leaven has been working even while it seemed to sleep. The nobles are already combined in factions. Neither patriotism nor religion nor honour are now their motives, but only an equal share in power. Pre-eminence or distinction of any kind insures the possessor the enmity of his fellows.

In "Henry VI." the factions of the nobles are swaying backwards and forwards, one ever strengthening itself by the destruction of another, according to the old saying, "Snake must devour snake if it would become a dragon," or, according to the Maori doctrine, that the warrior that eats another inherits all his prowess, a doctrine which Prince Hal seems to hold—

> " Percy is but my factor, good my lord,
> To engross up glorious deeds on my behalf ;
> That he shall render every glory up,
> Or I will tear the reckoning from his heart."
> —1 *Henry IV.*, iii. 2.

And all this time one family is gradually rising. York bases his fortunes upon the mutinous people, and receives fresh strength by every blow that weakens any other faction. His three sons grow up in this dice-play of fortune, which eradicates from their minds every guiding principle but the balance of power. Life has become to them a rule-of-three sum, a calculation, and nothing else. For two of them, however, nature is too strong. Edward IV. and Clarence are under the sway of their passions and affections. The youngest, Richard of Gloucester, alone knows how to stifle every feeling, to ridicule every principle, and to guide himself simply by the arithmetical calculation of his own interest.

What germs of feeling and conscience remain in him are employed only to gain the mastery over others.

Richard III. is the opposite pole to Henry VI. Unscrupulous, unhesitating, applying his great capacity not to unravelling casuistical questions of right and wrong, but to discovering the readiest means to his determined ends, he is the natural, the fatal result of the degradation of the nobles, which is traced all through these plays. Under him the nobles change their nature. They are no longer a collection of petty princes fighting amongst themselves for supremacy. They have at length found their master, and his tyranny does not drive them to insurrection but to look out for a deliverer. Richard III. bases his power on the Commons, and snaps his fingers at the nobles; his defeat and death are the consequence of his personal crimes, not of his political tendency, for his successor continues in the same line. He is the victim of his own victims, whose curses consume his marrow. Henry VI. falls through weakness. Richard III. circumvents himself in his own policy.

The dramatist omits one reign, and in his last chronicle play exhibits to us the state of England such as it was in his own day. In "Henry VIII." we have a king inheriting the position which Richard had created and Henry VII. had developed; an autocrat among his peers, but feeling in some blind way his dependence on the Commons. The king no longer strengthens himself with the alliance of

dukes and earls, as powerful in their counties as he
is in his kingdom, but he surrounds himself with
able ministers whom he raises from low estate, and
uses as his instruments for the still further weaken-
ing and degrading of the nobles. Nash in 1589
reproaches Shakespeare with stealing conceits like
"Blood is a beggar" out of Seneca. Nash was
wrong in supposing that the dramatist required
Seneca to tell him this secret. It was the first
fact patent to the eye that looked into the Tudor
rule ; and the first three scenes of "Henry VIII."
are taken up in illustrating it.

Buckingham, the son of the duke that had been
Richard's tool for hoisting him into the throne,
courted while needed, broken when done with, is
now no longer necessary for anything but the
amusement of the sovereign. Henry is pleased
with his talk, admires his talents, but when he
becomes a nuisance to his minister he sends him,
in spite of the Queen's intercession, to the block.
King-makers have dwindled down to courtiers.
Their lives, which under the former dynasties could
only be taken by violence or lawless treachery, are
now game for the labyrinthian subtlety of intriguing
lawyers. The great families are ruined by being
brought to court, not to honour them, but to weigh
them down with expenditure. Young nobles are
encouraged to "break their backs with laying
manors on 'em." Cardinal Wolsey, the "butcher's
cur," the beggar whose "book outworths a noble's

blood," omnipotent under the king, makes and mars, sets up and pulls down nobles as he lists, and pulls down, though he fails to set up, a queen. After Wolsey has fallen, another like him takes his place —Cranmer, like Wolsey raised from low estate to the highest ecclesiastical dignities; and Cranmer is simply a ministerial tool for carrying out the king's designs about the divorce.

Now it is noticeable that in assigning this characteristic to the Tudor times, and in the lament implied in the terms " Blood is a beggar " which he expresses, Shakespeare is taking the Catholic view of the Elizabethan era. It was one of the charges made against the Queen in the Bull of Pius V. that " she had dismissed the royal council of English nobles, and filled their places with obscure men and heretics." Father Parsons, according to whom the only purpose of the rebellion of 1569 was to restore their due influence to the old nobles, traces the plebeian origin of the Queen's five councillors, Bacon, Cecil, Dudley, Hatton, and Walsingham, and declares that in the whole bench of Anglican bishops there was scarce a drop of noble blood, while the ministry was filled up with beggars' brats.[1] It is to be remarked that this feeling in Shakespeare marks his party clearly. Raleigh's friends complained indeed that except a man were of noble blood he had no chance of promotion in

---

[1] Philopater, *Resp. ad. ii. Edict. Elizabethæ*, 2 *et seq.* Lugduni, 1593.

Elizabeth's court. But it was not mere court favour that Shakespeare desired for the nobility; he wanted power, such power as would make them balance the crown and obstruct its despotism. It was easy for Elizabeth to combine a narrow and senseless love of caste with a determination to destroy aristocratic privileges and to break the nobles as an independent power in the State.

Though Shakespeare evidently felt the regrets which Allen as well as Parsons express, he was not theorist enough to think that the old state of things could be restored by edict. He had traced the progress of decay through centuries, and knew that neither Pope's Bull, nor Act of Parliament, nor Royal Proclamation, could recall the dead to life. Nevertheless, he looked back to the past wistfully, and felt that he and his dearest friends were misplaced in the times when they were living :—

> "Why should he live, now Nature bankrupt is,
>   Beggared of blood ?
> Tired with all these, for restful death I cry,
> With needy nothing trimmed in jollity,
> And gilded honour shamefully misplaced,
> And strength by limping sway disabled."

Shakespeare's conception of Henry VIII. shows how he judged him. Henry would fain have been absolute monarch, to whom the least presumption of independence was present death, as the prejudged and murdered Buckingham felt to his sorrow; but knowing that he could not discontent the Commons

M

with impunity, Henry rebuked his favourite minister for oppressing them.   Queen Catherine patronised the Commons out of charity, the king out of policy. Wolsey, whose consummate art is only administrative, who has none other but personal ends, revenge and ambition, will oppress them when he may, and pretend to be their friend when oppression is forbidden.   Thus the king, sitting in the seat of Richard III., but raised to it by peaceable succession, not by war and murder, has to maintain himself there by other weapons.

Remorseless as Richard and libertine as Edward IV., he is yet a peaceful monarch, and must, apparently at least, confine himself within the limits of law and conscience.   The weapons of the barefaced usurper are denied him, but those of the hypocrite are in constant use.   Richard III. is an actor, a consummate hypocrite.   Henry is a more melodramatic, pretentious, arrogant, oily hypocrite, and his perpetual cry almost serves to characterise him—

"... Conscience, conscience,
O! 'tis a tender place, and I must leave her."

Shakespeare is not content with once saying this, the audience must not be allowed to forget it.   The marriage with the brother's widow had crept too near Henry's conscience—"No! his conscience has crept too near another lady," whose beauty was such and so tempting that, as one of the courtiers says, "I cannot blame his conscience."

It is for this hypocrisy that Cranmer is made necessary for Henry,—" with thy approach I know my comfort comes "; and till this comfort is administered no accusation shall stand between Cranmer and the king's favour. It is here that Shakespeare, supposing this scene to be his, for once condescends to borrow from " Foxe's Acts and Monuments " the first scene of the fifth act, where the king is convinced of Cranmer's honesty by his tears, and delivers him the ring which is to protect him against Gardiner and the rest of the Council. In the whole play the poet takes care to secure our interest successively for Henry's victims; for the noble but wilful Buckingham; for the repudiated Queen, one of the grandest, most touching, most constant, and purest figures that Shakespeare has drawn, and after his fall, for Wolsey himself.

In "Henry VI." the people first appear as a political force, in the rebellion of Jack Cade (1450). Shakespeare's treatment of that rising has been condemned by Mr. Wilkes, the American critic, as a deliberate perversion of every fact in the interest of falsehood, selfishness, and tyranny.[1] His account is indeed not historical, yet it accurately represents many features in the Lollard revolt under Wat Tyler in 1380, and is instructive as showing the bent of the poet's sympathies in religion no less than in politics. Those sympathies were certainly not with any Lollard movement. But Shakespeare is not to be considered

[1] " Shakespeare from an American Point of View," 239. 1877.

in consequence a blind worshipper of kings or nobles.
On the contrary, he fully recognised the bitter sufferings inflicted at times on the lower classes by the
injustice and tyranny of their rulers.   Hence the
indictment of Richard II. for the exorbitant taxation
of the Commons, and Catherine's speech on their
behalf in " Henry VIII.," where she declares that the
exactions, extending even to the sixth part of their
substance, were sapping the foundation of loyalty
and order in the kingdom.

> "Cold hearts freeze
> Allegiance in them ; their curses now
> Live where did their prayers."
> —*Henry VIII.*, i. 2.

So too in this very scene (in " Henry VI.") the
poet gives in Lord Say the portrait of a true noble-
man, just, generous, merciful, tender-hearted, wan
and worn in his judicial labours on behalf of the
poor and the afflicted, simple in his attire and tastes,
incapable of taking a bribe, a patron of learning,
the friend of poor scholars.   In this character he
pleads for his life—

> " Justice with favour have I always done ;
> Prayers and tears have mov'd me, gifts could never.
> When have I aught exacted at your hands,
> Kent to maintain, the king, the realm, and you ?
> Large gifts have I bestowed on learned clerks.
>
> . . . . . .
>
> Long sitting to determine poor men's causes
> Hath made me full of sickness and diseases.
> . . . . . .

Have I affected wealth or honour ; speak ?
Are my chests fill'd up with extorted gold ?
Is my apparel sumptuous to behold ?
Whom have I injur'd that ye seek my death ? "
—2 *Henry VI.*, iv. 7.

Shakespeare thus plainly regards the nobles as
the appointed guardians and defenders of the poor,
and he knows of no absolute title to rank or wealth
which is free from these obligations. For the poor
again, the lower classes, as such, he has none of the
old heathen contempt, the *odo profanum vulgus et
arceo*, the scorn which, as Mr. Devas has so well
pointed out,[1] Milton expresses in the "Samson
Agonistes."

" Nor do I name the men of common birth,
    That wandering loose about,
    Grow up and perish, like the summer flies,
    Heads without name, no more remembered."

For Shakespeare saw all men, and reverenced all,
whatever their exterior, as possessed of rational
souls, and made in the image of God. Thus some
of his highest examples of loyalty, fidelity, courage,
generosity, and affection are found in the lowest
grade of the social scale. Such are Corin the shepherd in " Winter's Tale," and Adam, Orlando's servant, in " As You Like It," and the servants of the
Duke of Gloucester, and the fool in " Lear," and the
groom of Richard II., already noticed. In these
cases sympathy with their superiors in affliction

---

[1] "Shakespeare as an Economist " (*Dublin Review*, vol. xiii.).

evokes, from the most uneducated, sentiments as graceful, appropriate, and attractive as any expressed by the most highly cultivated mind. So, too, Juliet's nurse, old Gobbo, and the gravedigger, each can speak to us of the dead in a way to move our hearts, because they speak the common tongue of faith.

But while Shakespeare held the equality of all men, both as regards their first beginning and their supernatural destiny, he scouted the idea of an absolute equality in natural gifts, attainments, or position. He would have found a fundamental political truth in the words of Burke, "Those who attempt to level never equalise. In all societies consisting of various descriptions of citizens, some description must be uppermost. The levellers only pervert the natural order of things, and the perfect equality they produce is of equal want, equal wretchedness, and equal beggary." [1] "They pull down what is above, they never raise what is below, and they depress high and low together below the level of what was originally the lowest." [2] So again, on the same principle, that society is built on a graduated scale, and that power is naturally vested in men of rank, wealth, and education, the poet did not believe in the infallibility of the multitude, or in the principle that "the majority of men, told by the head, constitute the people,

[1] "Revolution in France."
[2] "Thoughts on Scarcity."

and that their will is law." He thought, as he tells
us by Archbishop Scroop,

> " A habitation giddy and unsure
> Hath he that buildeth on the vulgar herd."
> —2 *Henry IV.*, i. 3.

Disbelief in what is now called Socialism is manifested in the fickleness of the mob in " Julius
Cæsar "; it is seen again in Coriolanus' disdain for
" the mutable, rank-scented many," and in the
repugnance he feels to appear as a candidate for
their votes. So too it is the conviction of the falseness of the cry of " The People," as popularly used,
and of the baseness of the demagogues who flatter
the multitude for their own ends, which explains
Shakespeare's treatment of Jack Cade's rebellion.

The main features of that rebellion, as drawn by
Shakespeare, are to be found, as we have said, in
the Lollard revolt, seventy years earlier than Cade's,
under Wat Tyler. That revolt originated with the
teaching of Wycliffe, and was in fact the popular
interpretation and expression of his doctrines. His
fundamental tenet in religion was the substitution
of the Bible, privately interpreted, for the authority
of the Church. The Church, in his creed, was the
synagogue of Satan, the Pope was Antichrist, or
the great Beast, and the Friars were his tail.
According to his theory of dominion, all authority
is founded on grace, and each individual in grace
possesses a dominion immediately from God, and

is himself to judge whether others are in grace or sin. The loss of grace entailed the forfeiture of all right to rule or possess. Hence, as the Church was, according to Wycliffe, essentially evil, her authority was to be rejected, and her goods confiscated.

From the spoliation of the Church to that of private individuals, the transition has always been easy and logical. Hence Socialism, or the denial of any difference of rank, and communism in property were openly advocated by John Ball, the quondam priest and half-crazed Lollard leader. "Good people," he said, "things will never go well in England as long as goods are not in common, and as long as there be villeins and gentlemen. By what right are they, whom we call lords, greater folk than we? On what grounds have they deserved it? Why do they hold us in serfage? If we all come of the same father and mother, of Adam and Eve, how can they say or prove that they are better than we, if it be not that they make us gain for them by our toil what they spend in their pride?"[1] And he inculcated his teaching by the popular rhyme—

> "When Adam delved and Eve span,
> Where was then the gentleman?"

Thus envy, discontent, class hatred, bitter and deep, were enkindled by specious but false shibboleths,

---

[1] Green's "History of the English People," 293.

all which are set forth almost verbally by Shakespeare. "It was never a merry world in England," says John, "since gentlemen came up." "Virtue," replies George, "is not regarded in handicraftsmen." Cade declares, "Then shall be in England seven halfpenny loaves sold for a penny; the three-hooped pot shall have ten hoops; and I will make it felony to drink small beer; all the realm shall be in common. . . . There shall be no money, all shall eat and drink on my score: and I will apparel them all in one livery, that they may agree like brothers, and worship me, their lord." Thus in the very moment that Cade proclaims universal socialism and communism, his own selfish greed and ambition are made apparent, no less than the gullibility of his dupes. To Cade's declaration, "And when I am king—as king I will be," all say "God save your Majesty." They were evidently but escaping from one tyranny to another more degrading and self-imposed.

Again, the poet reveals to us the morbid, unreal sentimentalism so often the accompaniment of democratic cries. Not only are lawyers to be killed and all "ink-horn mates," because they are the supporters of the existing order of things, and by their learning make themselves better than honest labourers, but also because they use the "skins of innocent lambs" for parchment—a cry we have heard echoed, though to other tunes, by anti-vivisectionists and other humanitarian reformers

in our own days.   It is to be observed that the
senseless hostility to education manifested in the
slaughter of the ink-horn men had a kindred origin
to the opposite cry for universal education in our
own day, as announced by some Socialist leaders.
In both cases the first principle is absolute equality.
There is to be no pre-eminence due to natural
talent, industry, or position, but the whole world
is to be one vast trades union, where all are kept
by law at the same dead level of ignorance or
knowledge.

The Lollard use of the Scriptures also finds its
place in Shakespeare.   Cade meets Stafford's reproach of his lowly parentage with the retort from
Ball's preaching "Adam was a gardener"; and
John's argument that the magistrates ought not to
be gentlemen, but taken solely from working men,
is proved from St. Paul's words, "Labour in thy
vocation."   So again George's speech, "Then sin is
struck down like an ox, and iniquity's throat cut
like a calf," in its rhythm and repetition manifestly
affects biblical phraseology.

The democratic morality, as exhibited in Cade's
proclamation of his future policy as king, is not of
a high order.   After declaring that a poll tax, like
that which had raised the rebellion, should now be
confined to the nobility alone, instead of coming
down to the daughters of blacksmiths who had
reached the age of fifteen, he proceeds, "Then shall
not a maid be married but she shall pay to me. . . .

Men shall hold of me *in capite*, and we charge and command that their wives should be as free as heart can wish or tongue can tell." Thus neither the maiden state nor the marriage tie are to be henceforth a protection against the legalised licentiousness of the new order. Is this return to universal corruption a libel on the Lollard morals or not?

Now we are possessed, fortunately, of very precise information on the subject. The Norfolk register, now in the archives of the diocese of Westminster, contains an account of the official examination of suspected Lollards by the Bishop of Norwich in his episcopal visitations of his diocese for the years 1428–30.[1] Besides the Wycliffian heresies already enumerated, the general character of the doctrines deposed to in the register exhibits a curious compound of Pietistic or Quaker tenets and undisguised licentiousness. On the one hand, the appeal to arms in behalf of the State or for any hereditary right, the recourse to legal redress, the taking of oaths or swearing in any form are alike declared unlawful; and on the other hand the doctrine of free love, as it is now termed, was openly advocated. Foxe says that the denial of matrimony only referred "as it is likely" to its being a sacrament, and that the papists "are but quarrel-pickers in the matter." The Wycliffian doctrine which

[1] By the kindness of Father Gasquet we have been enabled to examine his copies of these documents.

nearly all the Lollard prisoners held—that consent of the heart alone, or mutual love, sufficed for matrimony—might indeed mean no more than that the essence of the contract consisted in that mutual surrender.   But it is self-evident that a purely interior consent could never constitute any external bond, while it could be repudiated at any time, and did not necessarily imply more than a temporary union.   However, the evidence of William Colyn Skinner of Treyk, near Burnham Westgate, shows unmistakeably what the Lollard doctrine meant to his mind.   He advocated openly the community of women and the annulment of the marriage tie for the space of seven years, or at least some notable time.   Some of his statements connected with the subject are at once too blasphemous and coarse for quotation.

Of the fifty-three men and five women proceeded against as Lollards in these visitations, the greater number appear to have belonged to the artisan or small tradesmen class.   The list contains Tailors, Millers, Parchyn makers, Carpenters, Tylers, Sowters, Skynners, Glovers, Shipmen, Watermen, Cordwainers, all belonging therefore to the same social grade as Dick the Butcher, Smith the Weaver, and Cade the Clothier in Shakespeare's play.

The Norwich Lollards all accepted the public penances imposed and recanted their errors.   Their heresy and licentiousness they appear to have learnt in the first instance from the leaders of the movement, apostate priests, like William White, who, according to Foxe, "was as a morning star in the midst of a cloud," and "took unto him a goodly young woman to wife, named Joan."[1]

How far Lollardy was the lineal progenitor of the Reformation is a disputed point. The comparative apathy with which the movement was regarded by the country at large, the ease with which it was suppressed, and its almost complete disappearance towards the end of the fifteenth and beginning of the sixteenth centuries, have led many writers to regard the two movements as completely distinct. Yet the Lollard repudiation of authority both in Church and State may surely be regarded as preparing the way for the final revolt of the sixteenth century,[2] and Shakespeare's sketch of Cade's rebellion leaves little doubt of how he regarded the Reformation itself, or its precursors. It should also be noted that he must have been in all probability well acquainted with Foxe's book, for by a decree of Elizabeth, the first English edition of the work, in 1563, was placed in every chancel and vestry for the public to read; while Foxe himself was tutor to Sir Thomas Lucy of Charlecote, the father probably of Shakespeare's persecutor, not that persecutor himself, as Milner supposes.[3]   Foxe took the

[1] "Acts and Monuments," iii. 591. 1837.
[2] "With the appearance of the Lollards," Mr. Freeman says, "the Church and the Nation ceased to be fully one, and the puzzles and controversies of modern times had their beginning."—"Historical Essays," 123. 1871.   [3] "Life of Foxe," vi. 1837.

tutor's place in 1540, or twenty-four years before
Shakespeare's birth, and forty-one before the deer-
stealing incident.

Shakespeare's sentiments as to the Church and its
relations with the State, and the effect of its influence have been already in part set forth, in our study
of the character of Pandulph in " King John."   We
will now endeavour to trace them further, as they
appear in his views of " the Politicians," of liberty of
conscience, and lastly, in his portraits of individual
churchmen.

The Politicians were in Shakespeare's days regarded as a sect.   The name was first given to the
" liberal " Catholics or third party, which was formed
in France under Henry III., during the wars between
the Huguenots and Catholics.   The term is applied by
Davila [1] to those who hold that the State ought not
to recognise any essential difference between one religion and another.   According to Stapleton, "the Politicians hated zeal, winked at religious discords, and
declared that governments, not being charged with
the management of religion, had no right to endanger
the national welfare by attempts to suppress heresies." [2]
The odium in which they were held by Catholics is
seen by Fitzherbert's definition of them as " statists,
who prefer things less worthy before the more worthy,
inferior things before superior, corporal before
spiritual, temporal before eternal."   " Politikes," he

---

[1] *Storia delle Guerre civili in Francia*, lib. v., ad. an. 1573.
[2] *Sermo contra Politicos.*

says, "admitting in show all religions, have in truth no religion, denying God's providence in the affairs of men, which is the ground of all religion . . . acknowledge the necessity of religion for the State, but prefer in all things reason of State before reason of religion, as though religion were ordained only for service of commonwealth . . . use religion as a bugbear to frighten men into obedience to the law . . . care not greatly what religion is professed, so that people believe in a God who rewards and punishes."[1]

The Politiques then, properly defined, were those who, utterly indifferent to religion themselves, used it or discarded it, according to the exigencies of statecraft. They thus represented the modern school of Liberalism, as understood in its foreign sense, and as such were denounced by the earnest men of every creed. Their leading doctrines were condemned, three centuries later, by the Encyclical of Pius XI.

How, then, does Shakespeare regard them? If he were a broad-minded, vague rationalist, superior to theological dogmas of all kinds, a teacher of nature and nothing more, as he is so often represented, he would surely have gladly identified himself with their teaching. But, as a fact, his attitude towards them is exactly the reverse. He denounces them in no sparing terms. He makes Hotspur exclaim against the "vile politician Bolingbroke" ("1 Henry IV.," i. 3), and Hamlet talk

"Policy and Religion," vol. i. (1605), Pref. Nos. 1 and 2.

of the politician who "would circumvent God"
("Hamlet," v. 1). Policy is a "heretic," because it
"works on leases of short-numbered hours," instead
of working for eternity. Policy, in its general sense,
is the degradation of a moral act from its moral
purpose to some utilitarian end, and is used very
much as "Commodity" in "King John." With
Polonius it catches truth with false baits, and hence
the "scurvy politician" is said to "seem to see the
things he does not" ("Lear," iv. 6); "base and
rotten policy" will adopt any disguise that is not too
painful ("1 Henry IV.," i. 3); it will "beat his
offenceless dog to affright an imperious lion"
("Othello," ii. 3); and hence, when it "sits above
conscience," pity is dispensed with ("Timon," iii. 2).
Shakespeare, then, could not endure the principles of
the "Politiques," and denounced them as a party.

But if such were Shakespeare's opinion of the
Politicians, how, it may fairly be asked, did he
advocate, as he does, liberty of conscience, or universal toleration, which would seem to be one of
their leading principles? Liberty of conscience, then,
may be taken in two senses. It may mean that
there is no fixed truth or absolute right or wrong,
and that every man is free to teach or do as he
pleases, and that the State itself should be Godless.
In this sense the Politicians seem to have used it,
and in this sense it was condemned by Shakespeare,
who makes Sir Andrew Aguecheek say he had as
lief be a Brownist, or the wildest heretic, "as a

Politician." But liberty of conscience may also mean that every man has a right by nature to serve God, and obey His commands without let or hindrance, and so to attain his end. This is the liberty which the Apostles claimed, for which the first Christian Apologists ever contended, and the Martyrs shed their blood. Now it was this true liberty which the Tudor tyranny destroyed. Their axiom was *cujus regio, ejus et religio.* A man must be of the religion of his country, and as the Crown fixed that religion, the subject's conscience was not his own but the king's. And the king was himself, according to the post-Reformation theory, of divine right, absolute and infallible. "He made," as James I. said, "Law and Gospel," and he made both as his whim pleased him.

Against this degrading tyranny Shakespeare protested in Henry V.'s axiom that "every man's duty is the king's, but every man's conscience is his own." Not his own, that is, against the law of God, nor his own as against duly constituted civil authority within its own domain; but his own in matters spiritual, against the purely civil authority of a State, which had arrogated to itself the right to force its subjects to embrace the State creed. Now this is the very plea which Parsons puts forth contemporaneously with Shakespeare. " Neither breathing, nor the use of common air is more due unto good subjects, or common to all, than ought to be liberty of conscience to Christian

N

men, whereby each one liveth to God and to himself,
and without which he struggleth with the torment of
a continual, lingering death. . . . Let them show but
one only authority, example, or testimony out of
Scriptures, Fathers, or Councils, that we must obey
princes against our conscience and religion, and I
will grant he saith something to the purpose." [1]

This indeed was the common plea of all the
Elizabethan martyrs.   While they obeyed the State
in civil matters, they had a right to be free in
following a religion which did not interfere with
that civil obedience.   They did not say that the
State ought to be godless, or that a State without
religion was in the abstract the most perfect order
of government, which was then the theory of the
Politicians, as now of the Liberals.   But they maintained that when a new religion was being introduced, they had a right in nature to follow the
Christian faith of their fathers, if their conscience
bid them do so.

We come now to the third point—Shakespeare's
portraiture of the churchmen in the historical
plays.   The characters, as he has drawn them, of
Cardinal Beaufort and of Wolsey are often quoted
as decisive proof of Shakespeare's anti-Catholic
sentiments.

According to the great majority of critics, the
first part of " Henry VI." is an old play and not

---

[1] "The Judgment of a Catholic Englishman," 38, § 20, and 51,
§ 31.

Shakespeare's work, who, if he adopted it, at most retouched it here and there, and cannot, therefore, be held responsible for every line it contains. It is a relief that this is so, and that we are therefore not obliged to regard the repulsive caricature of the Maid of Orleans as by Shakespeare's hand. The character of Beaufort is equally unhistorical, especially the well-known death-scene. The Cardinal, in fact, retired from political life some years before his death, and lived in his See of Winchester, where he spent his money in works of charity, and founded and endowed the Hospital of St. Cross. By his own desire he was laid out before his death in the great Hall of his Palace, and had the Absolutions pronounced over him, which function, however eccentric, manifests a very opposite spirit to the reprobate, despairing end of the prelate in the play. The anachronisms in regard to him are also somewhat startling. In the first act, Beaufort is called a Cardinal, in order to introduce Gloucester's famous lines about trampling on the Cardinal's hat; yet he is not raised till the fifth act to the dignity of the Sacred College. But, granted for the sake of argument that Shakespeare must be held responsible for the play, since he allowed it to bear his name, the condemnatory terms applied to the Cardinal are only those which a Catholic might use of an unworthy, wicked prelate. The charges are all personal, not doctrinal.

There is only one line which seems to give countenance to the doctrine that the Church grants indulgences to commit sin. This line, which need not be quoted, refers absolutely to some disreputable houses, from the licensing of which the Bishops of Winchester drew some small portion of their income, and thus gave public scandal. The reproach, therefore, uttered by Gloucester, whether written by Shakespeare or allowed by him to remain, was both intrinsically probable and morally correct. Doubtless such licences were granted by the Bishops' agents, and secular governments do, in certain countries, grant such licences in our own day. Nevertheless, it was an undoubted abuse that a Bishop should derive any profit from such places, and the trafficking in them is wholly opposed to the legislative principles on this matter laid down in " Measure for Measure."

With regard to Wolsey, his faults and sins are precisely those which Catholics had to deplore in the worldly, ambitious, Erastian prelates of the time, because of the incalculable injury they inflicted on the Church. Wolsey's covetousness had led to the suppression of the smaller monasteries, and to the unjust taxation and misery of the people. His insatiable ambition had induced him to suggest the divorce of Henry from Catherine, in order to revenge himself on her nephew, the Emperor Charles V., for not supporting his pretensions to the Papacy. Finally, his greed of power and place made him descend to the " utter meanness " of advocating the

substitution of Anne Boleyn, whose licentiousness
he well knew, in the place of the noble and pure
Catherine of Arragon as Henry's wife. The denun-
ciation of the Cardinal by Catherine is not then more
severe than might have been fitly employed by any
Catholic historian.

Again, the reflection on the Cardinal's morality
(iii. 2) has been specified as an undoubted proof of
Shakespeare's Protestantism. But have Catholic
writers never censured the evil lives of churchmen
in high places? Have not Dante and Petrarch, for
instance, pronounced similar strictures? Of what
religion was St. Catherine of Siena, when she wrote
to Gregory XI.: " Our Lord holds in aversion these
detestable vices, impurity, avarice, and pride, and
they all reign in the Spouse of Christ, especially, at
least, among her prelates, who seek after nothing
but pleasures, honours, and riches. They see the
demons of hell carrying off the souls confided to
them, and they care nothing at all about it, because
they are wolves and traffic with divine grace." [1]
Blessed John Fisher admits, in answer to the
Lutheran objection, that the lives of the prelates
(*proceres*) at Rome were most diametrically opposed
to the life of Christ, and that their greed, vainglory,
luxury, and lust caused the name of Christ to be
everywhere blasphemed.[2]   But this, he says, only
confirms his argument for the indefectibility of

---

[1] Letter 41, Drane's "Life of S. Catherine of Siena," 246, 247.
1880.   [2] Opp. p. 1370. Wiceburg, 1597.

the faith of Peter and his successors, seeing that the preservation of Peter's See and of the Church founded thereon, notwithstanding all these scandals, proves the triumphant fulfilment of Christ's promises.

Shakespeare's adverse comment on Wolsey's moral character is not, then, inconsistent with his Catholicism; but further, his portrait of the Cardinal is actually copied from the description given of him by the B. Edmund Campion, the first Jesuit martyr.[1] "This Cardinal," says Hollinshed, "(as Edmund Campion in History of Ireland describeth him) was a man undoubtedly born to honour. 'I think,' said he, 'some prince's bastard, no butcher's son, exceeding wise, fair-spoken, high-minded, full of revenge, vicious of his body,[2] lofty to his enemies, were they never so big, to those that accepted and sought his friendship wonderful courteous; a ripe schoolman, thrall to affections, brought abed with flattery, insatiable to get and more princely in bestowing, as appeareth by his two Colleges at Ipswich and Oxenford, the one overthrown with his fall, the other unfinished, and as yet as it lieth, for an House of Students, considering all the appurtenances, incomparable through Christendom; a great preferrer of his servants and advancer of learning; stout in every quarrel; never happy till

---

[1] Hollinshed, "Chronicles of England," iii. 756. 1808. (Reprint of 1586.)

[2] "Vir magnificentissimus, cruciendus, confidens, scortator, simulator."—*Campioni opusc.*

his overthrow, wherein he showed such moderation and ended so perfectly, that the hour of his death did him more honour than all the pomp of his life passed.' Thus far Campion."

With this material before him, Shakespeare makes Catherine with Griffith speak of Wolsey as follows :—

> "*Catherine.* . . . He was a man
> Of an unbounded stomach, ever ranking
> Himself with princes ; one that by suggestion
> Tied all the kingdom : simony was fair play ;
> His own opinion was his law.   I' the presence
> He would say untruths ; and be ever double
> Both in his words and meaning.   He was never
> But where he meant to ruin, pitiful :
> His promises were, as he then was, mighty ;
> But his performance, as he is now, nothing.
> Of his own body he was ill, and gave
> The clergy ill example.
>   *Griffith.*   Noble Madam,
> Men's evil manners live in brass ; their virtues
> We write in water.   May it please your Highness
> To hear me speak his good now ?
>   *Catherine.*   Yes, good Griffith
> I were malicious else.
>   *Griffith.*   This Cardinal,
> Though from an humble stock, undoubtedly
> Was fashioned to much honour from his cradle.
> He was a scholar, and a ripe and good one :
> Exceeding wise, fair spoken, and persuading :
> Lofty and sour to them that loved him not,
> But to those men that sought him sweet as summer.
> And though he were unsatisfied in getting
> (Which was a sin), yet in bestowing, Madam,
> He was most princely : ever witness for him
> Those twins of learning that he raised in you,
> Ipswich and Oxford ! one of which fell with him,

> Unwilling to outlive the good that did it ;
> The other, though unfinished, yet so famous,
> So excellent in art, and still so rising,
> That Christendom shall ever speak his virtue.
> His overthrow heaped happiness upon him ;
> For then, and not till then, he felt himself,
> And found the blessedness of being little :
> And to add greater honours to his age
> Than man could give him, he died fearing God " (iv. 2).

But there is another churchman in " Henry VIII.," whose language is often quoted as decisive against Shakespeare's Catholicism.   This is Cranmer and his prophecy at the baptism of Elizabeth.

> "Good grows with her,
> In her days, every man shall eat in safety
> Under his own vine what he plants, and sing
> The merry songs of peace to all his neighbours :
> God shall be truly known " (v. 4).

Now this quotation, again, is really beside the mark, for the best critics agree that the fifth act, in which it occurs, with the exception of scene 1, is certainly not Shakespeare's, but an addition of Fletcher's.   Its genuineness is rejected on the grounds of its metre, style, and evident disconnection with the four previous acts.   The arguments on style would take us beyond our scope, but those regarding a metrical test are worth considering. The blank verse, as introduced by Surrey from Italy in the reign of Henry VIII., consisted of ten syllables of iambic measure, and to this metre Shakespeare more generally adhered.   Even in his later plays of "Cymbeline" and the "Winter's Tale," the proportion of lines, in which the eleventh or redundant syllable is employed, is on an average, according to Mr. Spedding, about one in three, while in the fifth act the average of the redundant lines is one in two. But by the same test no less than eight scenes of the four previous acts are declared ungenuine, and there only remain to Shakespeare, Act i. 1, 2; Act ii. 3, 4; Act iii. 2, to exit of the king. Act v. 1, altered by Shakespeare, the rest being all by Fletcher. This result is confirmed, in Mr. Spedding's judgment, by the peculiarities of style in the parts thus assigned to the respective poets. Now, while recognising Mr. Spedding's pre-eminent authority on this subject, it may be stated that there is an opinion on the other side advanced by H. Morley (Introduction to "Henry VIII.," p. xx.), that the redundant eleventh syllable was used intentionally to express by its cadence the idea of failure intended to be conveyed. Thus in Wolsey's speech—

"So farewell to the little good you bear *me*."

the redundant syllable breaks the pomp of each verse at the close, and gives to it a dying fall that suits the theme, the broken pomps of life, the wave that rolls to its full height, then bows its head and falls. If this be tenable, we are not obliged to surrender our traditional belief as to the Shakespearian origin of many of the finest passages from the plays.

More cogent, however, to us than the objection
from metre is that of the absolute estrangement of
the fifth act from the remainder of the play, and
from its expressed intention, as announced in both
prologue and epilogue. These two pieces, whoever
was their author, may be assumed to represent
correctly the contents of the drama to which they
are affixed.

The purpose of the play, then, according to the
prologue, is to tell the truth and to show the stern
but sad realities of life, " mightiness meeting misery."
The scenes depicted may cause pity and tears, but
not laughter. There may be a show or two but no
burlesque, no noise of targets, nor fellow in long
motley coat, guarded with yellow ; for truth is not
to be " mated with fool or fight." This is all literally adhered to in the first four acts, which contain
one pageant, the Field of the Cloth of Gold and
Anne Boleyn's marriage procession, but no burlesque ;
while in the fifth act there is a very coarse farce
between the porter and his men and the crowd for
the christening.

The epilogue, again, apologises for the mournful
tone of the concluded play, which contains neither
witticisms nor satire, and can hope for support only
" in the merciful construction of good women "—

"For such a one we showed them."

Now, Anne Boleyn could never have been called a
good woman, whatever other qualities may have

made her so attractive to Henry, and in the first
four acts she is kept well in the background.   On
the other hand, " the afflictions, the virtues, and the
patience of Catherine are," in Mr. Spedding's words,
" elaborately exhibited."   Our whole sympathy is
evoked exclusively in behalf of the deposed queen,
and our indignation is roused at the shameless
wrong done her.   Yet Henry, the perpetrator of the
iniquity, the ruthless sacrificer of a pure and noble
wife for a licentious caprice, euphemistically termed
his conscience; Anne, his accomplice in the evil
deed, " a spleeny Lutheran "; and Cranmer, the servile
minister of their passions under the cloak of religion,
the arch-heretic " who has crawled into favour," are
all three, without explanation, repentance, or any
justifying cause, crowned in the fifth act with the
full blaze of earthly glory and the promise of happiness to come.   " It is," says Mr. Spedding, " as if
Nathan's rebuke to David had ended, not with the
doom of death to the child just born, but with a
prophetic promise of the felicities of Solomon."

The fifth act, then, forms no part of the original
play, while the first four acts exhibit by themselves
a strict dramatic unity.   And the moral they teach
is exactly opposite to what would have been drawn
by any Protestant dramatist of the time.   Had
Fletcher, or Munday, or Marlowe written on such a
theme as Henry VIII., we should have beheld the
Reformation as the heroic act of his reign, and
Catherine and her daughter Mary would pale before

Anne Boleyn and her daughter Elizabeth. Shakespeare, as we have seen, places exactly the reverse
before us.   He exposes the Tudor tyranny in its
worst features, and its victims are in turn the
objects of our admiration.   Catherine is the heroine
of the piece; the despised Buckingham, and Wolsey,
after his fall, command our respect; while the martyred Sir Thomas More, whom Hall ridicules as "a
wise foolish man,"[1] and the courtier Hollinshed
describes as having forfeited God's grace, through
the misuse of the gifts he had received, and Donne
derided as an obstinate fanatic, is prayed for, as
follows, by Wolsey :—

> "May he do justice,
> For truth's sake, and his innocence, that his bones,
> When he has run his course and sleeps in blessings,
> May have a tomb of orphans' tears wept on them" (iii. 2).

The prayer is in truth a panegyric.   We need not
wonder that Dr. Döllinger should have said, as has
already been stated, that the play of "Henry VIII."
was a striking evidence of the Catholic opinions of
the poet.

How, then, it may be asked, was the fifth act
added ?   The original play was probably first acted
in 1603, the year of James' succession, when Catholics hoped for comparative toleration from him,
after the persecution of Elizabeth, and a piece conceived in an anti-Tudor spirit might hope for some

---

[1] Chronicles of England, 817.   1548.

chance of success. Too soon, however, it was found that James could oppress his Catholic subjects even more cruelly than his predecessors, and the play was dropped. In 1612 Shakespeare retired wholly from the stage, sold his plays and theatrical property to Alleyne, and the new piece, as adapted and altered, with the fifth act added to suit a Jacobean audience, was the work of Fletcher.

The portraiture of the remaining prelates in the historical plays, the scenes of which are laid in Catholic times, betrays nothing inconsistent with Shakespeare's Catholicism. "This group," remarks Thümmel,[1] "is recruited from the highest houses in England, and represents a stately array of political lords in priestly robes, of noble descent, true priests, and Englishmen to the backbone." They were statesmen, no doubt, for as spiritual peers they were legislators in the Upper House of the kingdom. Doubtless, also, their policy was not always disinterested and free from utilitarian motives. But these ecclesiastics bear no resemblance to the popular Protestant idea of a Catholic prelate, as the Bishop of Rochester in Drayton's play, or Munday's Sir John Oldcastle, or as Marlowe or Fletcher would have portrayed him, a serpentine, foreign intriguer, always bent on betraying the interests of his own country, to the supposed aggrandisement of Rome. At their head stands the loyal Bishop of Carlisle, who alone of the great nobles dared to resist the

---

[1] Shakespeare, *Jahrbuch*, 16, 361.

usurping Bolingbroke, and maintained the rights of
Richard—

> " I speak to subjects, and a subject speaks,
>   Stirred up by Heaven, thus boldly for his king.
>   My lord of Hereford here, whom you call king,
>   Is a foul traitor to proud Hereford's king."
>   —*Richard II.*, iv. 1.

And Bolingbroke, now Henry IV., in sentencing the
Bishop to a mild imprisonment, pays tribute to
one who, though ever his foe, had displayed " high
sparks of honour."

Again, with what dignity the learned and vene-
rable Archbishop Scroop defends himself against
Lord Westmoreland, for joining in the insurrection
against the same Henry IV. :—

> " I have in equal balance justly weighed
>   What wrongs our arms may do, what wrongs we suffer,
>   And find our griefs heavier than our offences.
>   We see which way the stream of time doth run,
>   And are enforced from our most quiet sphere
>   By the rough torrent of occasion ;
>   And have the summary of all our griefs,
>   When time shall serve, to show in articles ;
>   Which, long ere this, we offered to the king,
>   And might by no suit gain our audience :
>   When we are wronged, and would unfold our griefs,
>   We are denied access unto his person,
>   Even by those men that most have done us wrong.
>   The dangers of the days but nearly gone
>   (Whose memory is written on the earth
>   With yet appearing blood), and the examples
>   Of every minute's instance (present now),

Have put us to these ill-beseeming arms :
Not to break peace or any branch of it,
But to establish here a peace indeed,
Concurring both in name and quality."
—2 *Henry IV.*, iv. 1.

He was no partisan or turbulent agitator. The
injuries inflicted by the king's misrule were intolerable. Each household of the Commonwealth was
in suffering, and the Archbishop made each household's wrong his own. All constitutional means of
redress had proved useless, therefore he gave "the
seal divine" to the insurrection, not to break but to
establish peace. The whole tenor of the insurgent
manifesto is that of a solemn religious protest in
defence of the Church of Rome and England. The
document charges Henry with usurpation, treason,
perjury, unjust exactions, violation of the *privilegium
cleri*, trying clerics before the secular court. The
eighth article deposes that the King had ratified
" that most wicked statute (of *præmunire*) directed
against the power and principality of the Holy
Roman See as delivered by our Lord Jesus Christ
to the Blessed Peter and his successors." Then,
after proceeding to specify the abuses springing from
the royal patronage of benefices, such as the general,
simoniacal promotion of rude and unworthy persons
for the half or the third part of the benefices so
bestowed, it concludes by saying " that the same
most wicked statute is not only opposed to the
rights of St. Peter, but that it is destruction to the

clergy, to the knighthood and republic of the realm, because from one thing another always follows."[1] The framers of the complaint seem to have been convinced that the liberty of the Church guaranteed that of the State; and it was in defence of both realms, civil as well as spiritual, that the Archbishop gave his life. Shakespeare's treatment of the Archbishop is wholly in keeping with the facts of history and the popular cultus he afterwards received as a saint and martyr.

The two prelates in " Henry V.," Henry Chicheley, Archbishop of Canterbury, and the Bishop of Ely, are often instanced as examples of time-serving Churchmen who preferred a policy of utilitarian bloodshed to the interests of justice and peace. Their arguments on behalf of Henry's claims to the French crown are taken literally from Hollinshed, and their pleadings, however worldly, were first advocated by Edward III., and were held, in their own time, by the king and country at large. There is no reason, then, as Bishop Stubbs points out, why they, more than the lay Barons, who equally advocated an appeal to arms, should be made responsible for the war which followed. As a matter of fact, as the same author shows, Archbishop Chicheley was not present at the Parliament of Leicester;[2] but it is by no means improbable that the Bishops espoused the popular feeling in favour of the invasion of France, both as a means of uniting the country within and

---

[1] Foxe, iii. 233-255.   [2] Constitut. Hist , iii. 81.

of saving the Church from the threatened Spoliation Bill. Shakespeare, however, has profited by the prelates' speeches, as recorded in the Chronicles, not to expose their unworthy motives but to bring out the reverence felt by Henry V. for the Church. In the introductory discussion between the Archbishop of Canterbury and the Bishop of Ely, the king is described as full of grace and " fair regard," a true lover of Holy Church, suddenly changed from a wild prince, leagued with low associates, to a king as wise in counsel as if the crown had been his lifelong study, reasoning in divinity like a bishop, solving at once the most complicated cases in policy, so eloquent that his discourse on war seemed like

" A fearful battle, rendered you in music."

The strawberry thriving beneath the nettle, the summer grass growing fastest by night, are but images of this wonderful conversion; and Archbishop Chicheley concludes that some natural means must be admitted, " since miracles have ceased."

These last words, from the mouth of the first prelate of the kingdom, are taken both by Gervinus [1] and Kreysig [2] as evidence of the poet's rationalistic spirit, and of his freedom from the superstitions of his time. If so, most of the Fathers were equally enlightened, for the cessation of miracles is a common topic with them; and they explain the fact by show-

[1] iv. 420, cf. ii. 249.   [2] i. 281, quoted by Raich, 175.

O

ing that the utility of miracles would disappear were they of common occurrence, and that their purpose was attained when once the Church was established, itself a standing miracle.   But St. Augustine declares that his words as to the discontinuance of miracles are not to be taken as if they were no longer worked; for he had himself testified to the blind man who had recovered sight in the presence of the bodies of the Milanese martyrs, and he knew of many other miracles too numerous to be related.[1]

The Archbishop's words, interpreted by Lafeu's speech on the wonderful cure of the king in " All's Well that Ends Well," and the detailed account of the miracles worked by St. Edward in " Macbeth," are evidently to be taken comparatively, not absolutely, and bear no sceptical sense.   That the poet wished to represent the Archbishop as a conscientious priest, not an intriguing politician, is seen also from Henry's speech to him.   The king's words manifest both reverence for the prelate's office and an affectionate trust in a loved and faithful religious counsellor. He concludes :—

> " And we will hear, note, and believe in heart,
>   That what you speak is in your conscience washed
>   As pure as sin with baptism."—*Henry V.*, i. 2.

The Catholic doctrine of the justifying effects of the sacrament, *ex opere operato*, is here, we may note, clearly stated.

[1] Retract., i. 13

The three Bishops in "Richard III." occupy subordinate parts. The Archbishop of York behaves with becoming dignity, but Cardinal Bourchier shows himself weak and pliable in yielding at once the rights of sanctuary, by delivering the little Duke of York at Buckingham's demand; and the Bishop of Ely appears an obsequious courtier. Both these prelates are of a very inferior stamp to Carlisle and Archbishop Scroop and to the priest, Rutland's tutor in "Henry VI.," who is ready to imperil his life on his ward's behalf.

In the treason and necromancy of the Duchess of Gloucester three priests are concerned, Sir John Hume, her chaplain; Thomas Southwell, a canon of St. Stephen's, Westminster; and Roger Bolingbroke, chaplain to the Duke of Gloucester. The Duke of Gloucester, according to Æneas Sylvius, afterwards Pius II., had a European reputation for magic, and had probably attached Bolingbroke to himself on account of his astrological fame. The object of Dame Eleanor's conspiracy was doubtless to place her husband on the throne; and this her accomplices engaged to effect by procuring Henry's death. Their mode of action reveals an extraordinary combination of faith and superstition. Southwell said Mass, while a wax image of the king was exposed to a slow fire. As the wax melted, the health of the king, through the joint influence of Southwell's Masses and Bolingbroke's magic, was supposed to give way. The ceremony was apparently adapted from the Luciferarian Masses of the previous century, which are said to have been renewed in our own days. A graver ecclesiastical scandal could not well be imagined, but was the superstition favoured or countenanced by Church authorities? On the contrary, the prisoners were first tried before the Bishops' Court, composed of the Archbishop of Canterbury, Cardinal Beaufort, and the Bishop of London, and were handed over to the secular power. Southwell died in the Tower before his trial, but Bolingbroke publicly abjured his heresy, and was afterwards executed. Shakespeare only gives the carrying out of the sentence on Dame Eleanor, after she had been found guilty by the Bishops on the several indictments of necromancy, witchcraft, sorcery, heresy, and treason. The fourteenth and fifteenth centuries witnessed an extraordinary outburst of the Black Art in Europe. The Order of the Templars was suppressed by the Council of Vienne, in 1311, on charges similar to those advanced against Dame Eleanor. The practice of sorcery was condemned by John XXII. in two Bulls, in 1317 and 1327, again, in 1398, by Gerson and the Sorbonne. In the fifteenth century and later, those charged with sorcery were, as a rule, women. They were believed to have the power of producing storms and pestilences, changing the form of the human body, calling up spirits, and foretelling future events. The shameful condemnation of Joan of Arc, 1431, as a sorceress and impostor, was in part due to the readiness to believe in witchcraft; and Shakespeare, in introducing her trial and Dame Eleanor's in "Henry VI.," produces a special feature of the time. It is noteworthy that the English case of witchcraft should have taken place in the household of the freethinking Duke of Gloucester, a fact showing that superstition is begotten no less readily from scepticism than from faith. Foxe, in his desire to swell the list of his pseudo-martyrs, describes Dame Eleanor branded by the papists as a heretic for her love and desire of truth.[1] In defending himself against the criticisms of Alan Cope (Harpsfield), while declining to discuss the facts of her trial, he conjectures that she suffered, among other reasons, for being an adherent of Wycliff. In any case, Foxe's advocacy of the Duchess shows that he considered her no blind and superstitious papist, nor can Shakespeare's insertion of her trial be interpreted as implying any censure on the Catholic faith.

[1] "Acts and Monuments," iii. 709. 1837.

CHAPTER V.

IN considering the question of Shakespeare's religion the sonnets are of special importance. Their subject-matter is love. His views on this point present, in our opinion, the key to his philosophy of life. The sonnets are also singular in this, that they contain a purely personal element. His "Venus and Adonis," as well as his "Lucrece," though often classed with the sonnets, are not in fact lyrical compositions, but dramatic stories. They exhibit words and feelings wholly external to the poet, except so far as they were necessarily realised at first in his phantasy. The poet speaks throughout as a spectator, not as an actor. In his dramas he is personal only in the sense that the thoughts and feelings exhibited by his characters are all drawn ultimately from his own consciousness. They portray what the poet would be were he some one else, not what he is himself. Had Shakespeare been Othello or Hamlet or Falstaff he might have acted as they did in his drama. But Shakespeare was himself and not another. "I am that I am," he says. In the sonnets, however, he speaks not in character, but in his own person, and thus they furnish the most direct clue to his inner life.

The sonnets contain then, as we think, a revelation of the poet's self, though it must be admitted that the revelation is partial, fragmentary, disconnected, and obscure, and furnishes no data for a personal narrative. Every attempt at a literal interpretation of the sonnets meets with insurmountable difficulties. The poet speaks of himself as made lame by fortune's "dearest spite" (Sonnet 37), and of his "dead body," "the coward conquest of a butcher's knife" (Sonnet 74); yet there are no historical grounds for believing that he was either really lame or had actually been stabbed. Again, he speaks of journeys and pilgrimages "to limits far remote," "to the shores, furthest shores"; yet there is no sure evidence that he was ever out of England.

The indications of time are equally insoluble. In Sonnet 2 he fixes the age of forty as the time when the stage of decay has been reached. In Sonnet 62 he states of himself that he is "beated and chopped with tanned antiquity"; while in Sonnet 73 he declares that he has reached "the autumn and twilight of life." He must then, if these statements about himself are to be taken literally, have been at the time of writing his sonnets at least forty years old. That he was not forty years old at the time of writing his sonnets is made clear by his statement in Sonnet 104, that

three years had passed since he first became
acquainted with the friend to whom they are
addressed.   Now the friend to whom they are
addressed, in the opinion of Drake, Gervinus,
Kreysig, Mr. G. Massey, and others, is Henry
Wriothesley,[1] Earl of Southampton.   But Shakespeare had already made the acquaintance of the
Earl of Southampton at least as early as 1593, for
in that year he dedicated to him his "Venus and
Adonis."   Shakespeare then, if we take his statements literally, must have been forty years old in
1596.   But as a matter of fact he was not forty
years old till 1604, since he was born in the year
1564.

Even if it could be proved that W. H. was really
not Lord Southampton, it could still be shown that
Shakespeare was not forty years of age when he
composed the sonnets, seeing that Meres, writing
in 1598, speaks of Shakespeare's "sug'red sonnets"
"among his private friends."   Again, the last line of
Sonnet 94, "Lilies that fester smell far worse than
weeds," is quoted[2] in the play of "Edward III.,"

[1] W. H. are supposed to be the initials reversed.
[2] The speech in which the line occurs is one in which the Earl
of Warwick extols his daughter, the Countess of Salisbury, for
rejecting the shameful proposal of the King, Edward III.   The
speech consists of "a spacious field" of "eleven reasons" proving
that the malice of sin is in proportion to the rank or power or
knowledge of the sinner.   Each reason is condensed into an
aphorism, and the form of the whole speech is like one of Sancho
Panza's strings of Proverbs.   It is therefore a place where we
should least look for originality, and where an author would think

which was published in 1596, and was probably written in 1595 or 1594. The sonnets, then, were composed before 1596. Clearly, therefore, Shakespeare, was not forty years of age at the time of writing the sonnets, and his statements are not to be taken with literal exactness. Another proof that the sonnets are not to be taken in their literal exactness is found in the fact that Sonnets 72–86 declare that his praises of his friend and patron had become so notorious that others had emulated him, and one of them so successfully as to supplant him in his patron's favour—a statement whose inaccuracy appears from this, that critics have utterly failed to discover any such rival. The sonnets, then, though a lyrical composition, cannot be accepted as an autobiography.

But while we are forced to admit that we cannot expect to find in the sonnets accurate autobiographical data, we altogether dissent from the contention of those critics who maintain that the sonnets were written by Shakespeare solely to exhibit his versifying skill. Between the years 1591 and 1599 a vast number of sonnets appeared. Undoubtedly many of these sonnets were written for no better purpose than that of displaying their

---

least scorn of open plagiarism. For these reasons it seems more probable that the line in question was quoted from Shakespeare's Sonnets, already known in 1594 or 1595 among his private friends, than that it was afterwards adopted by Shakespeare from the play. *Cf.* Simpson, "Philosophy of Shakespeare's Sonnets," 76.

author's power in verbal fence, or were composed in a spirit of mere rivalry. This we freely grant. But at the same time we insist that many of the sonnets were inspired by a much higher motive. They treated of serious subjects in a manner suited to the dignity of their theme. No less than 500 sonnets were composed at this period on such grave topics as philosophy and religion.[1] The sonnets of Shakespeare, it is true, treat professedly neither of religion nor of philosophy, but of love. Yet this theme, however much it may have been degraded by the treatment of other sonneteers, was discussed from a pure and spiritual standpoint by such sonneteers as Surrey, Sidney, and Spenser. The presumption surely ought to be that Shakespeare would take his stand with such writers as these rather than with Marlowe, Greene, and Donne. But we have something more than presumption. A comparison of Shakespeare's theory on love with that which has found favour with the great Christian writers of every age will show the identity of his views on this subject with those of the leaders of religious thought.

The philosophy of love as taught first by Plato, and purified and completed by St. Augustine, Boetius, and St. Thomas, is a definite, comprehensive, and coherent system. In that philosophy the object of love is the good, the act of love is the tendency or the movement towards its

---

[1] S. Lee, "Life of Shakespeare," 441.

attainment, and in its secure possession love is perfected, *quies in bono*, "rest in good," being the essence of beatitude. In intellectual natures the good is apprehended by the intellect as true, and loved by the will as good. God, being infinitely intelligent, necessarily knows His Infinite Perfections in the Word, and from the mutual contemplation of the Father and the Word proceeds the Holy Spirit, their mutual love, the term of union in the Triune God. Thus Dante describes the Divine essence, *Luce intellettual pien d'amor*. From God's Infinite love of Himself proceeds freely His love of creatures, each of which is called into being to portray some special likeness of the Creator's Beauty, their graduated perfection being determined by their degree of resemblance to the Divine exemplar. Every kind of being by love, natural or supernatural, acquires its perfection. Thus the connatural attractiveness, which by the law of gravity binds the atoms in the stone and the stone in its place, may be called love. The vital principle of growth and increase in the plants, the action of the sensitive faculties in the animal world are respectively the law of self-preservation for each, or the love of their good. Man, as a reasonable being, finds his good in the love and acquisition of truth, and in the possession of absolute truth alone is his perfection attained.

Love, then, is the first beginning, the sustaining principle, and the final end of all things. All this is summed up in Dante's vision, in the depth of which he

> "Saw in one volume, clasped of love, whate'er
> The universe unfolds ; all properties
> Of substance and of accident, beheld
> Compounded, yet one individual light
> The whole.   And of such bond methinks I saw
> The universal form ; for that whene'er
> I do but speak of it my soul dilates
> Beyond her proper self."—*Par.* xxiii. 77.

So also Boetius had long since said—

> " Hanc rerum seriem ligat
> Terras et pelagas regens
> Et cœlo imperitans amor."
>   —*De Consol. Phil.,* xi. 8.

Now this love philosophy descended through Petrarch and others to the Italian Revivalists of the sixteenth century, and became a prominent subject in their literature.   From Italy it passed into England, and was taken up by Surrey and Spenser, and in the Hymns of the latter poet on love and beauty we find the theme treated on the lines of Catholic theology already given.   Love, then, according to Spenser, first produced order out of chaos, fixed all things in their different kingdoms, tempered, subordinated, and harmonised their constituent opposing forces, and quickened living things with the desire and power of increase.   Man, having an immortal mind, should love immortal beauty, and seek " to

enlarge his progeny not for lust's sake but for
eternity." Here comes the strife. False love or
lust persuades the "earthly-minded with dunghill
thoughts" to seek only the gratification of their
senses in the enjoyment of corporeal beauty. But the
pure, refined mind, by help of Heaven's grace, expels
all sordid baseness, and newly fashions the sense
image into a higher form, modelled on its divine
exemplar, "its God and King, its victor and its
guide." The love for this ideal must be sole and
sovereign. The fear of its loss is terrible suffering,
only to be surpassed by the joy experienced when
the loved one is possessed.

Such are the leading ideas of the hymns of earthly
love and beauty. The hymn of heavenly love tells
of the Procession of the Divine Persons and of creatures from the same source, "the blessed well of
love." The three great acts of divine love for
man are Creation, Redemption, and the Blessed
Sacrament.

> " Him first to love great right and reason is
> Who first to us our life and being gave,
> And after, when we farèd had amiss,
> Us wretches from the second death did save,
> And last, the food of life which now we have,
> Even He Himself, in his dear sacrament,
> To feed our hungry souls unto us lent."

Such love calls for the sacrifice of all else in return.

> " With all thy heart, with all thy soul and mind
> Thou must Him love, and His behests embrace.

> All other loves, with which the world doth blind
> Weak fancies, and stir up affections base,
> Thou must renounce, and utterly displace,
> And give thyself unto Him full and free
> That full and freely gave Himself to thee."

In the Hymn of Heavenly Beauty we are taught by ascending scale of beauty in creation, by the blinding brightness of the sun, to

> "Look at last up to that Sovereign light
> From whose pure beams all perfect beauty springs;
> That kindleth love in every godly spright,
> Even the love of God; which loathing things
> Of this vile world, and these gay seeming things
> With whose sweet pleasures being so possest,
> Thy straying thoughts henceforth for ever rest."

There are then, according to Spenser, two kinds of beauty, the corporeal and the spiritual. The first is the object of earthly, the second of spiritual love, and the work of the pure soul of true love is to fashion for itself and in itself from the earthly image that spiritual ideal which is the reflection of God Himself. In the process of transformation the better self, God's grace and God Himself, are constantly addressed in the same terms. This identity of love with the object is found in St. Paul's "Vivo ego jam non ego, sed Christus vivit in me," and is a leading thought with St. Augustine, "Anima plus ubi amat quam ubi vivit."

And now let us turn to the sonnets and see how they can be interpreted on the lines of the philosophy already sketched. The first series, 1-126,

is addressed to a youth idealised, described now
as a fair boy, now as an angel, the type of pure
love, leading the poet to higher things. The
second series, 127–156, is addressed to a woman,
the type of evil passion, whose only purpose is to
degrade and destroy the soul. The pure love and
the false the poet experiences in his own heart.

> " Two loves I have, of comfort and despair,
> Which, like two spirits, do suggest me still ;
> The better angel is a man right fair,
> The worser spirit, a woman coloured ill."

As love follows knowledge, the loveable object,
whether good or evil, is presented to the soul
through one of the three channels of human information. These are the outward senses, the inward
senses of the imagination and memory, and the
mind itself. Each of these, when actuated by the
object, proposes to the will a corresponding good.
The object of the outward senses is corporeal beauty.
The object of the inward senses is the imaginative
beauty created by the phantasies and memory.
The object of the intellect is the ideal beauty, the
perfect expression . of truth, and too spiritual and
intellectual to be set forth in any phantasm or outward form. As St. Augustine says, " Vera pulchritudo
ṭustitia est." This triple division is, then, found in
the sonnets.

Sonnets 1–45 treat of the imaginative love, which
is again subdivided by its object as represented

corporeally, by the memory or phantasy, or as an intellectual idea. In the first stage, goodness or beauty as seen through the outward senses forms the theme of twenty sonnets, which we proceed to summarise, the bracketed numbers indicating the sonnets referred to.

The opening lines declare that beauty or goodness should be perpetual, for the thought of coming decay and separation prevents any true enjoyment of the beloved object (1). Therefore he desires offspring for his friend (2). The child is the parent's reflection, and represents him in his prime. His beloved should not then be barren, but inspire the poet's soul with fitting conceptions of his worth, that he may live on in his rhyme (3, 4). As the rose, though dead, lives on in the fragrant water distilled from its leaves, so will his beloved in the verses of the poet. This simile is borrowed from Sidney's image of the rosewater in crystal-glass (5). The necessity of the spiritual marriage is reiterated and illustrated through the next four sonnets. "Summer defaced by winter's ragged hand," the sun's meridian glory adored with bowed head, but forgotten when it sets, typify the oblivion, the necessary heritage of a childless life (6, 7). Then follows an exquisite image from an acoustic phenomenon in music, recalling again the harmony found in every creature true to itself. As the two notes of a perfect triad, struck in complete accord, produce spontaneously a third, so should the poet's fruitful union with his beloved.

" Mark how one string, sweet husband to another,
   Strikes each on each by mutual ordering,
   Resembling sire, and child, and happy mother,
   Who, all in one, one pleasing note do sing ;
   Whose speechless song being many, seeming one,
   Say this to thee, 'Thou single wilt prove none ' " (8).

From this point the arguments become less
rhetorical, and appeal more directly to the feelings.
Do you keep single for fear of wetting a widow's
eye ? (9).   You cannot love others if you thus slay
yourself by singleness ; and here the poet urges his
suit by a personal appeal.

" Make thee another self for love of me,
   That beauty still may live in thine or thee " (10).

In conceptive power live wisdom, beauty, increase ;
without it, time would cease, and the world perish
in an age (11).   The visible decay of all things
warns us to prepare for death (12), and the only
preparation is to leave issue to posterity (13).   The
poet speaks, not as an augur or soothsayer from
weather signs, but from the principles of truth and
beauty seen in the " constant stars," the unchanging
light of his beloved's eyes (14).   The poet's verses,
inspired by this light, will immortalise his love,
though all other things, " cheered and checked by
the self-same sky," from memory pass (15).   If,
however, his friend would draw himself by his own
sweet skill, such a work would be more blessed than
the poet's barren rhyme (16).   Without such an
authentic declaration of the truth none would

P

believe in that beauty which is beyond compare
(17). But with this guarantee his love would live
through all time in his friend's verse and in his
own. Yet his unaided song shall sing his love's
praises, for Truth's eternal summer never fades (18).

> " Do thy worst, old Time, despite thy wrong,
>   My love shall in my verse be ever young " (19).

He then commences his praises of his love. His
beloved's beauty is the Creator's painting, not false
adornment of art. Yet its outward semblance
others may extol with what similes they will. Its
interior loveliness is the object of the poet's desire
(20, 21), and reclothed therein his youth is ever
renewed.

> " For all the beauty that doth cover thee
>   Is but the seemly raiment of my heart,
>   Which in thy breast doth live, as thine in me,
>   How can I then be elder than thou art ?" (22).

Notwithstanding his previous declaration to sing
his friend's praises at any cost, his love renders
him tongue-tied, like an actor who, through fear,
forgets his part. His beloved then must read in
his heart " what love hath writ." He holds there a
treasure. Earth's heroes and royal favourites live
in to-day's smile and expire in the morrow's frown.
His love and joy are eternal.

> " Then happy I that love and am beloved,
>   Where I may not remove, nor be removed " (25).

With Sonnet 26 we enter the second degree in

the scale of imaginative love, the phantastic representation of the beloved object. Again he asks
his friend to inspire his muse, confessing, as in
Sonnet 33, his own inability to do so. As the
internal senses are now alone operative he deplores
the bodily absence of his beloved, though the
memory of the ideal is with him day and night
(27), is brighter than the sun, and enlightens the
night.

> "How many a holy and obsequious tear
>   Hath dear religious love stol'n from mine eye,
>   As interest of the dead, which now appear
>   But things removed that hidden lie in thee " (31).

As he loves his friend truly, he can count on his
love in return, even though his "rude lines" be
outstripped by every pen (32). Again, though he
has to bear what seems inconstancy, if not disgrace,
even then the sorrow of pure love, the tears of true
contrition, procure their own pardon (34). To his
own faults must be attributed the loss of his love;
of himself he can do nothing, but if he can identify
himself with his ideal, his will be ideal beauty,
wealth, and wit (37).

The third stage of imaginative love begins at
Sonnet 38 with another prayer for inspiration. He
has again to deplore the trials of separation, for
he is now deprived even of the portrait drawn by
memory and imagination of his love (39). Yet
whatever his friend does, whatever injury he may

inflict, the poet's heart will be faithful.   He worships his beloved's will alone, and is one with it;
and as that will is perfect, so will he gain by his
very love (41, 42).   His beloved is indeed seen best
in the dark, when all other objects and earthly aims
are excluded (43), and but for the dull substance of
his flesh he would mount in thought and desire
to the presence of his beloved (44).   Were it not
for some tender embassies assuring him from time
to time of his ideal's reality and life he would sink
down and die (45).

The change to the ideal love is indicated in
Sonnet 46.   The object of this love being neither
outward beauty nor its pictured resemblance, but
an ideal purely interior and intellectual, self-know-
ledge is necessary. *Magister intus docet.*   The Master
teaches within, and we must know ourselves and
what speaks there, and distinguish our true motives
and aims, if we are to detect His voice.   The eye
and heart, the flesh and the spirit, the higher and
lower impulses are alike active and opposed in
mortal war.   Each claims possession of the soul.
The poet must then look into the inner depths of
his heart, "a closet never pierced save by crystal
eyes," and there decide by the higher principles of
reason, a jury impanelled by nature for that purpose,
the true province and function of sense and reason
in the representation of his beloved (46).

He finds then that sense and reason mutually co-
operate to teach us the truth.   The outward object

through the sense supplies the image whence the
heart obtains its ideal; and the phantasm of the
ideal again lives in the memory to refresh the soul
in the absence of its beloved (47). This he strove
to effect. But in spite of all his care to keep his
ideal uncorrupted "in sure wards of trust," locked
in his inner soul, it escaped and became "a prey
of every vulgar thief"; the distractions of outward
things (48). His own unworthiness then alone
accounts for his beloved's absence (49). His efforts
to rise to higher things are impeded by the flesh,
"the beast that bears me," "which plods dully on,"
and only answers with a groan to the bloody spur
(50). No carnal strength or power can help him
in his fiery race: and he dismisses his body with
contempt, and gives "his jade" leave to go, for he
would mount with a winged speed, to which the
mind itself is slow (51). In his heart's probation
only at times can he realise the presence of his
beloved. The visits of his beloved are rare and
solemn as annual feasts or "costly jewels," "captains
in the carcanet," or "state robes seldom worn" (52).
The best of earthly things, the most perfect type of
man or woman, Adonis or Helen, are in their beauty
but counterfeit imitations of the "One Fair." Spring-
tide in its promise, harvest in its abundance, are but
types of the beauty and bounty of his ideal, whose
unchanging truth or "constant heart" no earthly
image bears (53). This invisible truth is the essence
of all real perfection, and this shall live on in his

verse, though outward forms vanish from sight (54, 55).

Sonnet 56 gives expression to another state of soul; the lover pines for sensible consolation. The spirit is chilled by the " perpetual dulness " of his beloved's absence, whose coming would be welcome as summer after winter. But he has no right to be jealous or impatient; he is his beloved's slave, and can think no ill whate'er his master does (57). He must then wait, though waiting be hell (58). He will renew his courage by recalling how antique books and past sages have described his ideal (59). Its image, then, founded on truth, not feeling, will have a new and lasting birth (60). But may not the images thus awakened in his soul be merely his own creation? Have they an objective reality? His beloved cannot care to inspire them (61); yet he must have done so, for the poet sees himself to be so blackened and corrupt, " beated and chopped," by his own evil past, he could never form of himself any worthy conception of truth or beauty (62). His very deformity shall then be a foil and frame for his ideal's praise, as its beauty is seen in the poet's black lines, and shall live for all time; an image recalling the *nigra sed formosa* of the Canticles.

The poet, having now learnt to know himself, is enabled to pierce the mask of other things and to see them as they really are, and he expresses in Sonnet 66 his soul's disgust at the corruption

of his age.   Faith is forsworn, Virtue strumpeted,
Honour misplaced, the highest perfection disgraced,
Art tongue-tied by authority, evil everywhere trium-
phant, " captive good attending captain ill."

> " Tired with all these, from these I would be gone,
> Save that, to die, I leave my love alone."

If he dies of his own will, he neglects his duty and
abandons the cause of truth (66).

But why should his love live on in an age of
impiety and falsehood ?   The world, indeed, admits
its outward beauty, but slanders its thoughts and
motives; yet, since the world has ever slandered
truth, its enmity proves his love immaculate, as in
fact it is (68, 69, 70).

The poet now turns his thoughts to his own
death and its effects on the fame of his beloved.
His life has given much scandal.   His soul is like
a ruined choir or " twilight," showing traces of light
and beauty now gone.   Let not his friend attempt
to defend the poet's good name.   " His evil is his
own, his better part his love's "; therein was its
consecration (73, 74).   The thought of union with
his love is his only joy on earth, its praise his sole
theme (75, 76).   Again he asks that his muse be
fresh inspired, his brain is as a note-book of blank
leaves (77).

The next nine sonnets express the poet's jealous
indignation at the false praise and " strained touches
of rhetoric " and " gross painting " bestowed on his

subject by rival poets.   His object is truth.   Faith
in his ideal will compensate for lack of education
or skill.   He has not to ransack the universe for
comparisons, but only to say simply what he sees—
none can say more,

> " Than this rich praise, that you alone are you."

Such creation is the highest art ; its subject thereby
lives individualised and unique (78—86).

In the next nine sonnets the rivals seem to
prevail, which the poet explains by the same reason
as before—his own unworthiness.   But while in
Sonnet 49 he had admitted his own inferiority in
comparison with his ideal, he does so now in comparison with his rivals.   For the sake of his beloved
he will consent to be effaced, and confess whatever
faults may be laid to his charge.   Like Ophelia
in " Hamlet," he owns beforehand—

> " Thou canst not, love, disgrace me half so ill,
>   As I'll myself disgrace " (89).

But he begs that his dismissal, if determined on,
may be at once, when all the world is against
him, and not come as an after-blow to destroy his
only hope.   Whatever his fate, his love is always
" the only fair."   For a moment he seems to doubt
—what if his love were really false !   *Corruptio
optimi pessima*—the best, corrupted, is the worst.

> " For sweetest things turn sourest by their deeds,
>   Lilies that fester smell far worse than weeds" (94).

The second stage of ideal love has the same conclusion as that which terminates (36) the second
stage of imaginative love. For the same situations
recur, but ever in a higher significance.

In the third stage of ideal love, introduced in
Sonnet 97, all previous errors or adverse judgments
are rectified and the poet's scattered premises draw
to one conclusion. Before the beauty of his spiritual
ideal, fair nature pales. " Proud-pied April, dressed
in all his trim," renewing youth in all things ;
summer's story told by lays of birds and flowers
varying in scent and hue, all seemed winter compared to his beloved (98, 99). Then, after rebuking
his muse for her silence (100, 101), he excuses
it, because his theme is above its power. His
verse would only mar what it cannot mend, and his
love would be degraded by public praise (102, 103).
In Sonnet 104 commences his solemn and final
act of homage. He declares his love endowed
with perpetual youth. His ideal has passed through
three seasons—three being the image of completeness or eternity—and unites in itself the three
great elements of love, beauty, goodness, truth.
All the praise of beauty, chronicled in the past,
but prophesy his " only fair." Yet neither prophecy
of the past nor even his own reverential fear can
set bounds to his love (105, 106). Day by day,
then, he will repeat the " paternoster " of his love,
which loses not, but grows in time (107, 108).
After this act of homage begins his own Confiteor.

In words borrowed almost literally from the Church's commendation of the soul, he declares that though through nature's frailty he has erred, he was never really false at heart.   If he wandered, he returned again to the breast, his home of love, and was there cleansed anew.   All his past wildness, his actor's life, his wounded conscience "goring his own thoughts," his apparent estrangement from truth, have all proved to him more fully what was the heaven he had lost.

For the scandal he has caused, due much to his needy state and deteriorating surroundings, he begs pardon and will deem no penance harsh.   With his love's approval he cares not who condemns.   With sense and mind now purified, he can see all things in the light of the ideal and find goodness everywhere, save in his own deformity (109–114).   He retracts all previous expressions of uncertainty, " the marriage of true minds admits of no impediments." His soul now steers straight for the star.   " Strange love of other days but makes the true love stronger." He has drunk of siren tears, of alembics foul as hell, but *omnia cooperantur in bonum*—" better is by evil still made better."   He sees the justice of past chastisements inflicted by his beloved, though he still repudiates the slanders of evil tongues. His mind is no longer a blank leaf (77), but a lasting record of gifts received.   Subject no more to things of time, nor dependent like a heretic on the favour or frown of the passing hour, he stands

alone, unchanging himself, having fixed his heart on
what is unchangeable and eternal (124). One act
alone can adequately express his love and worship
—the sacrifice of all he is and all he has to its
true object; a poor offering, indeed, but voluntary
and complete.

> " No, let me be obsequious in thy heart,
> And take thou my oblation, poor but free,
> Which is not mixed with seconds, knows no art
> But mutual render, only me for thee" (125).

As the Paternoster was chosen to express his
former petition (108), so here the language of a yet
more solemn office is used. The outward sign of
the Eucharistic oblation is but wastel bread, the
inward effect the union of the creature with his
God—of the human love with the one ideal and
perfect exemplar. Then, as if remembering that he
had employed the words of a proscribed ritual, he
concludes—

> " Hence, thou suborned informer ! a true soul,
> When most impeached, stands least in thy control."

Sonnet 126 is merely an epilogue or appendix to
the series we have considered. That series is complete in its unity, and exhibits the ascent of the
soul by purifying love through the phases recognised both by mystical writers and sonneteers contemporary with Shakespeare. The leading idea is
often hard to trace, hidden as it is under a wealth
of imagery; but, when discovered, is ever found

advancing in its appointed grades, with precision and certainty, to its only legitimate conclusion.

In his second series of sonnets, the poet traces the descent of the soul in the "love of despair." Its object, instead of an angelic youth, *aliquid jam non carnis in carne*, is a gipsy-like woman, with black eyes and hair and complexion "coloured ill." He sees in her "beauty profaned," and, like Dante and the siren, is at first disgusted with the sight. But like Dante again, he lingers in the presence of the temptress. Sense attractions and his lower impulses stifle reason and conscience. No angel appears to save him as with his Tuscan prototype, and he surrenders himself to the painted charms. The delusion and disorder of the soul, a prey to temptation, the madness consequent on "the swallowed bait," and the repugnance and loathing resulting therefrom, when the heat of passion is passed, the close connection of sin with sin, the parentage of crime from crime—all these are then described in language alike psychologically and theologically accurate. No less profoundly true are the concluding lines, expressing the extraordinary power of temptation, even where experience has taught the misery of a fall.

> "All this the world well knows; yet none knows well
> To shun the heaven that leads men to this hell" (129).

These last lines explain how it is, that though he knows the real deformity of the temptress, he is still held captive by her. He groans under her tyranny, as St. Augustine under the iron chain that held him bound (*Conf.* viii. 10), but strives in vain for freedom. Absent from the accursed object, he has a lucid interval, and realises the extent of his delusion; but accounts for it by supposing that she is really fair without and only foul within (131), or that her pretended sympathy has won his heart (132). Nor has he only to deplore a moral fall; the image of purity, the type of his true love, is now effaced from his soul. This concludes the imaginative stage of sensual love, the inability to recall or picture the remembrance of what is good.

The ideal stage opens with the soul wholly materialised; and thus enslaved, the poet abandons himself and his friend to his mistress's yoke, under the symbol of the three Wills. Himself, W. S., his friend, W. H., are handed over to the Will and dominion of evil. The very fact of his previous high ideal and former purity makes him a valuable conquest in her eyes (136); while on his side he is so completely blinded by her " over-partial looks," that he regards as exclusively his own what is in truth "the wide world's common place" (137). Having thus attempted to justify false love by idealising it, he still further seeks excuses for his passion by painting its vices as virtues. In this his mistress joins, and thus the partners in evil flatter each other with falsehoods, and increase their mutual blindness. She calls his old age youth, he, her falsehood truth.

> " Therefore I lie with her, and she with me,
>   And in our faults by lies we flattered be " (138).

Nothing breaks the chain of his captivity. She is false and cruel to him to his face, and he knows it; yet she is able by her sensual dominion to keep him in slavery (139). She had better feign a little kindness, and make at least some profession of the love which she is incapable of feeling, or he may grow reckless, and speak out (140). He does so. Her face is hideous, her voice discordant, her touch freezes, her presence repels. She is no longer attractive but loathsome; yet having dethroned reason, and yielded to passion, he must be still " her venal wretch." His iniquity is indeed his torment; perhaps his bitter experience may be of future profit.

> " Only my plague thus far I count my gain
>   That she that makes me sin awards me pain " (141).

In their mutual and utter degradation they cannot reproach each other. Virtue and vice have changed places; love and hate have lost their true meaning. All things are perverted and confused. Their so-called honour is rooted in shame and treachery. Yet again he accuses her; false, pitiless, and heartless to him, if she ever want pity, may she be paid in her own coin, and seek it in vain.

> " If thou dost seek to have what thou dost hide,
> By self example may'st thou be denied " (142).

In her insatiable selfishness, fickleness, and vanity, she forgets the slave at her side, to pursue any one she thinks indifferent to her charms; just as a housewife drops her crying child to capture a stray chick. The conquest made, she returns to her helpless victim, plays the mother's part again, kisses him and is kind (143). All this he sees, for the good angel still wrestles with the devil in his soul, yet its accents are scarcely distinguishable to his seared conscience. He will not know what he truly is, till he finds himself a reprobate (144). She alternately tortures and coaxes, drives him away and calls him back; and he comes, for, fallen as he is, he lives only in her (145). In Sonnet 146 he apostrophises his soul, much after the language of St. Paul: " Infelix homo, quis me liberabit a corpore mortis." All the bodily indulgence, luxury, and sensual delight, with which his mistress pampers him, is, after all, only feeding on death (146), for "in a sort lechery eats itself " (" Troilus and Cressida," v. 4), yet his passion is as fever, longing for that which nurses the disease. He is past cure and past care, he is mad, frantic mad, and he knows it.

> " For I have sworn thee fair, and thought thee bright
> Who art as black as hell, as dark as night" (147).

Still he remains wilfully and voluntarily blind to his own foulness and to hers (148), and yields a complete and fawning submission to her every caprice. His self-respect is dead. The more he ought to hate, the more he loves her, yet wins her not. He has sold his conscience and abjured truth and reason for her sake. They are both perjured, but he the most, for he has sinned against light. He has worshipped an idol, and forsaken the only good.

> "For I have sworn thee fair, more perjured I
> To swear against the truth so foul a lie" (152).

Thus his downward steps had led him to the Inferno, and leave him there, Sonnets 153, 154, being probably only an appendix, as was 126 at the conclusion of the first series. A careful inspection shows that both series proceed upward and downward by analogous steps to their respective term; and that the whole collection exhibits the three great divisions of love as stimulated by the presentation of good through the senses, imagination and reason.

Such then, summarised, is Mr. Simpson's interpretation of the sonnets. We fully admit that only after repeated readings can the allegory be discovered, and that they must be studied in the light of that philosophy which gave them birth. That philosophy forms the basis alike of the dramas as of the sonnets, and read in conjunction they will be found to repeat the same teaching and to illustrate the same common principles. The ideal of true love is presented in Isabella in "Measure for Measure" on the same lines as in the portraiture of the better angel of the sonnets. Cleopatra or Cressida are counterparts of "the woman coloured ill." The alliance of sin with sin, of impurity and murder (129), is repeated in Pericles.

> "One sin I know another doth provoke,
> Murder's as near to lust, as flame to smoke ;
> Poison and treason are the hands of sin."

The sacrificial requirement of the higher love, the law that the flesh must die that the soul may live, as expressed in Sonnet 146,

> "Poor soul, the centre of my sinful earth,
> Why feed'st the rebel powers that thee array ?"

this same truth forms the moral of "Love's Labour's Lost," and is enforced in the penitential exercises imposed on the three lovers. The inferiority of imaginative love to that of reason, shown in the ascending scale of the first series, is the lesson taught in the playful satire of "Midsummer-Night's Dream." And so we might go on, finding every maxim of the sonnets confirmed in the poet's other works. This identity of teaching we think shows that the philosophical interpretation we have followed is neither fanciful nor arbitrary, but has a solid foundation.

We prefaced this chapter with the statement that the sonnets alone of Shakespeare's works furnish a clue to his own feeling, and we would here observe that in them we learn, as nowhere else in his writings, his intense antagonism to his times. Sonnet 66,

Q

already quoted, is a solemn impeachment of the
government of his day, of its oppression, falsehood,
and treachery.   All this invective finds additional
force and significance when we remember in whose
house and among what private friends " the sug'red
sonnets " were read, circulated, and discussed.   Henry
Wriothesley, Earl of Southampton, whether or no he
was " W. H.," was undoubtedly Shakespeare's one
literary patron, for there is not the slightest evidence of his having been in similar relations to
any other distinguished personage.   To Southampton he dedicated his " Venus and Adonis " in
1593, and his " Lucrece " in 1594, at the very
time the sonnets were, according to our com-
putation, in course of composition.   Both dedi-
cations are in terms of exclusive devotion.   That to
" Lucrece " is indeed recast in verse in Sonnet 26.[1]
There is then every reason for believing that it was
under Southampton's roof and among the earl's
friends that the sonnets first appeared.   Now
Southampton's town house, " Drury House," [2] was as

---

[1] Lee, "Life of Shakespeare," 127.

[2] Southampton House was never apparently the residence of the
poet's patron. This mansion, situated in Holborn, was one of the
chief resorts of Catholics and priests in London, and was repeatedly
searched for recusants. It was leased to Mr. Swithun Wells in
1591. Here F. Edmund Jennings was apprehended in his vestments
by Topcliffe after saying Mass, and with him were taken Polydore
Plasden and Eustachius White, also priests ; Brian Lacy, John Mason,
and Sydney Hodgson, laymen ; and Mrs. Wells. Mrs. Wells died in
prison. The rest were martyred at Tyburn. Mr. Swithun Wells
was hanged in Gray's Inn, opposite Southampton House, for having
allowed Mass to be said there.

we have seen the meeting-place of the Essex conspirators, amongst whom were so many of the poet's
country-folk and friends. Shakespeare's friendship
with Southampton may then, we think, throw some
light on the political allusions in the sonnets, though
we look upon the whole collection, as has been said,
as intended primarily to illustrate the course and
circumstances of love.

The laments over his time speak of " Bare ruined
choirs, where once the sweet birds sang," of

> " Unswept stone, besmeared with sluttish time.
> When wasteful war shall statues overturn,
> And broils root out the work of masonry."

of
—*Sonnet* lv. ;

> " Lofty towers down-razed,
> And brass eternal slave to mortal rage."
> —*Sonnet* lxiv. ;

an imagery singularly applicable to the sanctuaries
violated, and the brasses and images destroyed by
the Tudor rule. Such metaphors, as well as that
of the vestments and feasts already quoted, form a
fitting framework to the Catholic line of thought
traceable throughout the series.

Lastly, to return to Southampton. To what
library could a playwright have had access, suggestive of the following lines :—

> " Show me your image in some antique book,
> Since mind at first in character was framed,"

and

> " When in the chronicle of wasted time
> I see descriptions of the fairest wights,

And beauty making beautiful old rhyme
In praise of ladies dead and lovely knights ;
Then in the blazon of sweet beauty's best,
Of hand, of foot, of lip, of eye, of brow,
I see their antique pen would have expressed
Even such a beauty as you master now " ?

—*Sonnet* cvi.

Mr. S. Lee tells us that the collection of books presented by the Earl of Southampton to St. John's College, Cambridge, " largely consisted of illuminated manuscripts, books of hours, legends of the saints, and mediæval chronicles." [1]

[1] " Life of Shakespeare," 382.

CHAPTER VI.

THE LOVE PLAYS.

AMONG the various dissertations contained in "Troilus and Cressida," that on the origin and nature of intellectual knowledge forms a fitting preface to an examination of the love plays. The passage we are about to quote gives the philosophical principles of Shakespeare's teaching on love, and this philosophy explains an imagery otherwise unintelligible.

To Ulysses' question why it is that no man, however gifted, knows either himself, or what he has, or whence it comes, save by reflection, Achilles answers—

> " The beauty that is borne here in the face
> The bearer knows not, but commends itself
> To others' eyes. Nor doth the eye itself,
> That most pure spirit of sense, behold itself,
> Not going from itself ; but eye to eye opposed
> Salutes each other with each other's form.
> For speculation turns not to itself
> Till it hath travelled, and is married there
> Where it may see itself."
> —*Troilus and Cressida*, iii. 3.

The soul is thus an eye which sees not itself, " a mirror," a " glassy essence," a retina void of forms,

245

till it is actuated by the objects it reflects. Thus
all objective speculation becomes in Shakespeare's
terminology a "reverberation,"[1] "reflection,"[2] issuing
from the union of the knowing mind with the
known object. Without this union sense and mind
are in darkness and ignorance.

The term "marriage," as thus employed, is not
merely a poetical figure, but the correct, scholastic
expression for the mode in which knowledge is
obtained. For it is from the union of the object
to be known and the knowing mind that a
"concept" is begotten. The knowing mind is
united, not indeed with the substance of the thing
known or with its proper nature, but with its
likeness or species, which the poet correctly terms
its "form" (*forma intentionalis*), and which actuates
the intellectual faculty in the process of knowledge.
The intellect, thus actuated or informed, conceives
or begets the object in the ideal order. The object
thus conceived or known is termed, in the language
both of Shakespeare and of scholastic theology,
concept or "child" (Sonnet 59). Thus even material things are "married" to the soul, and become
assimilated to and one with it. "The soul sees
itself" in them, the *intellectus in actu* and the *in-
telligibile in actu* being, as S. Thomas, following
Aristotle, says in his "Summa," I. q. xiv. a. 2, one
and the same. Thus if Shakespeare follows Plato

---

[1] "Troilus and Cressida," iii. 3.
[2] "Julius Cæsar," i. 2.

in his doctrine of love, he is equally a disciple of Aristotle in his theory of knowledge.

Now we have seen in the interpretation given of the sonnets, that the true and adequate object of the soul, where " it knows even as it is known," is the ideal truth, goodness, and beauty, " marriage with which admits of no impediments " (Sonnet 116). In this ideal alone, mind and heart, thought and feeling, find at last their true term, and love and philosophy become identified in the knowledge of, and union with, the " only fair." Till that object is found and the soul is drawn out of itself in pursuit of its ideal, there can be no development of character, or art, learning, or love worthy of the name.

As love and philosophy are identical in the lower spheres of truth and love, so in the highest sphere of all, absolute truth and love are one. From this unity of principle, ordering all things in harmony, from the " smallest orb to the young-eyed cherubim," and guiding all to their one end, arises again the affinity between love and religion found in Shakespeare's plays. Beauty of face or form is but a reflection of the one exemplar, and the love inspired by created fairness should end in worship which, in itself and its object, is wholly spiritual.

It follows from what has been said that the religious allusions that abound in Shakespeare's love poetry are neither profane mockeries, nor metaphysical figures, but the expression of the poet's sense of the simple tendency of unimpeded love, of the real community between true love and true religion. Hence comes the importance of considering, as has been already pointed out, what form of religion Shakespeare adopts in his love plays. Does he make true love, when it uses religious language, speak the language of Protestantism, of the English Prayer-book and Homilies, or that of the old religion? Dramatic exigencies in no way hampered his choice. He need not have selected Catholic countries, or if he did, his reverence for the conventionalities of times or places was not sufficiently powerful to make him its slave. Thus, the "Merry Wives of Windsor" belongs to the days of Henry V.; yet Evans is a Protestant parson. Illyria, the scene of "Twelfth Night," could hardly be a Protestant country; yet the religious allusions in it are to a Protestant society. If Shakespeare had felt that it had been proper to make true love speak as a Protestant, he either would not have chosen the stories of "Romeo and Juliet" or the "Two Gentlemen of Verona," or if he had, he would boldly have made Romeo speak with the tongue of the Reformers.

With this much of preface, we will proceed with the examination of Shakespeare's love plays, beginning with "Love's Labour's Lost." According to the laws of chivalry, which were essentially religious, a knight had to prove his manhood by deeds of courage and endurance, his fidelity by prolonged absence and many tests of his constancy, before he could lay claim to the hand of his only fair. The practice of penance or of ascetic exercises in some form was thus regarded, according to the mediæval code of love, as a necessary condition for winning the affection of the beloved object. The same law is expressed in Shakespeare. The princess in " Love's Labour's Lost " sentences the king, if he would gain her, to spend a year in a hermitage, remote from all worldly pleasures, living austerely, " Nipped by frosts and fasts, hard lodging and thin weeds." Biron, too, is condemned by Rosaline to spend a year in a hospital as a penance for the presumption of his love, and as a test of his constancy.[1] The same practice appears in the "Two Gentlemen of Verona."

> " I have done penance for contemning love
> With bitter fasts, with penitential groans,
> With mighty tears and daily heartsore sighs" (ii. 4).

Among the trials proposed by Hamlet to Laertes as a test of their love was fasting. " Wilt fast ? " The practice is abused if exaggerated or undertaken without a worthy object and a reasonable hope of success. Cervantes satirised this abuse in his portrait of Don Quixote alone in the desert, stripped to the nude and meditating on Dulcinea, who was wholly ignorant of his affection. The purpose of " Love's Labour's Lost," then, is not to satirise the

[1] v. 2.

religious state, as some German critics have taught, but is to show the futility of undertaking penance, study, or solitude without an adequate motive, *viz.* the likelihood of attaining the beloved object. These things are not good in themselves but in their end. Without this end penance and solitude are but "pain purchasing pain," and study, without a higher light guiding it, is but to lose one's sight.

The comedy in "Love's Labour's Lost," like that in the "Merry Wives of Windsor," is meant to be Protestant. The pedant and the curate, Nathaniel and Holofernes, dread of speaking concerning the Fathers. "Tell me not of the Fathers; I do fear colourable colours" (iv. 2). Under their training, Costard catches the knack of pulpit oratory, already observed in Falstaff, and repeated, as we shall see, in Bottom. His formal discourse on the law-text, "in matter and form following" (i. 1), would be pointless were it not evidently a parody of the sermonizing of the day. The ministers themselves are exhibited, not indeed as vicious or corrupt, but as weak-minded pedants, timid and time-serving, and totally void both of that sturdy fidelity incapable of betraying "the devil to his fellow"—the attribute of the poet's true heroes—and of that versatility, fertile of expedients in difficulties, peculiar to his Friars.

In the "Two Gentlemen of Verona" the moral seems to be fidelity in love, based, as we have seen in the sonnets, on the conviction of the sovereign

truth, goodness, and beauty of the beloved mistress.
Thus Silvia says to Proteus :—

> "Thou hast no faith left now, unless thou hadst two,
> And that's far worse than none ; better have none
> Than plural faith, which is too much by one" (v. 3).

Constancy in love is the corner-stone of virtue in
Shakespeare's eyes.

> "O Heaven,
> Were man but constant, he were perfect ; that one error
> Fills him with faults, makes him run through all sins ;
> Inconstancy falls off e'er it begins" (v. 4).

That Shakespeare carried this feeling into religion
also is seen from the contempt with which he speaks
of those who go where grace is said "in any religion "
(" Measure for Measure," i. 2), and of that " past-
saving slave " Parolles, who offers to take the sacrament " how or which way you will " (" All's Well
that Ends Well," iv. 3), very much as we have seen
Ben Jonson did. Hence the sting of Beatrice's
taunt of Benedick ("Much Ado about Nothing," i. 1),
" He wears his faith but as the fashion of his hat.
It ever changes with the next block." On the
other hand, infidelity in love, the religion of the eye,
is heresy,[1] and the woman who causes it is said to
" found a sect." Even the true professions of a lover
who is rejected are called heresy,[2] for truth is not

---

[1] "Romeo and Juliet," i. 2, 93; "Cymbeline," iii. 4; "Merry
Wives of Windsor," iv. 4 ; "Midsummer-Night's Dream," ii. 3.
[2] "Twelfth Night," i. 5.

merely a subjective creation, but consists in the conformity of the thought and its object.

But there was a worship severely condemned in Shakespeare's day as idolatry. In the "Two Gentlemen of Verona" (iv. 2) he employs the word in its Protestant sense for all worship of images or relics. He qualifies it, however, by leaving us to infer that there is a good idolatry, as well as the bad one that worships false deities. So he makes Sylvia say, when she gives her picture to Proteus :—

> "I am very loth to be your idol, sir ;
> But since your falsehood shall become you well
> To worship shadows, and adore false shapes,
> Send to me in the morning, and I'll send it."
> —*Two Gentlemen of Verona*, iv. 2.

A few scenes afterwards, Julia addresses this picture :—

> "O thou senseless form,
> Thou shalt be worshipped, kissed, loved, and adored ;
> And were there sense in his idolatry,
> My substance should be statue in thy stead " (iv. 4).

Compare what Helena says of Bertram in "All's Well that Ends Well."

> "He's gone, and my idolatrous fancy
> Must sanctify his relics " (i. 1).

This employment, in a good sense, of a term generally used in mockery is the boldest form of approval of the principle attacked.

The moral of the "Two Gentlemen of Verona" is brought out in the contrast of the two characters of Valentine and Proteus. Valentine is the prototype of fidelity, his fancy being subjected to his reason—a type repeated in Bassanio and Henry V. Proteus represents inconstancy, for with him fancy commands reason, as in Romeo, Orsino in "Twelfth Night," and the two lovers in the "Midsummer-Night's Dream." The superior claims of pure friendship to love which terminates in marriage, a principle already enunciated in the sonnets, is enforced again in the readiness of Valentine to surrender Sylvia to Proteus (v. 4); and of Bassanio to sacrifice himself and his wife for Antonio ("Merchant of Venice," iv. 1). Proteus on the other hand, with a passion merely selfish, like that of Arcita in Chaucer, could not understand how friendship should be respected in love (v. 4).

The supernatural development of the love of friendship appears in the "Midsummer - Night's Dream" (i. 1), where human and divine love are compared, with the conclusion that, however happy the lot of the maiden loving and beloved, her happiness is more earthly than that of the thrice blessed nun, whose love is " dedicate to nothing temporal," but to God Himself. Charity thus eclipses all human loves, or rather embodies them in itself, transfigures and transubstantiates them into its own form and substance. We find something like this in " Hamlet " (i. 5). When he dedicates his life to performing the commands of his father's ghost, he casts out everything from his mind, except the one remembrance,

the one commandment, and at once, in obedience
to this resolution, sacrifices the love of Ophelia.
The sacrifice of a lower to a higher love is then
no breach of constancy, but rather a severe and
inexorable duty, imposed by the nature of the obligation already contracted.   Shakespeare's teaching
on this subject is thus, we see, in exact accordance
with the Church's doctrine of the imperative and
supreme claims of a religious vocation, in comparison
with those of the closest human ties.   The truth that
the stronger absorbs the weaker flame is embodied
in a proverbial expression often used by the poet,
" Fire drives out fire." [1]   The principle, when perverted, applies of course also to an evil passion, if
dominant; thus Lady Macbeth declared that her
ambition overrode any maternal instinct.

The manners in the " Two Gentlemen of Verona "
are Catholic, and some Catholic expressions are
used.   The metaphor of having " a month's mind "
is an old Catholic expression still in use and is
intended to designate the mass of requiem celebrated a month after a person's decease.   Sylvia
goes to Friar Patrick's cell for " holy confession ";
Julia compares her affection to the unwearied steps
of the time-devoted pilgrim.   Thurio and Proteus
are to meet at St. Gregory's Well, as in " Measure
for Measure " (iv. 3) the Duke desires Angelo to
meet him " at the consecrated fount a league below

[1] "Coriolanus," iv. 7 ; "Julius Cæsar," iii. 1 ; " King John,"
iii 1 ; " Romeo and Juliet," i. 2.

the city." Launce appropriately invokes St. Nicholas
to aid Speed to read, for this Saint was the patron
of scholars. Sir Eglamour had made a solemn vow
of chastity (iv. 3).

The "Comedy of Errors" is an early play of
Shakespeare's, and is remarkable as his adaptation
of Plautus to the English stage, representing the
Latin comedy as "Richard III." does the Greek tragedy. Both are adaptations rather than imitations
and as such, reveal to the inquirer many secrets
concerning Shakespeare's art. With regard to his
religious opinions the "Comedy of Errors" has not
much to tell us. We find it an amusing specimen
of Shakespeare's indifference to the conventionalities
of time and place already referred to, when he
endows the inhabitants of ancient Syracuse with
the habits and customs of Catholic countries, and
makes one of the Dromios call out for his beads
and cross himself (ii. 2); while Adriana offers to
shrive her husband (ii. 2). The theological jokes
about bailiffs (iv. 2, 3), and the jest of mistak-
ing the courtesan for the devil (iv. 3), all belong
to Shakespeare's day; so do the conjurations of
the cheating juggler Pinch, which belong to the
same class of magical cheats as the pretensions of
Glendower. But in this play Shakespeare is careful to distinguish between the illicit impostures of
Pinch "conjuring by all the saints in heaven"
(iv. 4) and the lawful and remedial exorcisms of
the Abbess—for Shakespeare will not deprive even

the Pagan Greeks of the benefits of the religious orders and of Christian charity.

> "I will not let him stir
> Till I have used the approvèd means I have
> With wholesome syrups, drugs and holy prayers,
> To make of him a formal man again :
> It is a branch and parcel of mine oath,
> A charitable duty of mine order" (v. 1).

But a duty of the effects of which poor Adriana complains.

> "Ill doth it beseem your holiness
> To separate the husband and the wife" (v. 1) ;

though her respect for the cloister will not allow her to force an entrance.

In this play, as in " Much Ado about Nothing," " Romeo and Juliet," and " Measure for Measure," the " religious," the Friar, and the Nun are not only patterns of personal purity, but centres of a soothing higher influence, in which the contradictions of the characters and the intricacies of the plot find their solution. But we shall have to return to this subject.

As Shakespeare in the " Comedy of Errors " has made Pagan Syracuse a Catholic city, so in the " Merry Wives of Windsor " he has made the England of Henry V. Protestant : at least, he has peopled it with Protestant ministers and laymen. The religious element here, however, begets not peace, but discord, and awakes the pungent harmonies of this stimulating *scherzo*. Parson Evans prays his Bible well, commends the virtue which resolves only to be "drunk in company with men who fear God" (i. 1); and through ignorance of Latin, condemns, as affected, quotations he should have recognised as biblical. Though he exerts a certain ministerial power, as when he bids Ford pray and not follow the imaginations of his own heart (iv. 2); yet in his peppery Welsh temper, his lax standard of morality, and his very unclerical duelling, feasting, and mumming, he still presents but a scurvy model of the Parson, very different from the Friars and Nuns of the plays above mentioned. In the " Merry Wives," the religion of the characters is all a chaos. It is " the Hundredth Psalm to the tune of ' Green Sleeves ' " (ii. 1). Mistress Quickly does not much exaggerate the prevailing confusion when she calls it " peevishness to be given to prayer " (i. 4), and encourages Falstaff to hope in Mrs. Page's compliance, because she is a " virtuous, civil, modest wife, and one that will not miss you morning nor evening prayer." And again, " Good hearts ! what ado there is to bring you together ; sure one of you does not serve Heaven well, that you are so crossed " (ii. 5). Most of these extremely satirical hits at the religion of the characters appear first in the remodelled play. They are fit only for persons who belong to a system where the principles of morals are obscured, and such a system can only be found in Calvinism or Lutheranism, or their

R

progeny. Even those who most condemn the dogmatic system of the mediæval Church, confess that she never obscured or perverted the principles of morals.

Mrs. Page has the cudgel wherewith Ford had beaten Falstaff "hallowed and hung o'er the altar" for its meritorious service (iv. 2). In the conversation between the two ladies about this beating—one affirming that it was pitifully done, and the other "most unpitifully"—there is a notable resemblance to Sir John Harrington's fine epigram on the execution of Essex, Blount, and Danvers—

> " Is't not great pity, think you. No! said I,
> There is no man of sense in all the city
> Will say 'tis great, but rather little pity." .

And the joke of Falstaff about Mr. Ford's "legions of angels" (i. 3) is found admirably developed in Harrington's character of Bishop Scory. The tale of Herne the hunter related by "the superstitious, idle-headed elf" is another instance of Shakespeare's contempt for unfounded stories of devilry.

Shakespeare in Fenton's defence of Anne Page's clandestine marriage lays down accurately the Catholic doctrine on the subject. The contracting parties have a right to perfect freedom of choice in the engagement they form. The wishes of the parents should indeed be consulted, and as far as possible followed. The children, however, are not bound to yield to parental injunctions which are unreason-

able, or are inspired by motives of worldly policy
or sordid interest. This is the pith of Fenton's
speech :—

> "*Fenton.*   Hear the truth of it.
> You would have married her most shamefully
> When there was no proportion held in love.
> The truth is, she and I, long since contracted,
> Are now so sure, that nothing can dissolve us.
> The offence is holy that she hath committed ;
> And this deceit loses the name of craft,
> Of disobedience, or unduteous title,
> Since therein she doth evil hate and shun
> A thousand irreligious cursed hours
> Which forcèd marriage would have brought upon her" (v. 5).

The "Midsummer-Night's Dream" exhibits love
in its second degree, when the object is created by
the fantasy, uncontrolled by reason. Love thus begotten is essentially short-lived, transitory, and fickle,
and becomes attached in turn to any object presented to the senses. This central idea is expressed
when Hippolyta, tired of Bottom's interlude, yawns
and says, "This is the silliest stuff." Theseus
answers, "The best in this kind are but shadows,
and the worst are no worse if imagination mend
them"; and she again replies, "It must be your
imagination then, and not theirs" (v. 1). Theseus,
in the opening speech of the fifth act, explains it
more fully. Plato (Phædrus, c. 47, p. 244) enumerates four inspired frenzies which supersede
reason ; that of Apollo, or prophecy ; of Dionysus,
ritualistic religion ; of the Muses, poetry ; and of

Gods, love. Shakespeare, leaving out religion, enumerates only three, the frenzy of the lunatic, of
the poet, and of the lover, and in them all he finds
one predominant quality. They are "of imagination
all compact." Their seething brains and shaping
fantasies "apprehend more than cool reason ever
comprehends"; for it is the nature of imagination
that if it would apprehend some joy, it must invent,
find, picture a cause or object, which is not necessarily reasonable. Imagination gives in one presentation both the feeling and the cause of the
feeling—the one is the apprehension, the other the
comprehension or *comes* (companion). The rational
judgment, summoned to take note of the proceeding,
authenticates the apprehension, or condemns it as
false, because devoid of any real objective prototype.
Shakespeare does not confine this stricture to the
imagination of madmen, poets, and lovers. He
generalises the doctrine, and assigns to imagination
everywhere the invention, not the discovery, of
causes, which are practically only hypotheses for the
cool reason to test.

The play is a comment on this text. It exhibits
a variety of persons with a strong feeling in their
"shaping fantasies," all constant to their own feeling, but most inconstant, since determined by the
merest accidents, as to their object. Thus Demetrius
nurses a passion, of which he first supposes Helena
to be the bringer. Then some accident makes him
substitute Hermia. At last Puck, by squeezing

lime-juice in his eye, makes his fancy revert to the first object. So Lysander has a plentiful fire of love. The fuel is first supposed to be Hermia, then Helena, then Hermia again. Titania's "shaping fantasy" is so strong that it can see an Hyperion in the ass-headed Bottom. So Bottom's play is wretched stuff, but the shaping imaginations of the spectators can make it as good as the best. In all these cases the apprehension, the internal feeling, is constant; but the comprehension, the judgment which affirms the cause or object of the feeling, and picks out the bringer (upholder, substantiator) of the joy is fickle, uncertain, the sport of chance and of the accidental perils which beset the course of love.

And yet this fickle judgment, this ungrounded, imaginative opinion which has no basis more relative than a little juice squeezed into the eye, affects the pompous title of reason, and pretends to have the right to sway the entire man. Thus Lysander, bewitched by Puck, fancies that he has just come to the use of reason.

> "The will of man is by his reason swayed,
> And reason says you are the worthier maid " (ii. 2).

And led by this false reason into a heresy in love, he moralises on his conversion, and declares the sudden and irrational hatred which he has conceived for his former love.

"The heresies that men do leave
Are hated most of them they did deceive" (ii. 3).

In the base mechanical drudges, Bottom and his crew, Shakespeare glances at some of the characteristics of the rabble of his day. They are no longer the socialist mob of Jack Cade, but a puritanical rabble whose itching ears have been caught by the psalmody of Sternhold and Hopkins, and by the profane scripturality of the pulpit. Thus (iii. 1) Quince wants the prologue written in eight and six; "make it eight and eight," says Bottom. This worthy, abashed by his new glory, protests. "I am a man as other men are"; and after his adventures with Titania, he can find no language so appropriate to describe his dream as an absurd travesty of St. Paul's words on heaven: "The eye of man hath not heard, the ear of man hath not seen, man's hand is not able to taste, his tongue to conceive, nor his heart to report what my dream was" (iv. 1). There we have the same sermonizing element already traced in Falstaff and Costard.

Even amongst the fun of the fairies we find traces of the poet's Catholic spirit. Oberon's blessing of the bridal chamber reads almost like a paraphrase of the *Benedictio Thalami* in the Church's Ritual, which is as follows: "Bless, O Lord, this bed. May all who dwell in it remain in Thy peace, abide in Thy will, grow to old age, and be multiplied to the length of days, and attain at

last to the kingdom of heaven. Through Christ
our Lord."

> "*Oberon.* To the best bride-bed will we,
> Which by us shall blessèd be.
> And the issue there create
> Ever shall be fortunate.
> So shall all the couples three
> Ever true and loving be.
> .   .   .   .   .   .
> With this field-dew consecrate,
> Every fairy take his gait ;
> And each several chamber bless
> Through this palace with sweet peace ;
> Ever shall't in safety rest
> And the owner of it blest" (v. 2).

According to the prologue, the moral of "Romeo
and Juliet" is the redeeming and atoning power of
dying for love. With their death their parents'
strife is ended, and an apparently implacable feud
is healed. But the poet sees deeper than this
external and adventitious action of love ; he ana-
tomises its core. Romeo's love for Rosaline was
but a passing fancy, and was therefore fickle and
accidental. It was merely a subjective feeling, and
belonged to that class of affections which thrives
best in solitude (i. 1). Hence Rosaline is purposely
kept out of sight, and Benvolio says of Romeo,
"blind is his love that best befits the dark," and
the Friar reproaches him for doting, not for loving
Rosaline, and for shedding so many tears "to
season love, that of it doth not taste." Romeo's
attachment to Juliet, on the other hand, had the

character of a violent, headstrong passion, enkindled and sustained by the object, and bent at all costs on its immediate possession.

The development hinges much on the action of Friar Laurence, one of Shakespeare's kindliest creations, which strikingly contrasts with the portrait drawn of the same character by A. Brook.

" One of Shakespeare's earliest plays," Knight says, " is 'Romeo and Juliet.' . . . Friar Laurence going forth from his cell in the morning twilight to fill his osier basket with weeds and flowers, and moralising on the properties of plants which at once yield poison and medicine, has all the truth of individual portraiture. But Friar Laurence is also the representation of a class ; the Infirmarian of a monastic house, who had charge of the sick brethren, was often, in the early days of medical science, their only physician. . . . In ' Much Ado About Nothing,' it is the Friar who, when Hero is unjustly accused . . . vindicates her reputation with as much sagacity as charitable zeal. . . . In ' Measure for Measure ' the whole plot is carried on by the Duke assuming the reverend manners, and professing the active benevolence of a Friar ; and his agents and confidants are Friar Thomas and Friar Peter. In an age when the prejudices of the multitude were flattered and stimulated by abuse and ridicule of the ancient ecclesiastical character, Shakespeare always exhibits it so as to command respect and affection. The poisoning of King John by a monk, 'a resolved villain,' is despatched by him with little more than an allusion." [1]

The fact is that Shakespeare has caught all the prominent features of the order in Friar Laurence; who is a much truer portrait of the historical friar, as brought out by Mr. Brewer (*Monumenta Franciscana*, Pref.), than Chaucer's caricatures. Dr. Ingram argues that Shakespeare must have been a Protestant, because he gives us " no worthy idealisation of the Catholic Priest," like Chaucer's Parson, or Manzoni's Cardinal. The argument might as well have been that Chaucer could not have been a Catholic, because he gives us no worthy picture of the Friar like Shakespeare's. The Franciscan was the natural philosopher of the middle ages; he was the Infirmarian or the hospitaller, not of his own convent only, but of the whole town population. The exigencies of the physician had led him to the study of alchemy, and in him lay all the knowledge of chemistry that the age possessed. Friar Bacon was in this respect only the flower of his order. He was an exceptional specimen, not in the line, but in the extent of his knowledge. The Franciscan was not a merely scholastic student of nature, but to his reading he added observation, " which with experimental seal did warrant the tenor of his book," as the Friar says in " Much Ado," iv. 1.

To appreciate rightly the action of Friar Laurence

[1] Knight's " Biography of Shakespeare," 183.

and the standard of morality exhibited in the play, it must be remembered that the plot is not of Shakespeare's creation. Its scheme came into his hands complete, even to its details. His power was shown in quickening the dead bones, and in the life they exhibit when they arise and speak under his magic touch. Unless this be borne in mind it might seem that the poet regarded suicide as a legitimate means for the attainment of such an important end as the extinction of a faction feud, and that in Juliet's case the Friar offered little, if any, opposition. We believe, however, that a careful consideration of the piece will show that the poet has never departed from the principle enunciated in " Hamlet," that " Heaven has fixed its canon against self-slaughter," and that the Friar's advice is always in accordance with the purest morality. He agrees to Romeo's marriage with Juliet, not as an intriguing match-maker, but as one who knows what human nature is, and that in the present case things had gone so far, no other course was possible. He also hoped their alliance might heal the deadly enmity existing between the Montagues and Capulets (ii. 4). At the same time he has his misgivings. He prays Heaven's blessing on the rite he is about to perform, lest its sequel bring misery to all concerned, himself included. In the same strain he rebukes Romeo's rapturous assurance that no subsequent misery could outweigh the joy of even a momentary union to Juliet with the grave warning—

"Violent delights have violent ends,
And in their triumph die, like fire and powder,
Which, as they kiss, consume" (ii. 6).

Love that lasts is measured and reasonable, and not a mere impulse of feeling.

Again, he shows the same varied knowledge of human nature, and his care for the purity of the souls entrusted to him, in insisting on the discipline of the Church, that the betrothed should not remain together alone in their clandestine relationship till their marriage was performed. He has been ridiculed for sophistry and sententiousness for offering to Romeo, when maddened with the news of his banishment, the consolation of "adversity's sweet milk, philosophy"; and Romeo's reply, "Hang up philosophy, unless philosophy can make a Juliet," is judged alike apposite and reasonable. But by philosophy was meant, not a system of syllogisms or metaphysics, but the heavenly wisdom, which is the only true comfort left, when earth's hopes are gone. The martyr S. Boetius' book *De Consideratione Philosophiæ* — a standard authority with Dante—composed in prison, like B. Thomas More's "Dialogue of Comfort under Tribulation," was a work from which many of Shakespeare's thoughts and expressions seem borrowed. In any case, the term would have naturally been employed and understood in the spiritual sense. The Friar's personality and character seem indeed to give a religious colouring to the persons or subjects he deals with. He is always regarded as the mender of ills and the physician of souls.　Thus Romeo, even when exasperated at the news of his exile, asks—

> " How hast thou the heart,
> Being a divine, a ghostly confessor,
> A sin absolver, and a friend professed,
> To mangle me with that word 'banished'? " (iii. 3).

In the Friar's presence Romeo continues to speak in the same religious strain.　Outside Verona, Juliet's home, is " purgatory, torture, hell itself" (iii. 3); and when he learns that he is " banished," he exclaims with complete theological accuracy—

> "Oh Friar, the damnèd use the word in hell ;
> Howlings attend it."

So, too, Paris leaves Juliet alone with the Friar, with the remark, " God shield I should disturb devotion " (iv. 1).　Similarly the remark of the nurse, " See where she comes from shrift with merry look"(iv. 2), indicates the cheering results and the consolation she attributes to the sacrament of penance.　Nor is all this confidence misplaced.　The Friar is frank, simple-minded, and high principled, as beseems his office.　He speaks out openly to Romeo his fears as to his past conduct with Rosaline (ii. 3), and will be satisfied with no equivocal explanation.

> " Be plain, good son, and homely in thy drift,
> Riddling confession finds but riddling shrift " (*Ibid.*).

He condemns with a holy indignation Romeo's thought of suicide as brutish, cowardly, effeminate, and unnatural. He devises the sleeping potion for Juliet, as the only escape from a hated union with Paris. He strives his utmost to shape for good the burden laid on his shoulders—the three lovers' unreasonable, incompatible, and impossible demands, the old Capulet's unwarrantable anger. At length, when all fails, he offers simply and readily the sacrifice of his own life—

" If aught in this miscarried of my fault" (v. 3).

The Friar's action, however, produced in the end a blessed result. The clandestine marriage terminates, after its own tragic conclusion, in the reconciliation of the warring factions.

With regard to other religious allusions in the play, we postpone to Chapter IX. the discussion of the Friar's speech on Nature, and the lesson it teaches. The line " Too early seen, unknown, and known too late " (i. 5) recalls the well-known prayer of St. Augustine, " Sero te cognovi, sero te amavi." This and other instances show that Shakespeare caught not only the echoes of Catholic doctrine, but the very phrases in which they were expressed. The fine line which Pericles addresses to Mariana, " Thou that beget'st him that did thee beget," recalls the opening of the 33rd Canto of the " Paradiso," " Virgine e madre Figlia del tuo Figlio." It is an echo also of the martyr Father Southwell's [1] contemporary lines in his hymn on the Nativity of Christ—

> " Behold the Father in his daughter's Son,
>   The bird that built the nest is hatched therein."

In like manner Mr. Douce finds the prototype of the passage in " Hamlet," " The cock that is the trumpet of the morn," &c., in a hymn from the " Salisbury Breviary"; and Cicero's observation in " Julius Cæsar " (i. 4)—

> "Men may construe things after their fashion
> Clean from the purpose of the things themselves,"

seems a reminiscence of an old English rhyme—

> " There the Bible is all myswrent
>   To jangle of Job or Jeremye,
>   That construen hit after her intent
>   For lewde lust of Lollardie."
>   —*Political Songs*, ii. 243.

Other specimens of Shakespeare's reproducing old English forms may be noted. Thus his line in Sonnet 104, " For as you were when first your eye I eyed," is simply a variation of Robert of Gloucester's rhythm, " Ar they iwar war "—ere they were aware; and Ben Jonson's instance of Shakespeare's want of sense removed by his editors, " Cæsar doth never wrong but with just cause," is only an echo of the Saxon

---

[1] Mr. S. Lee has brought to notice the fact that Father South-well's "Fourfolde Meditation" was dedicated like Shakespeare's Sonnets to W. H., whom he believes to have been merely a stationer's assistant.—*Life of Shakespeare*, 92.

Chronicle which describes William the Conqueror
as taking "by right, and with great unright."[1]
It is astonishing to note with what receptivity
Shakespeare's mind retained and recorded all such
undertones of traditional English thought and
expression.

The expression "Evening Mass" in "Romeo and
Juliet" iv. 1) is commonly held to show Shakespeare's rudimentary ignorance of the usages of
the Catholic Church, and is regarded as a strong
argument in favour of his Protestantism.   Various
explanations have been offered of the passage.
The late Bishop Clifford showed[2] that the term
"Mass" was used indifferently of various Church
offices.   Another correspondent of the *Tablet*[3] took
the word as a synonym for "mess," and gave
arguments in support of this reading.   The words
may, however, be justified in their ordinary sense.

First, we must observe "that in this play 'evening'" means afternoon, and no more.   "Is it good
den ?" asks the nurse; "Yes," says Mercutio, "the
hand of the dial is on the prick of noon" ("Romeo
and Juliet," ii. 4).   Here at least evening begins at
twelve o'clock.   Evening mass, then, need signify
only mass said after noon.

Next, according to Liturgical writers, there was
great latitude in ancient times as to the hour of

---

[1] Among Ray's proverbs we find a similar expression : " He'll do
justice, right or wrong."

[2] *Tablet,* vol. lix. 28.   [3] Vol. lx. 23.

mass. The time for celebration changed, Strabo[1] says, with the character of the feast. It might be before noon, about None, sometimes at Vespers, and sometimes at night. And Martene[2] gives notice of solemn masses said on fast-days at three o'clock, in Lent in the evening, and at night at Christmas, Easter Eve, St. John Baptist, and days of Ordination. As for low masses, he says, "we think they were said at any hour that did not interfere with the high mass." Of this he gives several examples, and then concludes: "This shows that low mass might be said at any hour—dawn, 8 A.M.; noon, after None (3 P.M.), evening, and after Compline (night). Even to this day (1699) in the church of St. Denis, the Bishop says the solemn mass for the Kings of France in the evening, and in the Church of Rouen on Ascension Day mass is often said in the evening."

S. Pius V. (1566–72) discountenanced and prohibited afternoon and evening masses. But the isolation of the English Clergy, owing to the then difficulty of communication, might have withheld from them the knowledge of this law for some considerable time.[3] It was so slow in penetrating Germany, that it had to be enforced by various councils, e.g. Prague in 1605, Constance in 1609, Salzburg in

[1] *De rebus ecclesiasticus*, c. 23.
[2] *De antiquis Ecclesiæ ritibus*, I. c. iii. Art. iii.
[3] *Navarr. lib. de Orat.*, c. 21, n. 31, *et Enchirid. Confess.*, c. 25, n. 85.

1616. Cardinal Bona (1672) seems to say that in his time high mass was sung in Lent and on Vigils at 3 P.M., instead of sunset, the ancient time.[1] And the remarkable thing is this, that according to the testimony of the Liturgical writer, Friedrich Brenner,[2] Verona was one of the places in which the forbidden custom lingered even to our own century. After quoting the precepts against it, he says, "Notwithstanding, evening masses are still said in several Italian churches, as at Vercelli on Christmas Eve by the Lateran Canons, at Venice by the same; moreover *in the Cathedral of Verona*, and even in the Papal Chapel at Rome." Since, then, notwithstanding the Papal prohibition, the custom of having evening masses lingered in Verona for nearly three centuries after Shakespeare's day, it becomes most probable that in his time it was an usual occurrence in England. But whether it were a usual occurrence in England or not, it was certainly so in Verona. To assert, then, as so many have done, that Shakespeare's mention of an evening mass argues in him an ignorance of Catholic customs, is to convict one's self of the very ignorance falsely ascribed to the poet. Afternoon and evening masses were, as we have seen, frequently celebrated. It is, however, a remarkable coincidence that in Verona, the scene of Shakespeare's evening

---

[1] *Rer. Liturg.*, lib. ii., 182-186 (Paris, 1672).

[2] *Geschichtliche Darstellung der Verrichtung der Eucharistie* (Bamberg, 1824), vol. iii., 346.

mass, the custom of celebrating late masses lasted longer than in any other city.

Another very special technical use of a word occurs in the same play—

> " I must up-fill this osier cage of *ours*
> With baleful weeds, and precious-juicèd flowers."
> —*Romeo and Juliet*, ii. 3.

"Ours" is not for the rhyme. It is the rule of the Franciscans, who have all property in common, to call whatever article of this property they use "ours," not "mine," *e.g.* "I must put on our shoes," "I must go to our cell."

"All's Well that Ends Well" is supposed not improbably to be the comedy coupled by Meres with "Love's Labour's Lost" under the title of "Love's Labour's Won." The former play exhibits the uselessness of a Quixotic asceticism and "taffeta courtliness in love." The latter shows how merit may win a husband, and self-sacrificing effort secure its beloved object. To modern notions there is something indelicate in Helen's forcing herself on a man averse to her affections. In an age, however, when the suitor paid his addresses not to his bride but to her father, a maiden might without unfitness appeal to the lord paramount of her beloved to secure the hand of his son. The Crown in Shakespeare's days disposed of its wards as absolutely as the king disposed of Bertram.

Bertram's opposition arises not only from his

pride, but from the fact that his affections were pre-engaged. He had, we learn afterwards, a fixed fancy for Lafeu's daughter that made all other objects contemned, warped the lines of all other favours, scorned fair colours, or only esteemed them as stolen from the one beloved object (v. 3). But this fixed fancy proves capable of gadding after Diana, and of being fooled by Helen herself into making sweet use of what it hated (iv. 4). In Helen, on the other hand, we see a determination to overcome, to which

> "All impediments in fancy's course
> Are motives of more fancy" (v. 3).

And as the deaths of Romeo and Juliet wash away the old feud of their houses, so does Helen's supposed death call into life the love of Bertram, and win from him the fixed affection which he had believed himself incapable of entertaining for her.

The Clown in this play is highly individualised. He is "a shrewd knave and unhappy" (iv. 5), one who had been "a wicked creature" (i. 3), and had become a cynic, doubting of all goodness, and accepting evil as his destiny. Into his mouth Shakespeare puts with perfect propriety such ideas as this—that Popery and Puritanism, however different in faith, are one in this, that in both marriages are equally unhappy—" Young Charbon (*Chaire bonne*) the Puritan, and old Poysam (*Poisson*) the Papist, howsome'er their hearts are severed in religion, their heads are both one." Or this, that "the nun's lip and friar's mouth" are a pair of things that are ordinarily coupled together, and fit each other naturally (ii. 2). It is for talk like this that his mistress calls him "a foul-mouthed and calumnious knave" (i. 3). Yet some persons have argued that Shakespeare in writing these passages meant to show that he was no Papist. On the contrary, it is remarkable that while he has put these scurrilities into the mouth of the unhappy Clown, the words of the Countess are decisive the other way. When she first learns that her son has renounced his wife, she says—

> "What angel shall
> Bless this unworthy husband? He cannot thrive
> Unless her prayers, whom Heaven delights to hear
> And loves to grant, reprieve him from the wrath
> Of greatest justice" (iii. 4).

Whose prayers are these? Not those of Helen, but of one greater than any angel, whose prayers God delights to hear, and loves to grant. This is exactly the way in which Catholics speak of the Blessed Virgin, and the lines will not apply to any one but her. The testimony is brief but decisive; Shakespeare in these lines affirms distinctly, but not contentiously, one of the most characteristic doctrines that distinguishes the Catholic Church from the Protestant communion.

It is quite in accordance with this that the line

of self-sacrifice adopted by Helen, on hearing of her husband's devotion, is a " bare-foot pilgrimage " (iii. 4), " which holy undertaking with most austere sanctimony she accomplished " (iv. 3). Shakespeare's additions to this play, says Professor Morley, are all designed to bring out the elevation of Helen's character and the dignity of her love. The Countess, Bertram's mother, is introduced to testify with the zeal of a noble woman to her praise, and the old Lord Lafeu brings his experience of honourable age in testimony of her worth. As regards her religious opinions, the language the poet makes his heroine hold regarding her professed remedy for the king's evil, and its mode of operation, is somewhat difficult to reconcile with the assertion that Shakespeare was an Agnostic or disbelieved in the miraculous or supernatural. While expressly condemning the practice of ascribing to Heaven remedies which may follow from merely natural causes (i. 2), Helen yet bids the king hope for his cure in the following words :—

> " He that of greatest works is finisher,
> Oft does them by the weakest minister.
> So Holy Writ in babes hath judgment shown,
> When judges have been babes : great floods have flown
> From simple sources ; and great seas have dried,
> When miracles have by the greatest been denied " (ii. 1).

So Lafeu's words, on hearing that the cure has been effected, seem again addressed to some professors of modern science—" They say miracles are past ;

and we have our philosophical persons to make
modern and familiar, things supernatural and
causeless (*i.e.* to be explained by no natural cause).
Hence it is that we make trifles of terrors (signs
of divine omnipotence) ensconcing ourselves into
seeming knowledge when we shall submit ourselves to an unknown fear (*i.e.* bow our head and
adore, ii. 3)."

In the "Taming of the Shrew," Shakespeare
makes Petruchio among his other antics knock down
the priest who was marrying him, kiss the bride in
church, quaff to her health and throw the sops in
the sexton's face.   It would be difficult, however, to
conclude from this that the poet himself approved
of such conduct, even when done in subservience to
so laudable an end as the frightening a shrew for
the purpose of taming her (iii. 2).   There is more
meaning in the passage where Gremio, presenting
Lucentio to Baptista as a tutor for his daughters,
calls him "a young scholar that hath been long
studying at Rheims; cunning in Greek, Latin, and
other languages" (ii. 1).   Rheims, it will be remembered, was then the seat of the English College
from which the greatest number of Seminary Priests
was sent over into England.   Against this seminary
legions of proclamations and placards had been
issued, warning parents not to allow their sons to
proceed thither, and denouncing the doctrine taught
there.   It was little short of impudence in Shakespeare to choose Rheims for the pretended *alma*

mater of Lucentio, the gentleman, though not the hero of his drama.

In "Much Ado about Nothing" we have another of Shakespeare's Friars, whose character is not developed like that of Romeo's Friar Laurence, but who is in all essential points from the same stock. The merciful view he takes of Hero from the first; his silence during the altercations of her accusers and relations; his judgment so decisive in her favour when at last he speaks, and his ready plans and counsel when he proposes a politic trap similar, except in its results, to that of Friar Laurence, are all points of resemblance between the two Friars. It is curious that the resources of the Friars in all the three plays, where the plot turns upon their help, should culminate in the very same contrivance—a pretended death. Juliet's sleeping draught, Hero's reported death, and the substitution of Ragozine's head for Claudio's in "Measure for Measure," are all variations of one theme. Perhaps Shakespeare wished to defend Friar Laurence's policy, and was determined to show that his stratagem, though in Juliet's case a failure, was a good policy in itself and deserved success. If some such simple explanation of the curious reiteration of the Friars' plots be unacceptable, some more recondite reason might be sought in the region of Spenserian allegory. Here we must also note that in other plots which turn on a temporary death or absence of the heroines, an influence analogous to that of a Friar is supposed to

govern them.   Thus Helena in " All's Well " gives
out that she is making a bare-foot pilgrimage to St.
James of Compostella ; and Portia in the " Merchant
of Venice " (v. 1), during her husband's absence,
proclaims that she " doth stray about by holy crosses,
where she kneels and prays," accompanied by " a
holy hermit and her maid."   It may be that Shakespeare wishes to show the efficacy even of a temporary
death in reconciling and reuniting the unravelled
strands of life, the atoning power of the pity excited by the mere idea of death, in the case of Hero
and Helena, just as the deaths of Romeo and Juliet
were the reconciliation of their families.   In all this
it is clear that Shakespeare is only following out the
Christian scale of love, and speaking of a lower kind
of love in terms that are only applicable in their full
meaning to the highest.   Hence, perhaps, the reason
why he surrounds their exhibition with the sacred
functions of religion.

In "Twelfth Night " the comedy is in the spirit
of the " Merry Wives of Windsor," or the Falstaffian
scenes of the historical play.   Indeed Sir Toby is
in some respects another edition of Falstaff, while
Sir Andrew and Malvolio remind one of Simple, or
Silence and Shallow.   The drama is supposed to
take place in a Catholic country, yet, as in the
" Merry Wives," the religious allusions are all to the
manners and opinions of the day, which, as in the
other comedy, are all treated without the slightest
semblance of respect.   The most important character

of the play is Malvolio the Puritan.[1] Humble and cringing with his superiors, Malvolio is churlish and tyrannical with his inferiors. He is further so inordinately vain that he falls a ready victim to the plot of Maria the serving-maid. The manner of his nemesis, confinement as a possessed person in a darkened room, is an evident satire on a case of alleged possession in a Puritan family named Starchie. The case is mentioned in Harsnett's "Puritan and Popish Impostures," and was of considerable notoriety in Shakespeare's time.

If Malvolio is to be taken as a representative Puritan, he is certainly made ridiculous as a gloomy, pompous, sanctimonious pedant. It is thus he appears in the well-known dialogue of Toby and the Clown with Malvolio: "Dost thou think, because thou art virtuous, there shall be no more cakes and ale? Yes, by St. Anne, and ginger shall be hot in the mouth too" (ii. 3). So again when Sir Andrew says that if he thought Malvolio was a Puritan he would beat him like a dog, we have an expression of the popular dislike of the sect.

The Clown's speech when he puts on the Curate's gown (iv. 2) is not very complimentary to the clergy, implying, as it does, their gradual change from scholars into housekeepers and husbands. "I'll put it on, I will dissemble in it; and I would

---

[1] We cannot agree with Mr. Simpson, who thinks that the poet in his treatment of this character intended to deal tenderly with that sect,

I were the first that ever dissembled in such a gown. I am not fat enough to become the function well; nor lean enough to be thought a good student: but to be said, an honest man and a good house-keeper, goes as fairly as to say a careful man and a great scholar." There are, besides, passages which seem to refer to the poet's private experiences. For instance when the Clown says he lives by the Church, but is no Churchman; for his house stands by the Church (iii. 1); or when Maria talks of Malvolio being " cross-gartered most villainously," like " a pedant that keeps school in the Church." Again, we have phrases which doubtless spoke to con-temporaries, as when she says that he behaves in a way that "no good Christian that means to be saved by believing rightly" could ever believe (iii. 2), or when Sir Andrew would "as lief be a Brownist as a politician."

The love argument of the play is the same as that of so many others; the sudden transfer of the fancy from one object to another; of Olivia from Cesario to Sebastian, of Orsino from Olivia to Viola.

Olivia in the following speech shows the rever-ence with which she regarded the priest, and the importance she attached to his presence at her marriage :—

> " *Oliv.* Now go with me, and with this holy man
> Into the chantry by : there before him,

And underneath that consecrated roof,
Plight me the full assurance of your faith ;
That my most jealous and too doubtful soul
May live at peace" (iv. 3).

The priest subsequently declares the indissoluble
nature of the bond then contracted, and expresses
accurately the Catholic doctrine that the contracting
parties are themselves the ministers of the sacrament of marriage, and that the priest is only the
appointed witness.

"A contract of eternal bond of love,
Confirmed by mutual joinder of your hands,
Attested by the holy close of lips,
Strengthened by interchangement of your rings,
And all the ceremony of this compact
Sealed in my function, by my testimony" (v. 1).

The two late plays, "As You Like It" and the
"Winter's Tale," though real comedies, have more
of the tragic element about them than any of those
as yet referred to. The pictures of the court of
the reigning Duke, and of the home of the unnatural brother in "As You Like It," are drawn with
such passionate feeling, that they seem not only
to be wrung from the poet's own heart, but to be
intended to go straight to the hearts and minds of
the audience. The tyrant to whom mistrust is
sufficient cause for the condemnation of a man,
and mere circumstance of birth sufficient motive
of mistrust, was a picture of English rulers applicable only to one party in the State. Duke
Frederick says to Rosalind, whom he banishes, "Let

it suffice thee that I trust thee not," and she replies, "Yet your mistrust cannot make me a traitor,"
and he again answers, "Thou art thy father's daughter; there's enough" (i. 3). Again, Adam says to
Orlando, who had been forced to fly from the Duke
for the same reasons, and from his own brother for
his unkindness :—

> "To some kind of men
> Their graces serve them but as enemies.
> . . . your virtues . . .
> Are sanctified and holy traitors unto you.
> O, what a world is this when what is comely
> Envenoms him that bears it !" (ii. 3).

Both these speeches must have reminded the audience of the class of Englishmen whom the law
made criminal by kind, and who were reckoned
the worse subjects, the more faithful they were to
their profession. In this sense must have been
understood Orlando's lament over the departure of
the antique world, when duty, not recompense, was
the motive of service (ii. 3). In the pastoral life
of the outlaws in the forest of Arden Shakespeare
finds the real remedy for the falsehoods of court;
and this idea is repeated in "Cymbeline." It is as
if the poet was comforting a class cut off from all
civil functions by showing them that their loss was
gain, and that their moral profit was more than
their material sacrifice. In the tyrannical court,
such as Shakespeare describes it here, even the
sacred privileges of the motley were suppressed—

as they might have been in Macbeth's gloomy castle. The fool was "whipped for taxation," and might no longer speak wisely what wise men did foolishly. But the poet found that nature provided a compensation—"Since the little wit that fools have was silenced, the little foolery that wise men have makes a great show" (i. 2). When Claudius had murdered sleep and mirth in the court of Denmark, the best fun left was the wisdom of the odious old fool Polonius.

In the forest, Touchstone has all the privileges of his bauble; while Jaques, who claims the same licence, fails to obtain it. His "taxation" would not be the froth of an infirm reason, but the gall of old disappointments, stored up in the brain of a philosopher, and vented under the false pretence of extemporaneous sallies. The keen winds of the outlaw's cave were not the proper atmosphere for a croaker. The fun of the forest could, however, make game of hedge-parsons like Sir Oliver Mar-text, of lack-latin priests, and of the fashionable travellers whose only point was to "disable all the benefits of your own country, be out of love with your nativity, and almost chide God for making you that countenance you are" (iv. 1). Among the bitters of the outlaw life the poet enumerates the being forced to live where no "bells knolled to church"—quite a characteristic of the state of the recusants, who were forbidden every external sign of their religion.

"As You Like It" is one of the dramas the unravelling of which is again due to a Friar. The usurping Duke hearing of the rustic court kept by his banished brother in the forest, marches out to entrap him, but is himself entrapped.

> "Meeting with an old religious man,
>   After some question with him, was converted,
>   Both from his enterprise, and from the world" (v. 4).

The banished Duke returns to his own court. Jaques alone changes masters, goes to Duke Frederick, who "hath put on a religious life," to question and to observe, because

> "Out of the convertites ·
> There is much matter to be heard and learned" (v. 4).

According to Hunter, "convertite" with Shakespeare signifies a relapsed person reconciled, and is therefore distinguished from "convert," who enters the Church from without. Thus in Act v. 1 of "King John" the Legate says to John repentant, "Since you are a gentle convertite."[1]

Rosalind's description of Orlando's kiss being as full of sanctity as the touch of "holy bread," has given rise to some controversy. Warburton reads "beard," but the former expression, however forcible, would in its sacramental sense be thoroughly in-

---

[1] "Illustrations of Shakespeare," ii. 14.

telligible to a Catholic. The sacred elements con-
secrate by their contact. The joy and gratitude of
Oliver, a true penitent comparing his present with
his past, is expressed almost in the same terms as
Henry V. after breaking with Falstaff—

> "'Twas I ; but 'tis not I : I do not shame
> To tell you what I was, since my conversion
> So sweetly tastes, being the thing I am."

And the concluding lines of the play express the
joy of the angels over a repentant sinner.

> " Then is there mirth in heaven,
> When earthly things made even
> Atone together."

" As You Like It " presents us with a view of the
lower orders very different from that exhibited in
" Henry VI." The degenerate rabble of Jack Cade
were one and all ignorant, discontented, embittered,
fickle, and cruel. Here Adam the old servant and
Corin the shepherd are very models of dignity,
loyalty, religion, and self-sacrifice. Adam returns
Oliver's abuse with a blessing. He follows Orlando
into exile, and gives him his hard-earned savings,
trusting " Him who doth the ravens feed " for
his life needs. Famished and dying through his
loyalty, he has only a loving farewell for his kind
master, and when rescued by the Duke is most
thankful, not for his own but for Orlando's sake.
Well he merits his master's praise, which refers him

to an order of things now past, and the loss of
which Shakespeare never ceases to regret.

> " O, good old man : how well in thee appears
> The constant service of the antique world,
> When service sweat for duty, not for need " (ii. 3).

And so with Corin. He has known what love
means, shepherd though he be, and he can open
his heart to give what he has, though he serves a
churlish master, who

> " Little seeks to find the way to heaven
> By doing deeds of hospitality " (ii. 4).

Here, by the way, we have the doctrine of merit
laid down in clear terms. Corin can meet Touchstone's quips and gibes with quiet dignity, and
shows his refinement in declaring that vulgarity only
begins in aping manners unbecoming a man's state.
"Good manners at the court are as ridiculous in
the country, as the behaviour of the country is
most mockable at the court." In his defence of
his own condition he manifests, what the Christian
alone realises, the true nobility of every honest
vocation. "Sir, I am a true labourer; I earn what
I eat, get that I wear; envy no man's happiness,
glad of other men's good, content with my harm "
(iii. 2).

In the " Winter's Tale " the treatment of royal
jealousy is almost as tragical as in "Othello." The
manners are supposed to be Pagan, but what

religious doctrines appear are Tridentine rather than Olympian. Thus the King of Sicily describes his own and his friend's boyish days:

> "We knew not
> The doctrine of ill-doing, nor dreamed
> That any did. Had we pursued that life,
> . . . we should have answered Heaven
> Boldly, 'Not guilty'—the imposition cleared " (i. 2).

Original sin, he seems to tell us, is nothing intrinsic to our nature, it is an "imposition" inherited by our descent. The innocence of childhood is real sinlessness, and if original sin is once cleared, enables the person conscious of it to plead boldly, "Not guilty," at God's judgment-seat. The same king tells his counsellor that he has imparted to him the things next his heart, and received cleansing from his "priest-like" services, and departed from him his "penitent reformed" (i. 2). And again, thinking Hermione dead, "has said many a prayer upon her grave" (v. 3). But the most remarkable instance of Catholic imagery in the play is when the poet goes out of his way to describe the Oracle of Delphi. Now it must be remembered that Rome was the Delphi of mediæval Europe. "The mystical city," says Mr. Bryce, "which was to mediæval Europe more than Delphi had been to the Greek, or Mecca to the Islamite, the Jerusalem of Christianity."[1] How then does he speak of the mystical city ?—all

---

[1] "Holy Roman Empire," 2nd edition, 299.

T

things combine in one grand harmony—the climate, the air, the Temple much surpassing the common praise it bears.   But says Cleomenes :—

> " I shall report,
> For most it caught me, the celestial habits
> (Methinks I so should term them) and the reverence
> Of the grave wearers.   O the sacrifice
> How ceremonious, solemn, and unearthly
> It was in ' the offering ' " (iii. 1).

If the idea of the sacrifice of the mass be here indirectly suggested, the language used is worth contrasting with that of the Thirty-nine Articles, where that sacrifice is termed " a blasphemous fable and a dangerous deceit " (Art. xxxi.).   Puritan (iv. 2) is used for soprano, and a soprano Puritan who sings psalms to hornpipes signifies a Puritan in nothing but his treble pipes.

The " Tempest " we suppose to be the last of Shakespeare's comedies.   In it he seems to take his leave of the stage and to renounce his potent sway over nature, history, and men's hearts.   He bids farewell to the elves and demi-puppets.

> " By whose aid,
> Weak masters though ye be, I have bedimmed
> The noon-tide sun, called forth the mutinous winds,
> And 'twixt the green sea and the azure vault
> Set mutinous war : to the dread rattling thunder
> Have I given fire, and rifted Jove's stout oak
> With his own bolt : the strong based promontory
> Have I made shake, and by the spurs plucked up
> The pine and cedar : graves at my command

> Have waked their sleepers, oped and let them forth
> By my so potent art. But this rough magic
> I here abjure, and, when I have required
> Some heavenly music . . .
> . . . I'll break my staff,
> Bury it certain fathoms in the earth,
> And deeper than did ever plummet sound,
> I'll drown my book."

These exploits are too general to refer only to Prospero's doings in the play. They seem to allude to the whole cycle of his dramas, to the storm of passions he has swayed, to our ancient sovereigns whom he has raised from their graves, to make the age "joy in their joy and tremble at their rage."

> " While the plebeian imp from lofty throne
> Creates and rules a world, and works upon
> Mankind by secret engines."[1]

He has, he tells us, worked miracles with weak instruments, but he has done. He is retiring to Milan, to his midland home in Warwickshire, where "every third thought shall be my grave" (v. 1).

The epilogue spoken by Prospero continues in the same solemn strain—

> " Now I want
> Spirits to enforce, art to enchant,
> And my ending is despair,
> Unless I be relieved by prayer,
> Which pierces so that it assaults
> Mercy itself, and frees from faults.
> As you from crimes would pardoned be,
> Let your indulgence set me free."

---

[1] Verses on Shakespeare, by I. M. S., in the second folio.

From the midst of this unearthly sunset his voice comes for the last time to the rulers in recommendation of mercy. Prospero, by a great effort, throws off all desire of revenge against his usurping brother and the traitors who have wronged him. He is moved by Ariel's pity, and says—

> " Hast thou, which art but air, a touch, a feeling
> Of their affliction, and shall not myself,
> One of their kind, that relish all as sharply
> Passion as they, be kindlier moved than thou art?
> Though with their high wrongs I am struck to the quick,
> Yet with my nobler reason 'gainst my fury
> Do I take part : The rarer action is
> In virtue than in vengeance : they being penitent,
> The sole drift of my purpose doth extend
> Not a frown further " (v. i.).

The play presents two Dantesque images, Ariel confined in a cloven pine, an idea repeated in Prospero's threat—

> "If thou more murmurest, I will rend an oak,
> And peg thee in his knotty entrails, till
> Thou hast howled away twelve winters" (i. 2).

Both passages recall the forest of suicides, where souls are imprisoned in trees inhabited by harpies (*Inferno*, xiii.). Again, in Stephano, Trinculo, and Caliban immersed

> "I' the filthy mantled pool beyond your cell,
> There dancing up to the chins, that the foul lake
> O'erstunk their feet" (iv. 1),

we see a reproduction of the violent "naked and

wild mire o'erspread in the Stygian marsh" (*Inferno*,
vii. 115), or of "the sullen" "engulphed in boiling
slime, carrying a foul and lazy mist within" (*Ibid.*,
vii. 124). And in the description of the power of
Miranda's prayer—

> "You have not sought her help; of whose soft grace
> For the like loss I have her sovereign aid,
> And rest content" (v. 1),

we have an echo of St. Bernard's prayer to Our
Lady—

> "So mighty art thou, Lady, and so great,
> That he who grace desireth and comes not
> To thee for aidence, fain would have desire
> Fly without wings."—*Paradiso*, xxxii. 16.

In Ferdinand's love being tested by hard penance
and the power of a loved object to render sweet an
otherwise odious and bitter task, we find principles
already noted, repeated. Prospero's grave warning
of the reverence to be paid to Miranda till

> "All sanctimonious ceremonies may
> With full and holy rite be ministered,"

and Ferdinand's promise to respect his trust, manifest again the sanctity in the poet's eyes of the
marriage sacrament, and the somewhat baser teaching in "Measure for Measure" must be corrected by
the lessons here inculcated. The whole play is in
tone very solemn. The last thoughts with which
Shakespeare steps from the stage are forgiveness,

meditation of death, and prayer—thoughts quite out of tune with the triumphant and persecuting Protestantism of his age.

Our view of the "Tempest" as Shakespeare's last production is not inconsistent with Hunter's highly probable identification of the play with the "Love's Labour's Won" mentioned by Meres in 1596. We have only to suppose that Shakespeare revived it in 1611, and again perhaps in 1613 for the wedding of the Princess Elizabeth, each time with corrections and augmentations, which have left it as it was published in 1623. The epilogue and the burial of the wand may still be the swan-song of the great poet.

CHAPTER VII

TRAGEDIES.

WE come now to the last division of Shakespeare's plays—his tragedies. These may be classed apart, because their purpose is rather to develop the central character than to illustrate moral and political theories such as those discussed in the preceding plays. We will begin with "Hamlet," apparently Shakespeare's most valued child, named after his own son, whom he had lost in 1596, submitted to recensions, and always kept open for new additions and alterations.[1]

---

[1] The various theories in the interpretation of Hamlet's character form a literature of themselves, the discussion of which would be beyond our present scope. It is sufficient here to note that Hamlet, according to Dr. Plumptre, in his conviction of "the vanity of life," suggests a parallelism with Ecclesiastes.[1] Mr. Jacob Feis[2] believes that "Hamlet" was composed to reproduce the position assumed by Montaigne in his essays, that of a Catholic in religious conviction and of a sceptic in philosophy, and to show that scepticism is the result of Catholicism. Hamlet, like Montaigne, according to this author, was trained in the Catholic faith, but being sent to Wittenberg, the home of Lutheranism, he there learned first to try to think for himself, and to grapple with the mysteries of life. The soul-enslaving faith, however, to which he still clung,

---

[1] Kolcheth, Appendix, 231 *et seq.*
[2] "Shakespeare and Montaigne," 81, 82, 85. 1884.

Hamlet presents a disposition naturally open, developed into a character of impenetrable reserve. The dread charge laid upon him necessitates the habitual concealment of his thoughts and feelings; and this he endeavours to effect by exaggerating them to the extent that his reason seems impaired. In his advice to the players Hamlet condemns as a fault, according to Shakespeare's usual irony, the very practice he himself pursues. As the player, by tearing a passion to tatters, and overstepping the modesty of nature, offends his audience instead of winning their sympathies, so did Hamlet aim at deception by his very excess of truth. To make men sceptical he gives them too much evidence. He convinces all observers that he has lost his reason, by exhibiting too much sense. His own mental disturbance arose from an over subtle, per-

rendered him powerless to do so, and his tortured conscience was the necessary result. Father Darlington, S.J.,[1] on the other hand, considers that Shakespeare intentionally sent Hamlet to Wittenberg to portray in his perplexed soul the result of the false Platonism and fatalism there inculcated. Mr. Simpson, it will be seen, regards Hamlet as the presentation of a highly sensitive mind distraught with the scruples which to such a disposition would necessarily arise from the dread retributive task imposed upon him. Mr. Simpson finds the indications of Catholicism in the religious allusion occurring throughout the play rather than in any special delineation of Hamlet's character. Wittenberg, he says, became the cant name for any university, partly because of its signification, "the place where wit grows," as Chettle has it in Hoffman, partly as the school of Faustus, and perhaps of Luther. Nash was accused of meaning Oxford by Wittenberg in the life of Jack Wilton.

[1] *New Ireland Review,* January 1898.

plexed conscience. The general principles of morals and religion he never questions. His difficulty lay in their application in his strange circumstances. After having seen and conversed with his father's spirit, he still refuses to own that any traveller ever returned from the other world. He thinks it may be the devil. Even after the conduct of the king at the play had proved the truth of the ghost's story, he was still doubtful as to which world the spirit belonged; his father was cut off with all his crimes broad blown.

> "And how his audit stands who knows save heaven?
> But in our circumstance and course of thought
> 'Tis heavy with him" (iii. 3).

The ghost had indeed most distinctly said that he was safely landed in Purgatory.

> "I am thy father's spirit
> Doomed for a *certain term* to walk the night,
> And for the day confined to fast in fires
> *Till* the foul crimes done in my days of nature
> Are burnt and purged away" (i. 5).

But then, how could a blest spirit—"canonised bones" implies this (i. 4)—as he had at first considered him, so fiercely inculcate revenge?

> "Revenge his foul and most unnatural murder" (i. 5).

Yet Hamlet at once embraces the commission, though it is so contrary to his whole being that he feels it must utterly change him, and wipe out

from the table of his memory "all trivial fond
records, all saws of books, all forms, all impres-
sions of youth and observation" (i. 5); but this was
easier to promise than to perform. As soon as his
first passion cools he is overwhelmed with the
difficulty of the problem set him.

> "The time is out of joint! O! cursed spite
> That ever I was born to set it right" (i. 5).

For he is a man who could act only in the mad
whirl of passion, or in the full conviction of reason ;
and both conditions were enormously difficult to one
of his character. His conduct from this moment is
devoted to the problem of executing his father's
commands either in a paroxysm of excitement or
with a conviction fully formed. To inflame his
passion and brace his nerves for action he sedu-
lously cultivates his inner germ of madness, and
strips himself unsparingly of every other affection.
To form his conscience he sifts to the uttermost the
veracity of the ghost, who, he says,

> "May be the devil : and the devil hath power
> To assume a pleasing shape : yea, and perhaps
> Out of my weakness and my melancholy—
> As he is very potent with such spirits—
> Abuses me to damn me. I'll have grounds
> More relative than this" (ii. 2).

His speech when he finds the king praying
iii. 3) shows that though now convinced of the

ghost's veracity, he yet doubted the rectitude of his command. Revenge is measure for measure; eye for eye, tooth for tooth. To send a murderer to heaven was no revenge for the murdered man who had been sent to hell. Hamlet had clearly thought out the terms of the command; and the very frightfulness of the conclusion explains and justifies his inability to fulfil it in practice. He fears the canon which the Eternal has fixed against slaughter, and the future consequences of its transgression. The native hue of his resolution "is sicklied o'er" with the pale cast of their reflected rays. The currents of his enterprise are diverted, and his resolve, but now unalterably fixed, fades into a sterile velleity.

After all the preparation he had made, it would only be congruous to execute justice upon the king in a public and judicial manner, as in fact it was, though through an accident, finally accomplished. To slay him as a mere assassin was repugnant to his views, and to kill him at his private devotions, besides being liable to the objections which he states, might wear a sacrilegious aspect, like killing a man in church, and was a deed possible for Laertes, but not for Hamlet (iv. 7).

His great soliloquies point to these two difficulties. The wonderful "To be, or not to be" exhibits the vain struggle between the desire to escape from his sea of troubles by death and the voice of conscience forbidding the act. The almost equally powerful "O! what a rogue and peasant slave am I," expresses Hamlet's sense of his own apathy, the weakness of his passions, or the difficulty of maintaining them in a state of excitement necessary for action. And the speech (iv. 4), "How all occasions do inform against me," is another protest against the dulness of his passions, and the slow, methodical march of his critical intellect, and its therefore sluggish response to the double "excitement of his reason and his blood." This speech shows the character of his mind. He is no Abraham, to accept without question the command to slay his son. Hamlet would have promised to obey one moment, and the next would have said that God could not contradict Himself, and denied the authority of the bidder. His scruples spring, as has been said, from a perplexed conscience.

If Shakespeare had been blamed for making a blessed soul in Purgatory cry out for revenge, he might have shown the objector the text in the Apocalypse which tells of the souls under the altar crying out, "How long, O Lord, dost Thou not avenge our blood!" or if he had been blamed for exacting this vengeance, not by judicial authority but by a private hand, he might have shown the impossibility of a legal, public process, and have pointed out that Hamlet, as the legitimate king, was the proper person in whom both the right and the duty of exacting the punishment due to the murderer, tyrant, and usurper were vested.

Hamlet was aware that his hesitation might be

"Some craven scruple
Of thinking too precisely on the event,
A thought which, quartered, hath but one part wisdom
And even three parts coward " (iv. 4).

But wisdom or cowardice, it was ingrained, and he felt that he could not tear the scruple from his soul. It was not till his return from England with the proofs that the king had tried to get him murdered there, that he deliberately and finally made up his mind to do the deed. He had, indeed, once roused himself to a sudden paroxysm of anger, and had killed Polonius, whom he had taken for the king; and on his return from England he had found that he was further steeped in blood than he had intended to be. The alteration of the despatch to the King of England, and the substitution of the names of Rosencrantz and Guildenstern for his own, was not a final and unalterable act till he had boarded the pirate ship and was carried away. While he was with them he might always make another change, or interfere in some other way with its execution. But once separated from them the deed was irrevocable; and the considerations by which he justified it to his conscience, helped him to make his final resolution to kill the king. Added to this, the time left for deliberation was but short. It must be done before the messengers could return from England.

It was now, not then so much a question of revenge or of public policy as of self-preservation, and the last consideration mainly influences him. After saying that Rosencrantz and Guildenstern stand not near his conscience, because they "made love to the employment, and their defeat is their own fault," he speaks of the king.

> " Does it not, think'st thee, stand me now upon—
> He that hath killed my king and whored my mother,
> Popped in between the election and my hopes,
> Thrown out the angle for my proper life,
> And with such cozenage—is't not perfect conscience
> To quit him with this arm ? and is't not to be damned
> To let this canker of our nature come
> For further evil ?
>   *Hor.* It must be shortly known from England
> What is the issue of the business there.
>   *Ham.* It will be short : the interview is mine,
> And a man's life no more than to say 'One'" (v. 2).

But we anticipate. If Hamlet is to undertake the task, he must nerve himself for it. All other passions, all other excitements must be subject to this one end. This one end must be now his primitive love, to the exclusion of all else. Such is the doctrine of Shakespeare as we have seen in his sonnets. There can be but one sovereign love in man; all other loves are reduced to mere adjuncts of this; but in this all lesser loves revive to a new life, all contribute their strength to swell the fulness of the chief love, till it has

devoured and assimilated all lesser passions, and
turned them into its own substance.

> " Thou art the grave where buried love doth live,
> Hung with the trophies of my lovers gone,
> Who all their parts of me to thee did give ;
> That due of many now is thine alone :
>   Their images I loved I view in thee,
>   And thou, all they, hast all the all of me." [1]
> —*Sonnet* xxxi.

Hamlet has enough clear reason to see that he
must give up Ophelia, and his heart prompts him
to do so in the way least wounding to her feelings.
He might effect his purpose by convincing her of
the existence of some secret insuperable obstacle
on his side to their union.   The sage advice of
Laertes to his sister, backed by the injunctions of
Polonius to return all Hamlet's letters, give him
an opportunity of separation which a less perfect gentleman would have snatched at.   But he
cannot drop Ophelia in this way.   She must be
made to realise that he is not the kind of man
for her, that her only course is to obliterate, if not
her love, at least her election of him, and that
her marriage with him is impossible.   Hence his
behaviour to her.   His great parting in dumb-
show, described by her (ii. 1), in which he took a
passionate farewell, exhibiting traces of madness
which she, tutored by Polonius, misinterprets as the

---

[1] "And thou, all they," signifies "Thou art to me now all they
once were."

effects of his love, was in reality his act of renun-
ciation. After this, when she is used by Polonius
as a mere bait to get the truth out of Hamlet, he
treats her as one quite estranged! His mother's
shame has changed his opinion about all women.
He did love Ophelia once, and traces of it remain,
as is seen in his desire for her prayers. But now
the only advice he has to give her is to go to a
nunnery. She is not to think of him. He is too
evil for her. He is "very proud, revengeful, ambitious, with more offences at his beck than he has
thoughts to put them in, imagination to give them
shape, or time to act them in." And besides, he
has renounced womankind, for they only make
fools of men (iii. 1). Later on, at the play before
the king, he speaks to her with a coarseness intentionally revolting, and which would have revolted
her had she believed him sane. But this same
coarseness finally convinced her of his madness,
exhibiting, as it seemed to do, the ruin of his
sovereign reason and more sovereign heart, and
was essentially the cause of her own unfeigned
madness (iii. 2). This too explains the corresponding coarseness in the scraps of old songs she
sings in her lunacy. In this most subtle manner,
the cause of her lunacy is shown. Her father's
death crushes her as a fact. But Hamlet's madness and the consequent degradation of his mind
has become to her a contagion, an atmosphere, a
new vitiated life. She is degraded in and with

him. Her reason is buried in the same grave where she sees his entombed. After her death Hamlet can exhibit all the reality of his affection, and declare with truth "forty thousand brothers could not, with all their quantity of love, make up my sum" (v. 1).

Hamlet's character is, in fact, the most exhaustive study of Brutus' generalised observation in "Julius Cæsar" (ii. 1).

> " Between the acting of a dreadful thing
> And the first motion, all the interim is
> Like a phantasma, or a hideous dream ;
> The Genius and the mortal instruments
> Are then in council ; and the state of man
> Like to a little kingdom, suffers then
> The nature of an insurrection."

There is another speech of Brutus which will throw further light on Hamlet's character. We have already supposed that Hamlet wished to impart a kind of solemn judicial character to his father's revenge. This appears rather from the preparation he makes for it, and his exclusive devotion to this one object, than from anything that he says. It is apparently the sense of the disproportion between this all-embracing preparation, and the cowardly secret performance of stabbing the king at his prayers, that prompts Hamlet to make that curdling "Now might I do it pat" (iii. 3). He wishes to do the thing solemnly, judicially, sacrificially, with due intensity of thought and complication

U

of circumstance.　The daggers that he uses he wants
to be balanced by the daggers that he utters.　The
judicial sentence is with him as important as the
execution.　His mother indeed is only to be sentenced,
not executed.

> " Soft, now to my mother.
> O heart, lose not thy nature ; let not ever
> The soul of Nero enter this firm bosom,
> Let me be cruel, not unnatural :
> I will speak daggers to her, but use none ;
> My tongue and soul in this be hypocrites ;
> Now in my words soever she be shent,
> To give them seals never, my soul, consent !" (iii. 2).

Now it is exactly this solemn judicial feeling which
Brutus is careful to impress upon his fellow-con-
spirators.

> " Let us be sacrificers, but not butchers, Caius . . .
> Let's kill him boldly, but not wrathfully ;
> Let's carve him as a dish fit for the gods,
> Not hew him as a carcase fit for hounds ;
> And let our hearts, as subtle masters do,
> Stir up their servants to an act of rage,
> And after seem to chide them."—*Julius Cæsar*, ii. 1.

Claudius was but carrion for hounds ; in other
respects the feeling of Brutus seems the counterpart of Hamlet's, and the key for comprehending its
acts.　Othello strives in like manner to maintain
the solemn judicial feeling ; he says to Desdemona
just before killing her—

> " O perjured woman, thou dost stone my heart,
> And makest me call what I intend to do
> A murder, which I thought a sacrifice."
> 　　　　　　　　　—*Othello*, v. 2.

Hamlet is a conspirator, urged to revenge by policy and by the sense of personal injury, and only kept back by what he impatiently calls the craven scruples of religion and conscience.   Othello is likewise a conspirator, though his act is not treason, but more nearly allied to " petit treason."   He has this in common with the conspirator, that to right himself, to do what seems justice and to revenge what seems sin, he takes the law into his own hands, and becomes legislator, juryman, and judge in one.

In examining Shakespeare's physiology of conspiracy we must again recall the circumstances of his age and home.   He lived among conspirators, as they were then reckoned; among men whose political and religious opinions prevented their feeling that content with things as they were, which was required, under the name of loyalty, by the rulers.   In 1584 he must have been in the midst of the panic caused by the apprehension of Somerville and Arden; in 1601 he was intimate with the Essex conspirators, several of whom were his near neighbours at Stratford, who were again implicated in the Gunpowder Plot of 1605.   The conspirators in these cases considered that the measures which they undertook, even though they were measures of revenge, were of a judicial character.

A passage which at first sight seems irreconcilable with any great moral depth in Hamlet, is the famous one where he makes his mother compare her former and her present husbands.   The deed which had

blasted all morality, made religion a rhapsody, and
darkened the face of nature, seems to be simply
marrying after she had lost a handsome husband.
Such is the plain sense of the speech, "Look here
upon this picture, and on this"—and it may be
asked why such a contrast should scarify a conscience.   It is a great social lapse, but not in itself
a moral fall if the widow of Hyperion marries a
negro.   Yet the Queen, without waiting for Hamlet
to explain the real criminality of her action, as he
afterwards does, is moved to confess herself a sinner
for this very crime which is no crime at all.

> " O Hamlet, speak no more :
> Thou turn'st mine eyes into my very soul
> And there I see such black and grainèd spots ·
> As will not leave their tinct " (iii. 4).

Lady Macbeth, steeped to the lips in blood, could
say no more.   She could not wash the stain from
her hands.   The explanation is, that in art, to
Shakespeare, as has been shown in the sonnets,
the outward beauty is but a sign of inward virtue.
" Ad ognuno è palese," says Crescimbeni, " che la
bellezza del corpo sia sicuro argomento, anche
naturalmente, della bellezza dell' anima." [1]   The
front of Jove, the eye of Mars, the poise of Mercury,
" the combination and form " in Hamlet's father,

> " Where every god did give assurance of a man,"

were but the exterior pledge of the spiritual gifts

[1] *Della Bellezza*, 93.

within, the passions subject to reason, and reason to grace. His stepfather was, compared to this mountain, a moor, not because his features were misshapen and his stature dwarfed, but because his inward soul was deformed. He was " a murderer, a villain, and a slave, a vice of kings, a cutpurse of the empire and the rule." The truth that corporeal beauty should bespeak inner worth is axiomatic with the poet.

Thus Miranda says of Ferdinand—

> " There's nothing ill can dwell in such a temple ;
> If the ill spirit have so fair a house
> Good things will strive to dwell with it."
>
> —*Tempest*, i. 2 ;

and Pericles of Marina—

> " Falseness cannot come from thee : for thou look'st
> Modest as justice, and thou seem'st a palace
> For the crowned truth to dwell in."

It is Desdemona's purity, apparent in her whole presence, which makes his suspicion of her so terrible to Othello.

> " Look where she comes !
> If she be false, O then Heaven mocks itself.
> I'll not believe it " (iii. 3).

But this is a doctrine which love accepts spontaneously at first, but must often unlearn ; and then it cries out, " Thy sweet virtue answers not thy show " (Shakespeare, Sonnet 93). It is a doctrine

too of which age and experience of the world become
sceptical ; thus Duncan can say—

> " There's no art
> To find the mind's construction in the face."
> —*Macbeth*, i. 4.

But this disenchantment is wholly due to man's
perversity, the disorder of sin, and is wholly contrary
to the Creator's design, which is the ideal of the
poet and of all true art.

A similar observation must be made with regard
to the suicidal tendency of the tragedy.   This is
an artistic necessity, as has been said of the close
of "Romeo and Juliet "; all tragedy is necessarily
sacrificial, in a sense suicidal ; for in tragedy, the actor
risks all upon one die.   He devotes himself soul and
body to one enterprise, which exhausts him, consumes
all the wine of life, and leaves nothing but the lees
for the empty vault to brag of.   When the hero sur-
vives the tragical catastrophe, he takes himself out
of tragedy and makes himself a comic personage.
When Claudio in " Much Ado about Nothing " walks
away safe and sound, leaving Hero for dead, nothing
can remove a certain impression of an anti-climax,
an impression which remains, notwithstanding the
vivacity of the latter part of the play, and which
helps to make Benedick the true hero of the drama.
A vengeance which does not involve self-destruction
is not properly tragic.   A tragic purpose is one
which straitens the whole man till it be accom-

plished, welds him together, hardens him, points him to one great act, in doing which he dies. Tragedy is devotion, sacrifice; it moves as much by what it does not say as by what it does openly. It speaks only of the earthly, and to the sense, its term is the grave; but it is without meaning if the mind does not transcend this limit, and see the act illumined by the reflection of a world beyond the grave. No sorrow, however deep, is really tragical which receives its consolation here and now. Cibber turned "Lear" into a comedy by saving Lear and Cordelia. "Hamlet" would be Cibberised if a sixth act were added, in which he was revived to be king, with Horatio for prime minister, and Ophelia's cousin for his queen!

The moral difficulties of "Hamlet" then disappear when it is viewed as a work of dramatic art. And after clearing these difficulties, none need be felt about its religious significance. In it the same spirit is manifested which we shall find in "Cymbeline"; a spirit that clings to religious traditions, because in religion it prefers the old to the new;—the old which may be an echo of a revelation, to the new which certainly is a product of human reflection and thought. Hence the relevancy of the conversation between Horatio and Marcellus.

> "*Hor.* I have heard,
> The cock, that is the trumpet of the morn,
> Doth with his lofty and shrill-sounding throat
> Awake the god of day ; and at his warning,

Whether in sea or fire, in earth or air,
Th' extravagant and erring spirit hies
To his confine. . . .
   Mar. Some say that ever, 'gainst that season comes
Wherein our Saviour's birth is celebrated,
This bird of dawning singeth all night long,
And then, they say, no spirit dares stir abroad :
The nights are wholesome ; then no planets strike,
No fairy takes, nor witch has power to charm,
So hallowed and so gracious is the time.
   Hor. So have I heard, and do in part believe it " (i. 1).

Douce finds the original of this passage in a Salisbury hymn, printed in Pynson's collection. In the first quarto, instead of the ghost first "starting like a guilty thing" (line 148), and then "fading" (line 157), it "faded" in both cases. The ghost fading away seems much more congruous for a being "so majestical" than starting; besides, the pallor of guilt upon a fearful summons is more characteristic than the spasmodic start which is common to all surprise. The ghost's description of his state points unmistakeably to the doctrine of Purgatory, which Shakespeare, if he had been a Protestant, ought to have regarded "as a fond thing vainly invented, grounded on no warranty of Scripture, but rather repugnant to the word of God."

      "Mine hour is almost come
When I to sulphurous and tormenting flames
Must render up myself. . . .
. . . I am thy father's spirit ;
Doomed for a certain time to walk the night,
And for the day confined to fast in fires,
Till the foul crimes done in my days of nature

Are burned and purged away. But that I am forbid
To tell the secrets of my prison-house
I could a tale unfold whose lightest word
Would harrow up thy soul, freeze thy young blood,
Make thy two eyes, like stars, start from their spheres,
Thy knotted and combinèd locks to part,
And each particular hair to stand on end
Like quills upon the fretful porcupine :
But this eternal blazon must not be
To ears of flesh and blood.
. . . Thus was I . . .
Cut off even in the blossoms of my sin,
Unhousel'd, disappointed, unanel'd,
No reckoning made, but sent to my account
With all my imperfections on my head " (i. 5).

" Unhousel'd," is without the Communion ; " disappointed," is not in a fit state, not appointed or
prepared by absolution ; " unanel'd," is without the
unction ; "no reckoning made," is without confession. These ceremonies omitted, man goes to his
account with all his imperfections on his head.
Performed, they take him out of the world with
all possible helps. They give him a share in the
treasury of the Church, they bring him into company with those who relieve him of some of his
burden. Such is the doctrine implied in Shakespeare's words, which were added to the play in
the edition of 1604, and are not found in that
of 1603.

In the same scene (line 136) Hamlet swears—
" Yes, by St. Patrick." Oaths of this kind are
scattered broadcast through the plays, and they
contribute their quota to the determination of

the poet's opinions. "Were it not an idolatrous oath I would swear by sweet St. George," says Greene in that "Groat's Worth of Wit" in which he makes his famous attack on Shakespeare as the Johannes Factotum. Hamlet's injunctions to Ophelia, "Get thee to a nunnery" (iii. 1), chime in with Shakespeare's recognised approval of monasticism—an approval which Dr. Flathe (*Shakespeare in seiner Wirklichkeit*, i. 85) seeks to disprove by two texts, in one of which Rosalind says of the man she had cured of love by driving him mad, that she had made him "forswear the full stream of the world, and to live in a nook merely monastic" ("As You Like It," iii. 2); while in the other, Venus tries to seduce Adonis by talking to him of

> "Love-lacking vestals and self-loving nuns
> That on the earth would breed a scarcity
> And barren dearth of daughters and of sons."
> —*Venus and Adonis*, 752.

Venus' argument is indeed that of many non-Catholics, but it was not Shakespeare's.

Hamlet says to his mother, "Confess yourself to heaven; repent what's past; avoid what is to come" (iii. 4), a mode of speech which might be indifferently Protestant or Catholic; but when a few lines farther on she says, "O Hamlet, thou hast cleft my heart in twain," and he answers, "O throw away the worser part of it, and live the purer with the other half," there is a very sensible mark of the sacrificial form of religion. The king's order to bring Polonius' body into the chapel is more consonant to Catholic than to Protestant practice. The feelings which come out so naturally in Ophelia's madness are Catholic—"They say he made a good end—God ha' mercy on his soul, and of all Christian souls, I pray God " (iv. 5).

We have already noticed how natural, graceful, and noble Shakespeare makes Catholic feelings appear in his great historical portraits, such as " Richard II." A like remark may be added touching his portraits of the mad, the uneducated, the common people, who have, in their own way, the naturalness and simplicity of field-flowers, which a master like Shakespeare can make as attractive as the richer qualities of the more cultivated kinds. Now it is worth while to notice the part which Prayer for the Dead plays in creating this attractiveness. Read the mad scene of Ophelia—look at Juliet's nurse—

> "Susan and she—God rest all Christian souls !—
> Were of an age : well, Susan is with God ;
> She was too good for me."—*Romeo and Juliet*, i. 3,

or at old Gobbo ("Merchant of Venice," ii. 2) to his son who had reported his own death—" Alack the day, I know you not, young gentleman; but I pray you tell me, is my boy, God rest his soul, dead or alive ? " — or the gravemaker who tells Hamlet that he is digging a

grave for "One that was a woman, but, rest her
soul, she's dead" ("Hamlet," v. 1).   Not that
Shakespeare at all confines this ejaculation to the
uneducated; he makes Macduff cry out on hearing
of the murder of his wife and children, "Heaven
rest them now!" ("Macbeth," iv. 3).   Warwick,
when he finds his brother dead, cries out, "Sweet
rest his soul" ("3 Henry VI.," v. 2), and Horatio
to Hamlet just dead, "Flights of angels sing thee
to thy rest" ("Hamlet," v. 2).   On this subject we
may quote the passage when Laertes demands more
funeral honour for his sister, than can be allowed.
"What ceremony else?" he asks, to which the
Priest answers—

> "Her obsequies have been as far enlarged
> As we have warranties; her death was doubtful;
> And, but that great command o'ersways the order,
> She should in ground unsanctified have lodged
> Till the last trumpet; for charitable prayers,
> Shards, flints, and pebbles should be thrown on her,
> Yet here she is allowed her virgin rites,
> Her maiden strewments, and the bringing home
> Of bell and burial.
>   *Laer.*   Must there no more be done?
>   *Priest.*   No more be done:
> We should profane the service of the dead
> To sing a requiem and such rest to her
> As to peace-parted souls."

And Laertes rejoins—

> "I tell thee, churlish priest,
> A ministering angel shall my sister be
> When thou liest howling" (v. 1).

In the quarto of 1603 the Priest, instead of saying that she cannot have Requiem sung, says that she has had Dirge sung for her; the Dirge is the simple prayer and psalmody, the Vespers and Matins; the Requiem is the solemn sacrifice.

> "My Lord, we have done all that lies in us,
> And more than well the Church can tolerate,
> She hath had a Dirge sung for her maiden soul :
> And but for favour of the King and you,
> She had been buried in the open fields
> Where now she is allowed Christian burial."

Shakespeare has a more personal approval of prayer for the dead in his poem on the Phœnix and Turtle—

> " Let the priest in surplice white
> That defunctive music can
> Be the death-divining swan,
> Lest the Requiem lack his right

And again—

> " To this urn let those repair
> That are either true or fair :
> For these dead birds breathe a prayer."

Another stage of this Threnos is remarkable in connection with Shakespeare's opinions about monasticism, celibacy, and kindred doctrines; he says of the persons whom he celebrates under the names of the two birds—

> " Death is now the phœnix' nest ;
> And the turtle's loyal breast

> To eternity doth rest,
> Leaving no posterity.
> 'Twas not their infirmity,
> It was married chastity."

As a comment on these two lines, we may quote a passage from the *Saturday Review* of October 1, 1864, upon a "Cornish Mystery" published in the Transactions of the Philological Society of that year: "Such a passage as this could hardly have been written since the Reformation. After the murder of Cain, Adam says—

> 'Therefore after this,
> Chastely will we live together,
> And carnal joy in this world
> We will together deny us.'

It does not directly contradict any Protestant dogma, but is much more in the natural vein of an ante-Reformation poet."

In "Hamlet," as it had always been performed in Elizabeth's reign, the foolish old statesman was called Corambis; in the edition of 1604 the name is changed to Polonius. The wisdom of Lord Burghley is a dogma of such strong traditional credit that it may look overbold to say that he was glanced at in this character. The points, however, which serve to identify him are, first, the advice to Laertes (i. 3), which corresponds to Burghley's advice to his son; next, Polonius' care in his choice of words in "expostulating" (*i.e.*

expostillate) " matters of State," and his obtrusive
artificiality in covering nonsense with a robe of
seeming sense, as befits men " of wisdom and of
reach." The man who could write to Sir Geo. Cary :
" I thank you for your last letters, by which I was
glad to perceive your prestness to enter into
Scotland . . . I think the dulceness used to the
Duke proceedeth of the apparence of the King's
own humour, which if it come of mildness of nature
I am glad, and if it come of the counterfeited
provisableness of the Duke with pleasing, I hope
time will spend those concepts," &c., would certainly, especially when he grew a little older, speak
in the vein of Polonius.

Those who have had occasion to look over many
of the documents in the State Paper office, which
passed through Burghley's hands, will remember
with what diligence he dashed and noted the
peregrinate and inflated words that his corres-
pondents wrote to him, such as the " prestness "
and " dulceness " of the above scrap. He would
certainly have made Polonius' criticism " mobbed
queen is good." We do not mean to confine
Polonius to Burghley. Burghley was an avatar
of Polonius' spirit, as Leicester was of Claudius',
Elizabeth of Lettice's, the Countess of Leicester of
Hamlet's mother's, and Essex of Hamlet's. The
possibilities of Shakespeare's types go far beyond
the realities of any given individuals.

Shakespeare also gives Polonius somewhat of the

scriptural formalism or preachiness of his Falstaff,
Bottom, Costard, &c. When Polonius describes the
stages of Hamlet's malady—

> " Fell into a sadness, then into a fast,
> Thence to a watch, thence into a weakness,
> Thence to a lightness, and by this declension
> Into the madness wherein now he raves " (ii. 2),

he surely has in his eyes St. Paul's scale of repentance in the Corinthians. Then his politic
baiting of mouse-traps, as he describes them (ii. 5)
to Reynaldo, and his confession—

> " We are oft to blame in this—
> 'Tis too much proved—that with devotion's visage
> And pious action, we do sugar o'er
> The devil himself" (iii. 1),

which is singularly applicable to the story current
of Lord Burghley, that he owed his safety under
Queen Mary to the diligence with which he mani-
pulated a monstrous set of beads every morning
in Wimbledon Church.

Hunter finds a parallel to the Ghost in Hamlet
in a ghost story current in the families of Stourton
and Arundell (of Wardour) and consequently in the
kindred houses of Derby, Montague, and Southampton, in 1588. It is related in More's " History
of the English Province of the Society of Jesus "
(Lib. V. No. xi. p. 171): " The Lord Stourton, whose
widow married with Lord Arundell, was a Catholic
at heart, but externally conformed to the established

religion, preferring the preservation of his property
to the use and fruit of the Sacraments; but for
fear he might be taken off unprepared in this grave
neglect, he kept at his house two priests, and
ordered that one should always be at home by day
and by night; but by the secret judgment of God
his precautions proved vain in his last sickness, for
both were absent, and no other priest could be
found. He called, therefore, his wife (a daughter
of Edward, Earl of Derby, and sister to the Stanley
whose epitaph Shakespeare wrote), and with many
tears explained to them his exceeding grief, that
whereas he supremely desired to have the last rites
of the Church, he was balked of the gift; at the
same time he acknowledged his grievous fault of
pretended conformity, and humbly begged pardon
for all that weighed on his dying soul, and died.
The affair was referred to Father Cornelius. He
was asked whether one might pray for the man who
had so died? 'You both may, and you must,' he
replied. The next day as he was saying Mass, and
making commemoration of the dead, the man just
dead stood on the Gospel side of the altar, clothed
in his usual cloak, and asked the Father to have
pity on him, for he was burning in purgatorial
fires; he then opened his garment, and showed his
burnt side; he then asked to be recommended to
those present. Cornelius, turning his face towards
the ghost, remained so long praying, that he was
reminded by the server that he would never end.

After Mass, he exhorted the congregation to persevere in prayer for the soul of Lord Stourton;
for he was roasting in the fires of Purgatory, and
demanded the assistance of the living.   Some say
that the vision occurred at the commemoration of
the living; others that it was seen by the server
as well as the priest; but the affair was universally
talked about, and is to this day a fixed tradition in
the families of Stourton and Arundell."   So wrote
More in 1660.   Challoner in his "Memoirs of
Missionary Priests," vol. i. p. 310 (ed. Richardson,
Derby, 1843) gives a similar account on still earlier
authority: "When Mr. Cornelius was saying Mass
for the soul of John, Lord Stourton (who had died
unreconciled, but with great desire of the sacraments,
and more than ordinary marks of sorrow and
repentance), he had a vision, after the consecration
and elevation of the chalice (*i.e.* at the commemoration of the dead), of the soul of the said Lord
Stourton, then in Purgatory, desiring him to pray
for him, and to request of the lady, his mother,
to cause masses to be said for his soul.   This vision
was also seen at the same time by Patrick Salmon,
a good religious soul, who was then serving Mr.
Cornelius at Mass."

We subjoin the following parallel between Hamlet
and Essex, as showing how the poet is discovered to
reflect in detail the history of his time. " Has it ever
been hinted that the poet may have conceived his
characters of Hamlet from Essex, and Horatio

from Southampton? If not, it might be well to consider the indications which would point to such a conclusion. They are not few, perhaps, whether regard be paid to the external or the personal facts. It will suffice here to suggest a line of inquiry. To the common people Essex was a prince. He was descended through his father from Edward III., and through his mother was the immediate kinsman of Elizabeth. Many persons, most absurdly, imagined his title to the throne a better one than the Queen's. In person, for he had his father's beauty, he was all that Shakespeare has described the Prince of Denmark to have been. Then, again, his mother had been tempted from her duty while her gracious and noble husband was alive. That handsome and generous husband was supposed to have been poisoned by the guilty pair. After the father's murder the seducer had married the mother. The father had not perished in his prime without feeling and expressing some doubt that foul play had been used against him, yet sending his forgiveness to the guilty woman who had sacrificed his honour, perhaps taken away his life. There is indeed an exceeding singularity of agreement in the facts of the case and the incidents of the play. The relation of Claudius to Hamlet are the same as those of Leicester to Essex: under pretence of fatherly friendship he was suspicious of his motives, jealous of his actions; kept him much in the country and at college; let him see little of his mother; and clouded his prospects

in the world by an appearance of benignant favour.
Gertrude's relations with her son were much like
those of Lettice to Robert Devereux. Then, again,
in his moodiness, in his college learning, in his love
for the theatre and the players, in his desire for the
fiery action for which his nature was most unfit,
there are many characteristics of Essex which recall
the image of the Danish prince." [1]

As "Hamlet" is the physiology of justifiable
treason, so "Lear" is the development of the doctrine which was involved in Henry VIII.'s theory
of Empire, and was broadly stated in the days of
James I.—*uni et univoce.* The monarch has the
monopoly of loyalty and obedience, and whoever
gives only a divided allegiance is a traitor. Lear,
the king and father, demands complete submission
from his daughters. Goneril and Regan, while
professing to grant it, give the king less than his
due. Cordelia, while refusing to grant it, respects
in practice the sovereign and paternal rights.
Regan puts the problem to be solved in the play
thus—

> "How in one house
> Should many people, under two commands,
> Hold amity? 'Tis hard, almost impossible" (ii. 4).

It is to be noted that this idea is Shakespeare's
own; neither the play nor the old chronicle makes
Cordelia say that the reason why she cannot exclu-

---

[1] "Court and Society from Elizabeth to Anne," by the Duke of
Manchester, i. 297.

sively love her father, is because it may be her duty to love another as much. Shakespeare alone points out the distinction of duties—

> "Haply when I shall wed,
> That lord whose hand must take my plight shall carry
> Half my love with him, half my care and duty—
> Sure, I shall never marry like my sisters
> To love my father all" (i. 1).

Lear would have all, and those who promise all end by giving none. Regan and Goneril find that in promising all they have promised the impossible.

The religious allusions are few but suggestive. Goneril, whose profession pleased her father, exhibits a true Protestant dislike to the text which teaches that branches lopped off from the vine will wither, and must be burned. When Albany says to her—

> "She that herself will sliver and disbranch
> From her maternal sap, perforce must wither,
> And come to deadly use."

She replies, " No more ; the text is foolish "; and he answers, " Wisdom and goodness to the vile seem vile : filths savour but themselves " (iv. 2).

Cordelia, as Queen of France, is put in the position of a Catholic, and the terms used of her in the gentleman's description of her bearing,

> "She shook
> The holy water from her heavenly eyes" (iv. 3),

have a Catholic tone about them—and the motives

which keep Lear from Cordelia are much the same
as those which were supposed to keep the English
government from reconciling itself with the English
Catholics.

> " A sovereign shame so elbows him ; his own unkindness
> That stripped her from his benediction, turned her
> To foreign casualties, gave her dear rights
> To his dog-hearted daughters, these things sting
> His mind so venomously, that burning shame
> Detains him from Cordelia " (iv. 3).

Lear had already learned that the absolute submission professed by his daughters, and their readiness
" To say ' ay ' and ' no ' to everything I said ! ' Ay '
and ' no ' too, was no good divinity " (iv. 6). The
true theology is built on " distinctions " whose fan
winnows away the bad and leaves the good.

Lear, on first seeing Cordelia, cries out, as if from
Purgatory—

> " You do me wrong to take me out o' the grave :
> Thou art a soul in bliss ; but I am bound
> Upon a wheel of fire, that mine own tears
> Do scald like molten lead " (iv. 7).

And when he had overcome his shame, and had
fully reconciled himself to Cordelia, then his joy puts
on the solemn utterance of religion, and he gladly
makes the sacrifice of life.

> " Come, let's away to prison,
> We two alone will sing like birds i' the cage.
> When thou dost ask me blessing, I'll kneel down
> And ask of thee forgiveness : so we'll live,

> And pray, and sing, and tell old tales, and laugh
> At gilded butterflies, and hear poor rogues
> Talk of court news ; and we'll talk with them too,
> Who loses and who wins ; who's in, who's out ;
> And take upon's the mystery of things
> As if we were God's spies ; and we'll wear out,
> In a walled prison, packs and sects of great ones
> That ebb and flow by the moon . . .
> Upon such sacrifice, my Cordelia,
> The gods themselves throw incense " (v. 3).

The times to which the drama refers are characterised by Gloucester, " 'Tis the times' plague, when
madmen lead the blind " (iv. 1); and by Albany at
the end :—

> " The weight of this sad time we must obey,
> Speak what we feel, not what we ought to say.
> The oldest hath borne most : we that are young
> Shall never see so much, nor live so long " (v. 3).

And the conclusion is like that of Shakespeare's
sacrificial tragedies, such as " Romeo and Juliet,"
where the death of the chief actors has its effect
in the conversion of the survivors.   Albany is
of the faction of Lear's two daughters, he fights
against him and Cordelia; yet at the conclusion he
is left as the true representative of Lear, whose
cause is triumphant, though to secure its triumph
he and Cordelia perish.

But an objection to Shakespeare's Catholicism
requiring a somewhat detailed examination is commonly found in Edgar's feigned madness; the names
he gives to his supposed devil being the same as

those uttered by the possessed persons who were exorcised by Father William Weston, S.J. The exorcisms in question took place chiefly at Sir George Peckham's at Denham, near Uxbridge, and at Lord Vaux's at Hackney, and were made known to the world in Harsnet's "Popish Impostures," in the account there given of the trial of the parties concerned in the Ecclesiastical Court. Harsnet held successively the sees of Chichester, Norwich, and York, and in his capacity first of secretary then of judge in the Ecclesiastical Court, he seems to have accepted any witness, however worthless and false, who would help to obtain the verdict he desired. His book is full of the vilest calumnies. A true account of the possessions was given by Father Weston himself in his autobiography, edited by Father Morris, S.J.[1] Our business, however, is only to inquire into the nature of Shakespeare's belief in good and evil spirits, as set forth in his writings, and to see whether the nomenclature of Edgar's devils is an argument in favour of his Protestantism.

The belief in good and evil spirits forms an essential part of the Christian revelation, and was held by Puritans and Protestants as well as by Catholics in Shakespeare's time. Harsnett in fact prosecuted Darrell the preacher for exorcising seven persons in the Puritan family of Starchie, and Hartley was put to death for exorcising in the same

---

[1] "Troubles of our Catholic Forefathers," chap. vii., 2nd series.

household. The 72nd canon of the English Church forbidding exorcisms was passed in consequence of the Darrell case. Belief in evil spirits, like every other doctrine of faith, is open to superstitious corruption and to abuse for servile ends. From the days of Simon Magus there have been conjuring quacks, and true exorcists; simulated cases of possession, and real demoniacs. But superstition points to a basis of fact, and it is proper to a sound judgment to be able to distinguish truth from imposture by the character of the evidence adduced. Thus, Blessed Thomás More, as shrewd, learned, and experienced a lawyer as any in the England of the sixteenth century, after recounting the pretended cure of Simcox (" 2 Henry IV.," ii. 1) already related, proceeds to say that as false jewels do not disprove the existence of precious stones, but show the necessity of precaution in judging them, and of applying proper tests, so it is with miracles. " You do not," he says, " mistrust St. Peter for Judas ;" and he proceeds to relate a case of possession in the person of a daughter of Sir Roger Wentworth, who was cured by Our Lady of Ipswich under circumstances which, in his judgment, attested its reality. " There was," he says, " in this matter no pretext of begging ; no possibility of counterfeiting ; no simpleness in the seers, her father, and others right honourable and rich, sore abashed at seeing such sad changes in their children. The great number of witnesses, many of great worship, wisdom, and good experience, and the maid herself, too young to feign, and the fashion itself too strange for any man to feign.   Finally, the virgin herself was so moved in mind by the miracle" that for aught her father could do, "she forsook the world, and professed religion in a very good and noble company of the Minoresses, where she hath lived well and virtuously ever since."[1]

Now we think Shakespeare's view of preternatural manifestation was like that of More.   He knows how to condemn and expose the false conjuring of Pinch, or the pretended sorceries of Southwell and Bolingbroke.   He may complain with Hotspur that such "skimble skamble" credulity as Glendower's "puts him from the faith," or is a scandal to religion, or through the mouth of Mrs. Page he may expose the old wives' tales how

> " The superstitious idle-headed elf
>   Received, and did deliver to our age,
>   This tale of Herne the Hunter for a truth."
> —*Merry Wives of Windsor*, iv. 4.

He can embody, in the comic, good-natured satire of "Midsummer-Night's Dream," the popular belief in beneficent elves and fairies, or weave into the woof of his tragedy the superstitions prevalent on witch-craft.   Yet he can speak with unfeigned respect of the remedial exorcisms of the Abbess, and make the whole action of his mightiest drama hinge on

[1] Works, 137.

the apparition of a blessed spirit.   He can recount
as an attested fact the numberless cures worked by
St. Edward and the cure of the king by Helena's aid.
Nor are these merely chance poetic expressions.
Shakespeare's belief in the spiritual world is attested
by the fact that the functions he assigns to the angels
are in strict accordance with Catholic theology.
Their songs are the harmony of Heaven, and " they
tune the music of the spheres" ("Merchant of Venice,"
v. 1).   They are invoked as " blessed ministers from
above " (" Measure for Measure," v. 1), as " ministers
of grace " (" Hamlet," i. 4), as " heavenly guards "
(" Hamlet," iii. 4) ; though in constant conflict with
evil, they remain unstained.   Their love for men, pure,
disinterested, divine, furnishes the type of Catherine's
conjugal fidelity.

> " He counsels a divorce : a loss of her
> That like a jewel has hung twenty years
> About his neck yet never lost her lustre ;
> Of her, that loves him with that excellence
> That *angels love good men* with, even of her
> That when the greatest stroke of fortune falls
> Will bless the king."—*Henry VIII.*, ii. 2.

They shed tears on the crimes and disorders of man,

> " But man, proud man !
> Drest in a little brief authority,
> Most ignorant of what he's most assured,
> His glassy essence, like an angry ape,
> Plays such fantastic tricks before high heaven
> As make the angels weep."
> —*Measure for Measure*, ii. 2 ;

and they rejoice over his repentance.

> " Then there is mirth in heaven,
>   When earthly things made even
>   Atone together."—*As You Like It*, v. 4.

They inspire the soul with the spirit of prayer, and
though the heart be hard as strings of steel, they
make it soft as new-born babe's (" Hamlet," iii. 3).
Lastly, they watch by man in his agony, and sing him
to rest (" Hamlet," v. 2).

Nor is Shakespeare less accurate with regard to
the nature and functions of the evil spirits. As
Henry V. has a good angel ever about him, so Falstaff follows him like his evil angel " up and down "
(" 2 Henry IV.," i. 2). Similarly Antony, as a heathen,
has his demon, and the witches in Macbeth pander
to man's curiosity, and serve him solely with· mali-
cious intent, that he may " dwindle, peak, and pine "
(" Macbeth," 1. 3). The devils can assume all shapes
that man goes up and down in, from " fourscore to
thirteen " (" Timon of Athens," ii. 2). They can
present themselves in pleasing forms, and they suggest the worst temptations under some appearance
of holiness.

> " When devils will their blackest sins put on,
>   They do suggest at first with heavenly shows."
>   —*Othello*, ii. 3.

Thus, too, they put man off his guard and suggest
a motive for sin, by quoting Scripture, applying
some accepted truth in a false sense, or luring him
by honest trifles they " betray us in deepest conse-

quence " (" Macbeth," i. 3). If Shakespeare thus seriously attributes all the power to evil spirits accorded to them by Catholic doctrine, we see no reason why his allusion in Edgar's speech to the "possessed" at Sir G. Peckham's should be regarded as a caricature of the Church's belief. The evidence of such men as Fathers Weston and Cornelius, the latter a martyr for the Faith, was surely as unimpeachable as that which satisfied Sir T. More.

Another phase of belief in the preternatural current in Shakespeare's time, was the significance attached to natural portents, as signs of the divine displeasure at the changes being wrought in Church and State. The sudden rise of the Thames and Trent, and the consequent floods on the day of Blessed Campion's death, were then regarded as nature's protest against the murderous deed. Thus Poundes wrote :—

> " The scowling skies did stream and puff apace,
>   They could not bear the wrong that malice wrought,
> The sun drew in his shining purple face.
>   The moistened clouds shed brinish tears for thought,
> The river Thames awhile astonished stood
>   To count the drops of Campion's sacred blood.
> Nature with tears bewailed her heavy loss,
>   Honesty feared herself should shortly die ;
> Religion saw her champion on the cross,
>   Angels and Saints desirèd leave to cry ;
> E'en Heresy, the eldest child of Hell,
>   Began to blush and thought she did not well."

" All which accidents," says Parsons, speaking of the

same occurrence, "though some will compute to other causes, yet happening when so open and unnatural injustice was done, they cannot but be interpreted as tokens of God's indignation."[1] Now Shakespeare is continually calling attention to such occurrences as omens of the king's death or of the kingdom's overthrow :—

> " The seasons change their manner as the year
>   Had found some months asleep, and leaped them over,
>   The river hath thrice flow'd, no ebb between ;
>   And the old folk, time's doting chronicles,
>   Say it did so, a little time before
>   That our great grandsire, Edward, sick'd and died."
> —2 *Henry IV.*, iv. 4.

So Hubert tells John—

> " They say five moons were seen to-night,
>   Old men, and beldams, in the streets
>   Do prophesy upon it dangerously."
> —*King John*, iv. 2.

So before the fall of Richard II.—

> " The bay-trees in our country are all wither'd,
>   And meteors fright the fixèd stars of heaven :
>   The pale-faced moon looks bloody on the earth,
>   And lean-looked prophets whisper fearful change."
> —*Richard II.*, ii. 4.

And in the same play, Act ii. 2, the presentiments of the queen and the presages of Bagot show a

[1] " Epistles of Comfort to Priests," c. 15. 1882.

preternatural cast of thought as the citizen says in Richard III. :—

> " Before the days of change, still is it so,
> By a divine instinct men's minds mistrust
> Pursuing danger."—*Richard III.*, ii. 3.

Mr. Tyler discovers in these passages and "the wide world's prophetic soul" of the sonnets, evidence of Shakespeare's pantheism.[1] But as we have seen, this "finding of signs in the heavens" accurately portrays Catholic feeling prevalent in the poet's time, and is based on the Gospel teaching. Shakespeare's own opinions of signs and wonders may be gauged on the one hand by Lafeu's warning, already quoted against making trifles of terrors, " ensconcing ourselves in seeming knowledge when we should submit ourselves to an unknown fear "; and on the other hand by Edmund's speech, " that it is the foppery of the world to make the stars guilty of disasters which we have brought on ourselves by our own misconduct." The attitude of mind thus indicated is the mean betwixt superstition and scepticism or intelligent discriminating faith.

In "Othello" it is the deep moral lesson which gives the play its absorbing interest, and that we shall consider in Chapter IX. The religious allusions are on the side of Catholicism. Shakespeare generally makes the woman the embodiment of the religious conscience. If so, Iago's perpetual mistrust of

[1] Shakespeare's Sonnets, c. 11. 1890.

woman's honour, and confidence of his power of leading her astray, is simply the representation of the Machiavellian idea of religion; and his assurances of Desdemona's fickleness in her faith are no more trustworthy than his confidence in the unreasoning blindness of Othello's love—

> "For her
> To win the Moor—were't to renounce his baptism,
> All seals and symbols of redeemèd sin—
> His soul is so enfettered to her love
> That she may make, unmake, do what she list" (ii. 3).

Thus Othello is represented by Shakespeare as a Catholic. Witness again the regimen he prescribes for Desdemona's imaginary wanderings—

> "This hand of yours requires
> A sequester from liberty, fasting, and prayer,
> Much castigation, exercise devout;
> For here's a young and sweating devil here
> That commonly rebels" (iii. 4).

If there is anything seeming to savour of Reformed doctrine, he puts it into the mouth of Iago, or the drunken Cassio, who in his cups informs us in somewhat Calvinistic manner—"God's above all; and there be souls must be saved, and there be souls must not be saved;" and in reply to Iago's hope to be saved, says; "Ay, but by your leave, not before me; the lieutenant is to be saved before the ancient" (ii. 3)—a strange dream, as if predestination made salvation a matter of seniority, and a consequence of rank: and again Othello says before he murders her—

> "If you bethink yourself of any crime
> Unreconciled as yet to heaven and grace,
> Solicit for it straight. . . .
> I would not kill thy unprepared spirit ;
> No, heaven forfend, I would not kill thy soul" (v. 2).

And Gratiano says of Brabantio—

> "This right would make him do a desperate turn,
> Yea, curse his better angel from his side
> And fall to reprobation" (v. 2).

Y

CHAPTER VIII.

DIDACTIC PLAYS.

MR. SIMPSON believes that in the plays classed in the following chapter as didactic there may be traced, besides the primary moral lesson, certain covert political allusions bearing on the religious situation of the poet's time. Commentators of the realistic school deny that Shakespeare ever employed allegory in his drama. The penetration and soundness of his judgment was seen, they say, in the avoidance of all theories, whether on politics or religion, and in confining himself exclusively to the psychological development of character. Now, the faithful portraiture of character was doubtless the poet's primary intention; but the absolute denial of the possibility of any secondary or figurative application of his plays shows a complete misunderstanding of both Shakespeare and his times.

Allegory was, indeed, universally employed in the Elizabethan age. Spenser's "Faerie Queene" was simply one long allegorical eulogy of Elizabeth, whose praise was the common theme of writers of the day. This kind of poetry was specially serviceable for purposes of attack. Under the veil of trope, the dramatist could satirise the object of his dislike, whether social, political, religious, even the Government itself, without fear of losing his ears. Thus Bale and Fletcher, and the other dramatists mentioned in Chapter II., attacked the Papists. Lily, Marlowe, Greene, and Nash were engaged by Archbishop Whitgift, through Bancroft, to caricature the Puritans in revenge for the Marprelate Tracts. Further, a whole series of plays—"Gorbeduc" (1561), by Norton; "Damon and Pythias" (before 1568), by Walton; "The Woman in the Moon" (1597), "Midas" (1592), both by Lily; Marlowe's "Tamburlaine" (1587), aimed at exposing the abuses of the Government, the exactions and covetousness of ministers, the manœuvres of Elizabeth and her favourites, or the despotism of Philip II. or of James of Scotland. Shakespeare was no exception to the general rule. If, as he tells us himself, his purpose was to "hold the mirror up to Nature," it must have been reflected first from existing individuals, men and women, who were reproduced as universal types by his own genius. A thorough grasp of the real involves no exclusion of the universal and ideal. In truth, the more thoroughly the real is apprehended, the more easy is it to conceive the universal, which always has its basis on the real.

That the contemporary public believed in his allegory and unhesitatingly interpreted it, there is no doubt. Elizabeth saw herself in Richard II.,

Lucy was recognised in Shallow, Cobham in Falstaff.
"This author's comedies," says the preface to the
first edition of "Troilus and Cressida" in 1609,
"are so framed to the life, that they serve for the
most common commentaries of all the actions of our
lives." So again Sir C. Scroop wrote before 1686:—

> "When Shakespeare, Jonson, Fletcher, ruled the stage,
> They took so bold a freedom with the age
> That there was scarce a knave or fool in town
> Of any note but had his fortune shown."
> —*Rochester's Works*, 96. 1714.

"They wrote," says Towers (1657), "in their neighbours' dialect, and brought their birthplace on the
stage. They gathered humours from all kinds of
people. Dogberry was a constable at Hendon,
Shallow was Lucy with additions and variations.
They did not spare the highest game." The Lord
Chamberlain's players (Shakespeare's company) took
a memorable part in Essex's conspiracy. They were
called madmen, because under feigned persons they
censured their sovereign.[1] The French ambassador
declared (April 5, 1606) that they treated James in
the most unseemly way, making him curse and swear
and beat a gentleman who had called the hounds
off the scent and made him lose a bird, and representing him as drunk at least once a day. And
Chamberlain writes to Winwood about the trouble
they got into for acting the Gowrie conspiracy and
"playing princes on the stage in their lifetime."[2]

[1] MS. Sloane, 3543, fol. 20.　　[2] Von Raumer, ii. 219.

The possible application of some at least of Shakespeare's plays in a figurative sense must, then, we think, be admitted. But such an interpretation offers no direct or cogent evidence as to his religious opinions. Simpson's readings of the following allegories are given because they are ingenious and interesting in themselves, and may have been in the author's mind as a possible application of his plot, but they are not put forth as any proof or support of his Catholicism. For that we need direct evidence.

According to Simpson, then, some of Shakespeare's plays may be termed didactic, because the philosophical or metaphysical principle on which they are founded outweighs the imaginative, passionate, and poetical elements conspicuous in most of his dramas. In this class may be placed the " Merchant of Venice," " Measure for Measure," " Cymbeline," and " Troilus and Cressida." These all seem written for a political object and with controversial purpose. The " Merchant of Venice " appears to have been, in all probability, founded on another play called " The Jew," which set forth " the greediness of worldly choosers and the bloody mind of usurers." [1] Shakespeare's adaptation of it, while still enforcing its primary, obvious lesson, the evils of extortion or of extortionate contracts, presents secondarily and indirectly a plea for toleration. The argument is all the more forcible from being

[1] H. Morley, Introduction "Merchant of Venice," 6.

entirely indirect, like the Spartan argument against drunkenness from the exhibition of the drunken Helot. The persecuting spirit as exhibited in the Jew is made odious and monstrous, and yet appears the natural and inevitable consequence of the treatment he himself has undergone. Shylock thus becomes a kind of mirror, in which Christians may see reflected not only the consequences but the very manner and tendency of their own conduct. He is what he is, not only because their intolerance has provoked him to be so, but because his revenge is a direct imitation and reproduction of their intolerance.

Whatever may be thought of the allegorical interpretation of the play, it is clear that Shakespeare leaves his readers with mixed feelings about Shylock. He is by no means an object of universal detestation. He has enlisted the sympathy of many; and in the opinion of Hazlitt, Campbell, and others, he has distinctly the best of Antonio in such arguments as the following:—

"He hath disgraced me," says Shylock, "and hindered me half-a-million; laughed at my losses, mocked at my gains, scorned my nation, thwarted my bargains, cooled my friends, heated mine enemies; and what's his reason? I am a Jew. Hath not a Jew eyes? Hath not a Jew hands, organs, dimensions, senses, affections, passions? fed with the same food, hurt with the same weapons, subject to the same diseases, healed by the same means, warmed and cooled by the same summer and winter, as a Christian is? If you prick us, do we not bleed? If you tickle us, do we not laugh? If you poison us, do we not die? and if you wrong us, shall we not revenge? If we are like you in the rest, we will resemble you in that. If a Jew wrong a Christian, what is his humility? Revenge! If a Christian wrong a Jew, what should his suffrance be by Christian example! Why, revenge! The villany you will teach me, I will execute, and it shall go hard but I will better the instruction."—*Merchant of Venice*, iii. 1.

But it may be argued that Shakespeare could have had but a poor opinion of Catholics, if he pleads for them in the person of the Jew, and that Shylock's arguments for toleration are founded on his own evil passions, which, he suggests, it may be dangerous to inflame. The case, however, is argued not on any high principles of truth or justice, but simply on the mechanical principles of action and reaction. If you strike, shall we not return the blow, if we can? If all your Christian professions do not prevent you from injuring us, simply because we are what we are, you cannot expect us to be otherwise than what you take us to be, or rather will make us to be, unchristian in our revenges.

Whatever may be thought of this as a possible application of Shylock's part, the general tone of the play is decidedly Catholic. For instance, there is something very unprotestant in Portia's pretence—

> " I have towards heaven breathed a secret vow
> To live in prayer and contemplation. . . .
> There is a monastery not two miles off,
> And there will we abide" (iii. 4).

And in the belief of her attendants that she was "straying about by holy crosses, kneeling and praying for happy wedlock hours," accompanied by "a holy hermit and her maid" (v. 1).

But perhaps the most remarkable religious allusion of the play is Bassanio's speech before the Caskets. His theme is, "The world is still deceived by ornament." This he illustrates by the practice of the pleader who by his ornamental eloquence hides the taint and corruption of evil from the judge, and persuades him to acquit it. He then turns to religion—and where should we expect him to find his great example of religious deception by means of ornament? A faithful follower of the "Book of Common Prayer" would have referred to those ceremonies which the wisdom of our Reformers abolished, because though at first they were "of godly intent and purpose devised, yet at length turned to vanity and superstition." He would have been eloquent upon the "mummeries and trumperies" of beads, vestments, incense, lights, music, bells, processions, and imposing functions; but instead of this we have only—

> "In religion
> What damnèd error, but some sober brow
> Will bless it and approve it with a text
> Hiding the grossness with fair ornament?"

This is indeed the very opposite teaching. It is not, it appears, the Popish ceremonial but the

Protestant text divinity which is the false ornament in religion.   To a dramatist Catholicism
would indeed naturally commend itself as a ceremonial religion.   Thus Marlowe is reported to have
said " That if there be any God or true religion,
then it is with the Papists, because the service
of God is performed with more ceremonies, as
elevation of the mass, organs, singing men, shaven
crowns, &c., and that if Christ had instituted the
sacrament with more ceremonial reverence it would
have been had in more admiration." [1]   We have
already seen how largely Shakespeare's imagery is
drawn from Catholic sources, especially the solemn
ceremonial of the sacrifice in the " Winter's Tale."
But while Marlowe and Shakespeare were thus
agreed on the preference for Catholicism from this
point of view there was a wide difference between
their opinions.   Marlowe's was merely an æsthetic
preference unconnected with any moral or religious
principle.   In Shakespeare it is an organic member
of the body of his opinions and ideas, and harmonises
exactly with all that has been deduced from other
passages in his writings.

   This estimate of the deceptive character of the
scriptural argument of his day—which he calls
" the guiled shore to a most dangerous sea," the
" seeming truth which cunning times put on to
entrap the wisest " (iii. 2), gives point and application to other passages in the same play which have

   [1] Barnes' note on Marlowe's opinion.

generally been supposed to refer to the Puritans of
Shakespeare's day.   For instance—

> "There are a sort of men whose visages
> Do cream and mantle like a standing pond
> And do a wilful stillness entertain,
> With purpose to be dressed in an opinion
> Of wisdom, gravity, profound conceit,
> As who should say, 'I am Sir Oracle,
> And when I ope my mouth let no dog bark'" (i. 1).

or the passage (ii. 2) where Gratiano describes
the puritanic behaviour of "one well studied in
a sad ostent to please his grandam"; or Antonio's
reflection on Shylock—

> "The devil can cite Scripture for his purpose.
> An evil soul producing holy witness
> Is like a villain with a smiling cheek,
> A goodly apple rotten at the heart :
> O, what a goodly outside falsehood hath !" (i. 3).

It is instructive to see how in Shakespeare's mind
this devil quoting Scripture, this "sober - brow"
approving a damned error with a text (iii. 2),
was connected with his favourite image of a smiling
villain.   It adds a new meaning to the hypocrisy
of Richard III.—" I can smile, and murder while
I smile " (" 3 Hen. VI.," iii. 2); and to Hamlet's
great discovery of the possibilities of human nature
in Denmark at least — "A man may smile and
smile, and be a villain " (" Hamlet," i. 5).   The play,
then, is not only a triumphant argument against
persecution, but a satire upon hypocrisy, convicting

the religious pretenders of the time of the very vices which they charged to the Papists. To him who reads the play from the point of view of an Elizabethan Catholic, many fragments start into new life—as when Antonio says, in reference to his floating ventures—

"Should I go to church
And see the holy edifice of stone,
And not bethink me straight of dangerous rocks?" (i. 1).

And, when Portia says to Bassanio (iii. 2), "I fear you speak upon the rack, where men enforcèd do speak anything," is not this an expression of contemptuous disbelief in all the evidence upon which so many pretended Popish conspirators suffered the death of traitors in the days of Shakespeare? The scandalous use of the rack to get evidence for any mare's nest was complained of by Selden. "The rack is used nowhere as in England: in other countries it is used in judicature when there is a *semiplena probatio*, a half-proof against a man; then to see if they can make it full, they rack him if he will not confess; but here in England they take a man and rack him, I do not know why nor when—not in time of judicature, but when somebody bids." [1]

It is interesting to remark how throughout almost the whole play Shakespeare gives way to the didactic spirit. The characters are sententious, and deliver wise saws beyond precedent, and in the present

[1] Table Talk, *sub voce* "Trial."

instance they seem to extend the action of the play, after the dramatic interest has ceased. The conclusion of the play is the discomfiture of Shylock in Act iv. Act v. is a most charming and poetical idyll, tempered with philosophy; but it hangs fire after the dramatic passion of the trial scene, and is therefore generally omitted in acting. It contains, however, some gems of the kind proper to our subject. Lorenzo's discourses on the harmony of creation, audible to immortal souls, already quoted, and on the power of music (v. 1), are both in this act. So also is Portia's philosophy of respect. "Nothing is good without respect," or the true relation of a thing to its time, manner, circumstances, for by this alone things obtain their fitness, and fulfil their respective parts. The same axiom is repeated a few lines later. "Things by reason seasoned are to their right praise and true perfection." Both these speeches reiterate the doctrine of the necessity of priority, order, and degree in the political as in the natural order. In the scenes at the Caskets (ii. 7 and ii. 9), Shakespeare makes the proud Moorish prince and the "idiot" of Aragon discourse as wisely as Polonius to Laertes. It is to be noted that it is quite characteristic of Shakespeare to distinguish his fools, not by their foolish sayings, but by their foolish doings. This ideal of folly is not so much the inanity of Slender, Simple, or Sir Andrew Aguecheek, as a certain want of connection between the understanding and the practical reason, a sharp sight with a want of judgment to choose. Such as Portia describes—

> " O these deliberate fools ! When they do choose
> They have the wisdom by their wit to lose" (ii. 9).

" Measure for Measure " is another of the didactic plays, with a purpose similar to that of the " Merchant of Venice," for it is a kind of discussion on the penal code. As in " King John " the several theories of extraneous interference in the quarrels of a kingdom successively appear, and solve themselves by the mere progress of the history, so in " Measure for Measure " do several theories of penal law crop up to give rise to endless complications, and to refute themselves by their impracticability. " Measure for Measure " was acted twice before James I. and his court in the first year of his reign, at the time when the king was assailed on all sides, especially by the Catholics, with requests to mitigate the bloody laws of England. When James made his triumphal entry into London, Alleyne the actor recited to him the lines of Ben Jonson, where the coming of the new king was said to have

> " Made men see
> Once more the face of welcome liberty ; "

to have restored the golden age, rescued innocence from ravenous greatness, stayed the evictions of the peasantry, alleviated the fears of the rich to be made guilty for their wealth, and diminished the

murderous lust of vile spies.   When three days
later (March 19, 1603) he rode to Parliament for
the first time, Ben Jonson made Themis rehearse to
him " All the cunning tracts and thriving statutes,"
while afterwards

> " The bloody, base, and barbarous she did quote ;
>   Where laws were made to serve the tyrant's will,
>   Where sleeping they could save, and waking kill."

About the same time the Catholics of England
were preparing an address to James, protesting their
loyalty, and begging for a mitigation of the " cruel
persecution which had made England odious, caused
the decay of trade, the shedding of blood, and an
unprecedented increase of subsidies and taxes, and
discontented minds innumerable."   Let " the lenity
of a man," they said, " re-edify that which the unin-
formed anger of a woman destroyed."   One of the
advisers of the Catholics, whose letter is preserved
in the State Paper office, declared that one of the
first things to be done was to petition for liberty of
religion, and abrogation of those bloody laws, and also
to impress strongly on the king that nothing could
tend more to the security of his person and assurance
of his estate, than to show favour and grace to the
Catholics, by which he would cut off all practices
against his estate and person, seeing the Catholics,
by the cruelty of the bloody laws and intolerable
burden of persecution, had either just cause, or show
of just cause, to pursue their liberties by all means,

and with all princes, to the utmost of their power.
Whereas favour shown to the Catholics would not
only assure the king from all attempts of foreigners
who cannot take hold of England but by a party at
home, but also fortify the throne against the inso-
lence of the Puritans.[1]   Sir Walter Raleigh was an
advocate on the same side, as we may see from his
letter to Nottingham in Cayley's " Life of Raleigh." [2]
It will be seen that the reasoning just described is
exactly like that in the " Merchant of Venice—a
dissuasion from violence on the ground that it is
a game at which two can play.   The same argument was employed in Father Parsons' " Memorial "
(p. 248), and it reappears some two centuries later
as the main foundation of the famous letters of
Peter Plymley.

   It looks as if the play had been composed for
James.   When the Duke says—

> " I love the people,
> But do not like to stage me to their eyes :
> Though it do well, I do not relish well
> Their loud applause and Aves vehement :
> Nor do I think the man of safe discretion
> That does affect it " (i. 1).

It reminds one of the king's proclamation about the
throngs which pressed round him in his journey
from Scotland.

   The Duke's treatment of Lucio seems inconsistent

---

[1] Dom. James I., vol. vi. Nos. 56 and 63.
[2] Vol. ii. p. 11.

with the general scope of the argument, while the most atrocious criminals are let off free, or even rewarded. Lucio, the good-natured, hare-brained, is punished with something worse than "pressing to death, whipping and hanging," only because, as the Duke says, "slandering a prince deserves it" (v. 1). Yet this severity fits in so well with the notions of James about the sanctity of his royal person, that it would appear that Shakespeare must have introduced the glaring injustice for the purpose of satire. It is as if he said: I argue for relaxation of penalties for all crimes except slandering your sacred person, which is of so deep die, so murderous, so burglarious and wanton that the traitorous traducer deserves all you can lay upon him; as you are crazy on that point, I waive it. It is not to be denied, however, that Lucio's character is of the kind on which Shakespeare was always most severe. Licentious as Falstaff, of ungovernable tongue, and though willing enough to do friendly offices, in the end, from mere levity, he turns round on his friends, and bears false witness against the only witness who could entirely acquit them (v. 1).

The argument in "Measure for Measure" is not for the repeal of the penal laws, but for allowing them to lie dormant. The prerogative of the governor is said to be "so to enforce and qualify the laws as to his soul seems good" (i. 1), and James seems to be invited to commit his prerogative for a season to some upright viceroy, and himself to retire behind the scenes, and observe not only how his substitute behaves, but how the laws themselves suit the commonwealth. The dramatic interest of the play henceforth divides itself from its philosophic interest. Dramatically, it is the trial and fall of Angelo and the trial and triumph of Isabella. Philosophically, it is the trial and condemnation of the penal code.

The title " Measure for Measure " is the accurate summary of the theory of punishment which the poet advocates. In this world neither reward nor punishment should be given for what a man is, but only for what he does. " If our virtues did not go forth of us, 'twere all alike as if we had them not " (i. 1); and on the other side, " What's open made to justice, that justice seizes," " What we do not see, we do not think of " (ii. 1). To Shakespeare the great test of virtue is its inability to be hid, like the candle on the candlestick, or the city on the hill; hence his impatience under calumny, and under the loss of that "just pleasure" which follows the public recognition of worth.

> " 'Tis better to be vile than vile esteemed
> When not be, receives reproach of being;
> And the just pleasure lost, which is so deemed
> Not by our feeling, but by other's seeing."
> —*Sonnet* cxxi.

There are three propositions about the penal law which Shakespeare develops in this play. To be

z

punishable, a man must do something; he cannot be punished for what he is.   This, however, is not the theory of society.

> " We're nettles, some of us,
> And give offence by the act of springing up ;
> And if we leave the damp side of the wall,
> The hoes, of course, are on us."
> —Mrs. BROWNING, *Aurora Leigh*, p. 119, 1st ed.

Nor was it the theory of Elizabethan legislators. For them, to be a Catholic was to be guilty of misprision of treason ; to be a seminary priest was to be a traitor.   "Because he liketh mutton, therefore he hath stolen a sheep," said Campion at his trial, and for a priest to be caught in England was death. In other words, there was a kind of original sin in criminality.   Men grew guilty without doing anything.   To be a player was to be a rogue and a vagabond.   To be a vagrant was to be a rogue. As it was a crime against the Revolution of 1789 to be born noble, so it was treason against Elizabeth to be born a Catholic.   Some people were vermin by nature, and the sentence upon such a man was—

> " Let him die, in that he is a fox,
> By nature proved an enemy to the flock."
> —2 *Henry VI.*, iii. 1.

The next point is, to be punishable a man must not be merely a sinner, he must be a criminal. The sin comes not under the rod of the law.   " 'Tis

set down so in heaven, but not in earth " (ii. 4).
And next, the crime must be overt, it must be
done, not merely thought or intended. "Thoughts
are no subjects; intents but merely thoughts " (v. 1).
These two propositions are in exact accordance
with the Church's teaching on ecclesiastical as well
as civil jurisdiction. In the external forum, that
is, in any extra-sacramental tribunal, the Church
takes cognisance only of external acts. What is
internal, thought, desire, and purpose, belongs to the
forum conscientiæ, and is dealt with in secret in the
sacrament of penance, where the penitent alone is
his own accuser. Statesmen in Shakespeare's day
held exactly the opposite teaching, and claimed to
punish thought as well as act. James himself considered that he bore the sword to smite sin as well
as crime, and it was quite an inveterate notion
of Elizabeth's days that all Catholics being guilty
of treason in the first degree, that is, being necessarily discontented and hostile to the laws and the
regimen established, were punishable, though they
had never exhibited their disaffection in any overt
act.

It is with reference to the magistrate, punishing
sin as such, that Shakespeare in this play enunciates
the two extraordinary principles that' no one who
has committed an offence has a right to punish
another for an offence of the same kind, and that
no criminal should be punished capitally till he was
religiously prepared and ready to die.

(1) " He who the sword of heaven will bear
　　　Should be as holy as severe ;
　　　Pattern in himself to know ;
　　　Grace to stand, and virtue go ;
　　　More nor less to others paying
　　　Than by self offences weighing.
　　　Shame to him whose cruel striking
　　　Kills for faults of his own liking " (ii. 2).

This doctrine runs through the play.　Angelo says to Escalus—

" You may not so extenuate his offence
　For I have had such faults ; but rather tell me
　When I that censure him do so offend,
　Let mine own judgment pattern out my death,
　And nothing come in partial " (ii. 1).

Isabella pleads it to Angelo —

　" How would you be
If He which is the top of judgment, should
But judge you as you are ?" (ii. 2).

And in the last scene, the Duke pretends to disbelieve Isabella's story—

" It imports no reason,
That with such vehemency he should pursue
Faults proper to himself ; if he had so offended,
He would have weighed thy brother by himself,
And not have cut him off " (v. 1).

This doctrine becomes all the more pungent, supposing that the argument is for the mitigation of the penal laws, when we remember how James from time to time, all through his life, coquetted with the Pope.　This was not unknown to the Catholics.

Almost as soon as James ascended the throne, one Philip May, who, like Shakespeare himself, was one of the servants of Lord Chamberlain Hunsdon, was committed to the Tower for asserting that the King was a favourer of Catholics, and for using threats against him if he rejected the bills to be brought into Parliament for their toleration.[1] Father Parsons also wrote about "the sums of money and other presents" which he had "procured both from the King of Spain and Pope Gregory XIII. towards the maintenance of a guard for safety of his Majesty's person in Scotland" in the days of his trouble there.[2]

(2) The second corollary that Shakespeare deduces from the theory that penal law punishes sin as sin, is that no criminal can be put to death till he is spiritually prepared for it. The Duke finds Bernardine

> "A creature unprepared, unmeet for death,
> And to transport him in the mind he is,
> Were damnable" (iv. 3),

and in the end forgives his earthly faults, and commits him to Friar Peter to mend him (v. 1). He refuses to play into the devil's hand by sending the sinner, unrepenting, and unshriven, into the next world.

The story of Bernardine seems to be taken from the Life of St. Bernard,[3] when the saint saves a thief

---

[1] Dom. James I., vol. i. Nos. 31–35, 42, and 66, April 19, 1603.
[2] Ibid., No. 84.   [3] Vita. I. Lib. vii. c. xv. ed. Mabillon.

whom Count Theobald had ordered to be hanged. Bernard met the procession, and laid hold of the thief. "What are you doing?" said the Count; "why save from hell a criminal a thousand times condemned? You cannot save him, he is all devil. There is no cure for him but death. Let the son of perdition go to perdition, for his life is a peril to the lives of many." Bernard replied, "I know he is a villanous thief, and deserves every torture. I will not let him off; I mean to deliver him to the tormentors, and to punish him better, because longer. You had sentenced him to a momentary penalty; I will give him a lifelong death. You would have gibbeted him for a few days; I will make him live on the cross for many a year." Then he took him to Clairvaux and made a monk of him, and called him Brother Constantius; and he lived a holy life for thirty years in the Abbey, and died a saint.

The play of "Measure for Measure" is again Catholic in tone. Mr. Bohn, it is true, ventures to call it "distinctly anti-Romish."[1] It is difficult to see on what he founds his opinion, except it may be the second scene, where Lucio talks of the sanctimonius pirate, who went to sea with the ten commandments, but scraped one out of the table, "thou shalt not steal." Catholics had been accused of erasing a commandment, because they adopted a different division of them from that

[1] "Biography and Bibliography of Shakespeare," 278.

used by the Protestants. Lucio's remark does not apply to them; it rather applies to the argument of the play, which is in part that the guilty judge destroys the law wherein he is guilty, because he destroys his right to punish.

This is the only passage of the play which could by any possibility bear an anti-Catholic interpretation. In all the rest the tone is distinctly Catholic. Isabella's moral grandeur has been already discussed. The description of her as a fervent novice shows complete familiarity with the details of life in religion. She desires no more privileges, but rather wishes a more strict restraint upon the sisterhood, the votaries of St. Clare (i. 4), and she is distinctly said to be yet unsworn, in order to prepare for her wedding at the end.

> " You are yet unsworn.
> When you have vowed, you must not speak with men
> But in the presence of the Prioress ;
> Then if you speak, you must not show your face,
> Or if you show your face, you must not speak " (i. 4).

Religious and Catholic is her offer to bribe Angelo, not with gold,

> " But with true prayers
> That shall be up at heaven, and enter there
> E'er sunrise, prayers from preservèd souls,
> From fasting maids, whose minds are dedicate
> To nothing temporal " (ii. 2).

Then the Duke, disguised as a Friar, only exhibits

in his disguise to what honourable purposes the
Friars applied themselves—

> "Bound by my charity and my blest order
> I come to visit the afflicted spirits
> Here in the prison" (ii. 3).

And he catechises Mariana on the subject of penance
like a Catholic divine, while she answers him as a
Catholic penitent would—

> "I do repent me as it is an evil
> And bear the shame with joy" (ii. 3).

The distinction of repenting for the sin and re-
joicing at the temporal evil incurred by it is a
feature that would hardly have suggested itself to
a Protestant, unless, like Jeremy Taylor, he was
compiling from Catholic sources.

A pungent satire on the union of licentiousness
and Puritan cant is found in the list of prisoners
under Pompey's care, who are "all great doers in our
trade (scortatores), and are now in for the Lord's
sake" (iv. 3). .

Familiarity with Catholic forms of speech seems
also to manifest itself in the Duke's reply to Elbow's
"Bless you, good father friar," "And you, good brother
father" (iii. 2); and in Mrs. Overdone's declaration
that Lucio's child is a year old come Philip and
Jacob (iii. 2). It would be difficult to find a trace
of anti-Romish feeling in the Duke's description
of himself—

> "I am a brother
> Of gracious order, late come from the See
> On special business from his Holiness" (iii. 2) ;

or in the sketch of the times which he gives in that character : " There is so great a fever of goodness, that the dissolution of it must cure it ; novelty is only in request : and it is as dangerous to be aged in any kind of course, as it is virtuous to be constant in any undertaking. There is scarce truth enough alive to make societies secure ; but security enough to make fellowships accursed : much upon this riddle runs the wisdom of the world."

Isabella's doubt as to following the advice of the disguised Duke, and swearing that Angelo had achieved his purpose, is remarkable.

> "To speak so indirectly I am loth.
> I would say the truth . . .
> . . . yet I am advised to do it" (iv. 6),

because it must have reminded Shakespeare's audience of an incident that had been much talked of in 1595. In that year Blessed Robert Southwell, the Jesuit martyr, a poet of whom Ben Jonson spoke to Drummond with admiration, and to whose pieces Shakespeare paid the compliment of imitation, was tried for saying Mass at Mr. Bellamy's at Harrow-on-the-Hill. A servant girl of the family swore that he had not said Mass there. But her evidence broke down, and she then confessed that in swearing as she did she had acted on the advice of the Jesuit. Hereupon grave scandal arose ; the popular belief was encouraged that Catholics cared nothing for oaths or for the truth. What, then, were Shakespeare's views on the point ?

If his argument in "Measure for Measure" is that human law has nothing to do with sin, but only with crime, or injustice, he must necessarily have considered truth in its double aspect; as a debt owed to God by man, and as a debt owed by man to his neighbour. Prescinding for the moment from the first aspect of truth, under the second it is possible to inquire, whether truthfulness is a debt of justice to men who seek it to treat you unjustly ? If you are condemned for being what you are—Catholic or Puritan—you are not bound to criminate yourself by confessing what you are; and if your silence under interrogatories would condemn you, you have a right, so far as your oppressors are concerned, to give an ambiguous answer. Between man and man, unjust oppression is the natural parent of equivocation, and justifies it. Under all ordinary aspects of life I am bound to tell you the truth; but if you wish to compel me to tell the truth, in order to found on my confession your right to punish me unjustly, I have a right to let you be deceived. Such was Southwell's defence of what he had done. " I ask you, Mr. Attorney," said he, " if the French King were to invade the realm, and capture the city, and search for the Queen hidden in some corner of the palace, which you knew, and if you were taken, and examined upon oath where she was, what would

you do ?   To boggle is to tell; to refuse to swear
is to betray.   What would you say ?   You would
go and show the place! and would not everybody
call you a traitor ?   You would then, if you were
wise, swear you knew not, or that you knew
she was not there. . . . This is our state : the
Catholics are in jeopardy of goods, liberty, and life,
if they harbour a priest.   Who will prevent their
seeking safety in a doubtful answer ?   For in matters of this kind there are three things to be
regarded.   First, that injustice will be done if you
do not swear.   Next, that you are not bound to
answer every question; and lastly, that any oath is
lawful, if you can take it with truth, judgment, and
justice." [1]   The controversy reached its head in 1606,
after Father Garnet's trial, when he had said that
"equivocation" was not lying, but a peculiarity in
the use of certain propositions.   "For a man may
be asked of one who hath no authority to inter-
rogate, or examined concerning something that
belongeth not to his cognisance who asketh.   No
man may equivocate when he ought to tell the
truth : otherwise he may."

The Catholic doctrine, then, was that words are a
coin, which must in justice be sterling when we pay
our just debts with it, but which may be counterfeit
when we put it off on a thief.   An oath only adds
an additional sanction to an existing duty, but does
not change its nature.   What I may declare I may,

[1] More, *Hist. Prov. Anglic. Soc. Jes.*, Lib. v. No. 29.

if need be, swear. Before an unjust judge, or in presence of a tyrannical law, equivocation with oath is exactly as lawful as equivocation without oath; and under such circumstances it may be your duty to say what is only in one respect true, for perhaps you can only be true to those to whom you owe fidelity by thus veiling truth to others. This is the doctrine of Shakespeare in " Measure for Measure "; the very title of the play, moralised as it is in Act v. 1, implies it, and the words of the Duke (ii. 2), " pay with falsehood [equivocation], false exacting," formulate it with philosophical precision. To be true even by means of "falsehood" is a problem which he often makes his characters work out practically, and of which he makes Pandulph give, as we have seen, the theoretical demonstration (" King John," iii. 1, and Salisbury in " 2 Henry VI.," v. 1). " Cymbeline," according to Gervinus," is a parable on the doctrine of fidelity. Pisanio, the faithful follower, there speaks, " True to thee [Cloten] were to prove false, which I never will be, to him that is most true " (iii. 5); and again, " Wherein I am false I am honest: not true, to be true " (iv. 3). All this is distinctly on Southwell's side. Helena in " All's Well " is made to act much as Isabella in " Measure for Measure," and Desdemona, who dies declaring that she killed herself, elicits from Othello and Emilia the contradictory conclusions, " She's like a liar, gone to burning hell," and " O, the more angel she."

Shakespeare seems to contrast this deception for the sake of guarding fidelity with the political deception of the period which was used as a means of discovery.

> "*Pol.* Your bait of falsehood takes this carp of truth,
> And thus do we of wisdom and of reach
> With windlasses and with assays of bias
> By indirections find directions out."—*Hamlet*, ii. 1.

The rack was one of these windlasses, or winding, circumventing ways, where truth was drawn out of a man by untruth. A forged confession of an accomplice was propounded to him, and then he was racked till he confessed· or explained. " Some men," says Selden, " before they come to their trial are cozened to confess upon examination : upon this trick they are made to believe somebody has confessed before them, and then they think it a piece of honour to be clear and ingenuous, and that destroys them." This was the policy of the Cecils.

The Porter's speech in " Macbeth " has been taken as a protest against this doctrine of equivocation. The man supposes himself to be porter at hell's gate, and to be letting in the company; among them is an " equivocator, that could swear in both the scales against either scale, who committed treason enough for God's sake, yet could not equivocate to heaven " (" Macbeth," ii. 3). But this swearing in both the scales against either scale means the readiness under one and the same set of circumstances to swear indifferently whatever suits best, however false the matter might be, and does not therefore touch the case.   Richard lays down Father Garnett's doctrine in these terms—

> "An oath is of no moment, being not took
>   Before a true and lawful magistrate
>   That hath authority over him that swears.
>   Henry had none, but did usurp the place.
>   Then, seeing 'twas he that made you to depose,
>   Your oath, my lord, is vain and frivolous."
> —3 *Henry VI.*, i. 2.

The next, and perhaps the most important of Shakespeare's didactic plays, is "Cymbeline."   The story is taken from the fabulous British annals printed in Hollinshed, but with variations to adapt it to the times.   Thus the two shipwrecks that befell Julius' fleet on the English coast are an alteration of the account of Cassibelan's spiking the Thames and of Cæsar's ships being snagged upon the spikes, adapted to the recent history of Philip's two Armadas; and the end, the submission to the emperor after the victory over him, is a mere addition of Shakespeare, unhistorical, quite legendary, unnecessary for the drama, and simply didactic.

In its lessons "Cymbeline" has several points of comparison with "Measure for Measure."   Thus, Belarius' whole theory of political justice, expressed in the words "beaten for loyalty excited me to treason" (v. 5), is merely a subtle variation of the "Like doth quit like" of the former play, and the theory of truth, falsehood, and fidelity is absolutely the same, as the quotations given sufficiently testify. But the object of the play goes beyond that of " Measure for Measure." The latter play only ventured to urge the suppression of the penal laws by royal prerogative; " Cymbeline " recommends a reconciliation with Rome on certain concessions affecting the tribute and the franchise or liberties of the people, which Simpson takes to refer to the vexed question of Peter's pence, the provisos and the temporal suzerainty.

To the obvious objection that the grievances enumerated would apply only to the early Roman sway over Britain, and not at all to the Roman question such as it existed in the days of James I., it is answered, first, that, according to Shakespeare's doctrine, plays ought to take the stamp of the age, and exhibit the pressure of the time. Next, that the current Roman question in those days was of such paramount importance that common audiences could admit no other idea, and that all references to Rome were considered to allude more or less plainly to the circumstances of the day. This is clear by the prologue spoken by Envy in Ben Jonson's " Poetaster " :—

> "The scene is? ha!
> Rome? Rome? and Rome? . . .
>   . . . O my vext soul
> How might I force this to the present state?
> Are there here no spies who——could wrest
> Pervert, and poison all they hear and see
> With senseless glosses and allusions?"

Catholics as well as Protestants saw in Imperial
Rome an image of the Papacy, and the two failures
of Cæsar were a commonplace of the day. After
the failure of the Armada, Father Parsons reminded the Catholics that Julius and Henry VII.
had both been unlucky in their first attempts,
though they afterwards became lords of the country.
" The children of Israel (too) were twice beaten
with great loss in the war they had undertaken
by God's express command against the Benjamites :
it was not till the third attempt that they were
successful." [1]   And the attitude of James at that
time was such as to encourage the belief that
reconciliation with Rome was by no means impossible. Thus he told a prince of the House of
Lorraine who visited him, not without the knowledge of Paul V., that after all there was but little
difference between the two confessions. He thought
his own the better, and adopted it from conviction,
not from policy; still he liked to hear other opinions,
and as the calling of a council was impossible, he
would gladly see a convention of doctors to consult
on the means of reconciliation. If the Pope would
advance one step, he would advance four to meet
him. He also acknowledged the authority of the
holy Fathers; Augustine was to him of more weight
than Luther, Bernard than Calvin; nay, he saw in
the Roman Church, even in that of the day, the
true Church, the mother of all others; only she

---

[1] *Philopater ad Edict. repons.*, ss. 146, 147.

needed purification. He admitted, in confidence, that the Pope was the head of the Church, the supreme Bishop.[1]

Whether or no there be a political allegory in "Cymbeline," the religious allusions are again on the Catholic side. Imogen is the ideal of fidelity, and of religious fidelity—to be deceived neither by the foreign impostor who comes to her in her husband's name, nor by the ennobled clown who offers himself under the Queen's protection. "Stick to your journal course," she says to her brothers; "the breach of custom is the breach of all" (iv. 2). And she adheres to the old customs; the new gods of the Cloten dynasty had forbidden prayers for the dead, and the beads were baubles, and the rosary, with its "century of prayers," but a vain repetition in their eyes. Yet she begs Lucius to spare her till she has bedecked her husband's supposed grave,

> " And on it said a century of prayers
> Such as I can, twice o'er " (iv. 2).

This tenderness for old customs, understood or not, and for the religious traditions of past generations, is found also in the two lost princes: "We must lay his head to the east; my father hath a reason for it" (iv. 2). A few lines before Guiderius refused to sing, because his voice was choked; he would

[1] *Relazione del Sr. di Breval al Papa*, Ranke, ii. 86, 1847.

only say the dirge, it would be profanation to sing
it out of tune—

> " For notes of sorrow out of tune are worse
> Than priests and fanes that lie."

It is impossible to suppose that Shakespeare
really held that the singing of a *Miserere* a trifle
too sharp was worse than a hypocritical priesthood
and a false religion. Read ironically the text
means, " You talk of the lying priests and their
lying temples; I hold your vile psalm-singing to be
ten times worse."

The religious opinions of Posthumus are characterised in two places. In one he discourses of
Penance :—

> " My conscience, thou art fettered
> More than my shanks and wrists ; you good gods, give me
> The penitent instrument to pick that bolt,
> Then, free for ever !   Is't enough I am sorry ?
> So children temporal fathers do appease ;
> Gods are more full of mercy.   Must I repent ?
> I cannot do it better than in gyves,
> Desired more than constrained : to satisfy,
> If of my freedom 'tis the main part, take
> No stricter render of me than my all.
> I know you are more clement than vile men,
> Who of their broken debtors take a third,
> A sixth, a tenth, letting them thrive again
> On their abatement ; that's not my desire :
> For Imogen's dear life take mine ; and though
> 'Tis not so dear, yet 'tis a life " (v. 4).

Penance, he says, is in two degrees. One gains
pardon, the other makes satisfaction — " cancels
bonds " (v. 4). For Shakespeare, as my readers

may have seen before, was a stickler for the old
doctrine of merit.   In this very play he puts into
his dirge the line, " Home art gone to take thy
wages"; and it is this kind of penance which can
alone give confidence in death.   When Posthumus
declares that he knows where he is going after
death, the gaoler says to him : " You must either
be directed by some that take upon them to know,
or do take upon yourself that which I am sure you
do not know, or jump the after-inquiry at your own
peril."   And Posthumus replies : " I tell thee, fellow,
there are none want eyes to direct them the way
I am going, but such as wink and will not use
them " (v. 4).   This conversation recalls a controversial saying of Sir Thomas More : " Howbeit,
if so be that their way be not wrong, but they have
found out so easy a way to heaven as to take no
thought but make merry, nor take no penance
at all, but sit them down and drink well for the
Saviour's sake, sit cock-a-hoop, and fill in all the
cups at once, and then let Christ's passion pay for
all the shot, I am not he that will envy their good
hap, but surely counsel dare I give to no man to
adventure that way with them." [1]

Another characteristic of Posthumus is his par-
doning Iachimo :—

> " Kneel not to me :
> The power that I have on you is to spare you ;
> The malice towards you to forgive you ; live
> And deal with others better" (v. 5).

---

[1] Dialogue of Comfort, Works.   1177.

Did space admit, the aptness of the allegory might be traced into much minuter details. But we will only note that, as in "Measure for Measure," the character of the Duke is somewhat marred by his inconsistent severity to Lucio; so here, with the same barefaced irony, he makes Cymbeline threaten his preservers with death—one for having slain Cloten, a prince, though in self-defence; and the other for having said that Arviragus was in descent as good as the king: "And thou shalt die for it" (v. 5). Another sweetening sop which must have hidden much of the bitterness of this play from James, was the assumption of a natural and inherent superiority in princely blood.

> "O worthiness of nature ! breed of greatness !
> Cowards father cowards, and base things sire base :
> Nature hath meal and bran, contempt and grace" (iii. 2).

> "Their blood thinks scorn
> Till it fly out, and show them princes born" (iv. 4).

But Shakespeare has the same idea in other places. Perdita is an example. It cannot, then, be called mere flattery.

We will not spend much space on "Troilus and Cressida," a play which is recognised by the preface of the first edition to belong to the didactic series of the poet's dramas. It contains no doubt deep utterances upon questions of politics, and still deeper lessons on philosophy. It seems, however, to have been composed by occasion of some theatrical strife.

Witness Ulysses' description of Patroclus' acting in Achilles' tent—

> ". . . Like a strutting player,—whose conceit
> Lies in his hamstring, and doth think it rich
> To hear the wooden dialogue and sound
> 'Twixt his stretched footing and the scaffoldage."

A satire on actors is seen again in Troilus' " copper-nose " and in his speech—

> "Whilst some with cunning gild their copper crowns,
> With truth and plainness I do wear mine bare."

We have evidence of Shakespeare's intervention in one encounter of dramatists. In the "Return from Parnassus," 1602 (iv. 3), we read, "Ben Jonson is a pestilent fellow; he brought up Horace giving the poets a pill; but our fellow Shakespeare hath given him a purge that made him bewray his credit." This alludes to Jonson's "Poetaster," acted by children, the choir boys of the Chapel Royal, at the Blackfriars Theatre in 1601. It was written chiefly against Marston and Dekker, who replied to it in the "Satiromastix." Shakespeare, however, considered himself touched by it. He was so well known as the sweet, the honey-tongued, the English Ovid, that, in spite of some palpable inconsistencies, the public must have considered that he was attacked under that name in Jonson's play. His counter-hit is seen in "Hamlet," where Rosencrantz relates how the children have superseded the actors in public favour, "There is an aery of children, little eyases, that cry out on the top of the question, and are most tyrannically clapped for't: these are now the fashion, and so berattle the common stages— so they call them—that many wearing rapiers are afraid of goose-quills, and dare scarce come thither." This seems an allusion to Captain Tucca in the "Satiromastix," who says to Jonson, "We that are heads of legions and bands, and fear none but these same shoulder-clappers, shall fear you, you serpentine rascal?" Then Hamlet says that their writers (Jonson to wit) do the children wrong, "to make them exclaim against their own succession" —against the craft that they are for the most part destined to follow. Now this mild criticism can hardly be called "a purge to make Jonson bewray his credit"; Shakespeare probably administered a severer dose than this, and we think Thersites in "Troilus and Cressida" may have been meant for Ben. This view of the play as a concealed satire removes much of the difficulty which it presents as a drama in which the satirical purpose somewhat mars its artistic effect.[1] We will now consider those

---

[1] This may account for the difficulties in the date of this play. It was entered, as played by the Lord Chamberlain's men, in the Stationers' books, February 7, 1602, but when published in 1609 "it had never been staled with the stage, clapperclawed with the palms of the vulgar, or sullied with their smoky breath." It may have been played once, before some powerful person (the editor of 1609 had some ado to rescue it from the "grand possessor") and then forbidden. This was exactly the measure meted to Jonson's "Apology" for his "Poetaster," which was only once spoken on the stage, and then restrained from publication, by authority.

expressions in the play which seem to throw any light on the poet's religious opinions.

The reverence he had for the sacrificial ceremonies of religion peeps out in the words of Patroclus, where he says that the Greeks used to come to Achilles—

> " As humbly as they used to creep
> To holy altars " (iii. 3) ;

and in those of Troilus, where he expresses the deep feeling with which he delivers up Cressida to Diomede's hand, which he tells Paris to consider

> " An altar, and thy brother Troilus
> A priest there, offering to it his own heart " (iv. 3).

The religious sentiment is more generalised in Troilus' words to Cressida—

> " The blessed gods, as angry with my fancy,
> More bright in zeal than the devotion which
> Cold lips blow to their deities, take thee from me " (iv. 4) ;

and in Cassandra's to Hector—

> " The gods are deaf to hot and peevish vows :
> They are polluted offerings, more abhorred
> Than spotted livers in the sacrifice,"

though such utterances are useful as showing the sacrificial view which Shakespeare took of all religious devotion. True religion is a dedication of the best part of man to God, who will accept only supreme and absolute homage, and who is jealous of any one to whom a more zealous devotion is felt.

Hence the jealousy of a husband for his wife's purity of soul is called " a godly jealousy " (iv. 4); but, on the other hand, religion imposes no sacrifices which hurt other persons' rights.   It does not sacrifice the less good to the greater, to the real loss of the friend, but maintains both at once.

> " Do not count it holy
> To hurt by being just : it is as lawful,
> For we would give much, to use violent thefts
> And rob in the behalf of charity " (v. 3).

And again, " vows to every purpose must not hold " (v. 3).   As we have traced the preachy element in Falstaff, Bottom, and Holofernes, so we may find the same kind of genius in Thersites.   He reckons Ajax unable even " to learn a prayer without book " (ii. 1), and says, " I will buy nine sparrows for a penny, and his *pia mater* is not worth the ninth part of a sparrow " (ii. 1).   He opens the next scene with a kind of litany, and then says, " I have said my prayers, and devil Envy say Amen."   On the theory above suggested this would be an allusion to the prayerful prologue of Envy in the " Poetaster," just as the armed prologue of Shakespeare's play is an allusion to the prologue in armour of Ben Jonson's.   Thersites continues in the same strain, " Discipline come not near thee—Amen."   And then Ajax breaks in, "What! art thou devout? wast thou in prayer ? "   He replies, " Ay, the Heavens hear me."

A proof of Shakespeare's anti-Romish ideas of ritual is found in the passage—

> " 'Tis mad idolatry
> To make the service greater than the God " (ii. 2).[1]

The words occur in a speech where, in reply to Troilus's question, " What is aught, but as 'tis valued ? " Hector answers—

> " But value dwells not in particular will ;
> It holds his estimate and dignity
> As well wherein 'tis precious of itself
> As in the prizer : 'tis mad idolatry
> To make the service greater than the God,
> And the will dotes that is inclinable
> To what infectiously itself affects
> Without some image of the affected merit."

In other words, the value of any object depends not only on any individual's estimation of it, but on its own intrinsic worth.   It is idolatry to value the service more highly than the God.   And it is madness to love a thing for what our fancy attributes to it when it really has no such quality.   To use the language of the modern schools, Shakespeare is distinguishing the subjective and the objective elements in value.   And he says that it is folly to estimate a thing merely by our subjective feeling about it. Hence, in the illustration, " service " means not " ritual " but subjective feeling about God, as contrasted with the objective truth about Him.   And the lesson taught is that it is mad idolatry to set a

---

[1] *Edinburgh Review*, vol. cxxiii. 182.

higher value on our own devotional act or experiences than on God Himself, His truth, and His will, which are alone the end of all religion. The passage, in fact, condemns emotional religion, or the assurance of salvation through feeling, the doctrine not of Rome but of Calvin and Luther.[1]

The Reviewer asserts that the words " You are in a state of grace " ("Troilus," iii. 1), are taken from the Church of England Catechism, and present in consequence another proof of Shakespeare's Protestantism. The " Catechism," however, referred to existed only in part in 1601, when this play was published. Neither in the part then existing, nor in that added in 1603, is the phrase "state of grace" to be found. But though not found in the Anglican catechism, it is to be found in the Decrees of the Council of Trent (sess. vi. cap. iv.), and in the catechetical instruction founded thereupon, and thus the phrase has become proverbial and common among Catholics. Moreover, " state of grace" is a distinctively Catholic expression. The Protestants of the Reformation period, who denied grace to be a quality inherent in the Christian, and declared it to be only the external election of God concerning him, could not properly use such a phrase. Hence it was that the translators of the Anglican version altered the words of the angelic salutation in St. Luke, " Hail, full of grace," into " Hail, thou that art highly favoured." And it is

---

[1] *Edinburgh Review*, vol. cxxiii. 182.

because Shakespeare did not look upon grace as mere outward favour, but as an inward quality, that he uses the phrase "state of grace," and calls Edward the Confessor and Henry II. "full of grace" ("Macbeth," iv. 3 ; "Henry V.," i. 1).

What Shakespeare's doctrine on grace really was may be easily learned from a passage which occurs in the verses spoken by the Duke at the end of Act iii. of "Measure for Measure."

> "He who the sword of Heaven will bear
> Should be as holy as severe,
> Pattern in himself to know,
> Grace to stand, and virtue go."

The last line is noted by the Cambridge editors as corrupt. It is not so. The meaning is clear. The man should have the pattern or idea of holiness in himself to enable him to stand ; and virtue to enable him to advance. In the speech of Ulysses to Achilles in "Troilus and Cressida," we have the palm of virtues given to perseverance, or constancy.

> "Perseverance, dear my lord,
> Keeps honour bright—to have done is to hang
> Quite out of fashion, like a rusty nail
> In monumental mockery."

And this perseverance, constancy, or force to stand, he attributes to grace. The intellect may know what is good, the natural forces may be adequate to sallies of virtue, isolated acts of heroism, impulsive acts of good, but standing consistency or perseverance requires constant grace. This is the doctrine of the Council of Trent (sess. vi. cap. xiii.) and of S. Alphonsus ("On Prayer," cap. iii. sec. 3). It is the Catholic, as distinct from the Protestant doctrine of grace.

The Reviewer next produces a phrase from the litany ("Taming of the Shrew," i. 1): "From all such devils, good Lord deliver us"—an exclamation often used by Catholics who have never heard the Anglican litany in .their lives. That the litany form of prayer was in common use in Shakespeare's days is evident from the fact that Ben Jonson ends one of his plays ("Cynthia's Revels," 1600) with a formal litany in which the response runs, "Good Mercury, deliver us."

The Reviewer finds the origin of the lines—

> "His plausive words
> He scattered not in ears, but grafted them,
> To grow there and to bear."
> —*All's Well that Ends Well*, i. 2,

in a collect of the English Church. The collect which the Reviewer has in his mind is evidently that which runs, "that the words which we have heard with our outward ears may through thy grace be so grafted inwardly in our hearts, that," &c. The ideas in the two texts are quite distinct, and there is no proof that one is copied from the other. The expression *verbum insitum*—"engrafted word" —is scriptural (James i. 21), and is read in the epistle for Mass, fourth Sunday after Easter, and would have been known without the prayer-book, while the collect itself was probably taken from other sources.

Finally, the Reviewer quotes a phrase which he says is taken from the Anglican marriage service: "If either of you know of any inward impediment why you should not be conjoined, I charge you on your souls to declare it (" Much Ado about Nothing," iv. 1). But it is evident to any impartial student that the phrase, which is spoken, by the way, by Friar Francis, might just as easily have been taken from the York Manual, which runs, "I charge you on Goddes behalfe and holy Chirche, that if there be any of you that can say anythynge why these two may not be lawfully wedded togyder at this tyme, say it nowe, outher pryuely or appertly, in helpynge of your soules and theirs bothe;" or again, from the *Sarum Pontifical*, "Admoneo vos omnes, ut si quis ex vobis est qui aliquid sciat, quare isti adolescentes legitime contrahere non possint; modo confiteatur."[1]

The arguments of the Edinburgh Reviewer offer, we may take for granted, the strongest evidence the writer could discover for Shakespeare's Protestantism; yet on examination most of them are seen to be proofs of his Catholicism, while the rest are merely negative, and offer no sure ground for any conclusion respecting the sources of the poet's knowledge.

[1] Maskell, *Monumenta Ritual. Eccles. Anglic.*, i. 52. 1882.

In the first scene of Act iii. there is a short conversation which has been quoted as a proof of Shakespeare's familiarity with the formulas of the Anglican Church. The conversation in question seems a dangerous foundation for an argument to prove his Protestantism; such as it is, however, the advocates of that side are welcome to it.

> "*Servant.* I do depend upon the Lord (Paris).
> *Pandarus.* A noble gentleman—I must needs praise him.
> *Servant.* The Lord be praised.
> *Pandarus.* I am the Lord Pandarus.
> *Servant.* You are in a state of grace.
> *Pandarus.* Grace ? not so ; honour and lordship are my titles."

Luxury is used in the Catholic sense of impurity (v. 2); and to complete the catalogue of religious allusions in the play, pity is called a "hermit" (v. 3), as if it was a specially monastic virtue, and Hector quotes the Psalms of David—

> "Pleasure and revenge
> Have ears more deaf than adders to the voice
> Of any true decision" (ii. 2).

CHAPTER IX.

IN our opening chapter we endeavoured to trace the contrast between Shakespeare's philosophy and that of the Reform. We shall conclude by showing some of the salient points of difference between his teaching and that of some of the modern theorists whose doctrine is the logical offspring of Protestantism, on the subject of morals. The Reformers claimed to have emancipated human reason from all external authority through their asserted supremacy of the right of private judgment. Yet from their teaching of the utter corruption of man through the fall, and the hopeless wreck of his moral powers, it followed that he was merely a passive instrument for good or evil, as either principle predominated. Thus the freedom conferred on him without was taken from him within. A similar theory is advanced by modern rationalists. Professor Caird tells us that "as moderns we are all fighting under the banner of a free spirit. That is, we are all engaged, consciously or unconsciously, in the effort to free man's life from the yoke of extraneous authority, and we are learning that we can do this only as we discover in that life a principle in virtue of which it can be a law to itself," and for this view he claims the support of Shakespeare.   It is, according to this critic, the moving principle in his *dramatis personæ*,[1] "which inevitably in the long run comes to the surface, when the passion and character of the individual act on each other";[2] just as in the Darwinian theory, genera and species are necessarily developed through progressive steps by the combination at certain junctures and under certain conditions of environment and heredity.

The poet's genius, then, according to this estimate, is seen not simply in his marvellous power of sympathy with characters of the most diverse kinds, but also in his intuitive grasp of how each character must from certain beginnings arrive at its final issue.   Thus his tragedies present, *not* the operation of a free will or a decision of human choice, but the pure evolution of a catastrophe. As we gaze with bated breath at a tempest-driven ship grounding helplessly from rock to rock till it finally strikes and sinks, so is it with the action of Shakespeare's greatest tragedies.   Macbeth impelled by his first crime, Lear by his wilfulness, Hamlet fettered by his irresolution, each hopelessly and helplessly makes for his doom, "till the final blow of fate is felt as a kind of relief, and as the necessary solution of a contradiction which has become too great to subsist."

[1] *Contemporary Review*, lxx. 826.   [2] Ibid., 826.

Now, is this really Shakespeare's teaching, or merely that of Shakespeare's modern critic? We think it is certainly not his, and that he calls this evolutionary, or necessitarian, or fatalist doctrine, " excellent foppery " (" Lear," i. 2). Thus, in reply to Gloster's complaint that our misfortunes are but the sorry effect of natural causes—

"This," says Edmund, "is the excellent foppery of the world, that when we are sick in fortune, often the surfeit of our own behaviour, we make guilty of our disasters the sun, moon, and stars, as if we were villains by necessity; fools by heavenly compulsion; knaves, thieves, and, by spherical predominance, drunkards, liars, and adulterers, by an enforced obedience of planetary influence, and all that we are evil in, by a divine thrusting on—an admirable evasion."—*Lear*, i. 2.

Thus does the poet dismiss summarily the sophists of the day, and he lays down as explicitly by the mouth of Iago, another knave—for with him knaves at times speak the truth—the doctrine that free-will and reason, and not passion or nameless impulse of any kind, form each man's character. To Rodrigo's complaint that virtue could not cure him of his love, Iago replies—

"Virtue! a fig! 'tis in ourselves that we are thus or thus. Our bodies are gardens, to the which our wills are gardeners; so that if we will plant nettles, or sow lettuce; set hyssop and weed up thyme; supply it with one gender of herbs, or distract it with many; either to have it sterile with idleness,

2 B

or manured with industry; why the power and corrigible
authority of this lies in our wills. If the balance of our
lives had not one scale of reason to poise another of sensuality, the blood and baseness of our nature would conduct
us to most preposterous conclusions; but we have reason to
cool our raging motions, our carnal stings, our unbitted lusts,
whereof I take this that you call—love to be a sect or scion."
—*Othello*, i. 3.

And indeed if each character were necessarily determined by the moving principle within, or by circumstances, or by both, the whole interest, power, and
pathos of Shakespeare's plays would be gone.   If
Iago were a villain, Henry V. a hero, Isabel pure,
and Cressida stained, solely by necessity, how could
any measure of praise or blame be attributed to
them ?   They would be no more responsible for
their moral conduct than for the height of their
stature or the colour of their hair.   Virtue and vice
would be meaningless.   But Shakespeare's aim was
to show "virtue her own feature, scorn her own
image," and virtue and vice with him have a real
meaning.   Their very notion consists in the fact
that the agent in each case might have done the
opposite.   Isabella's purity is admirable because she
voluntarily preferred her own honour to her brother's
life.   Cressida lashes Troilus to desperation because
she was voluntarily forsworn.   She "is and is not
Cressida."
   Previous habits, as they are good or evil, do indeed
dispose the individual to either course of action;

the passions may warp the judgment, but the will has always the power in Shakespeare's philosophy of doing or not doing the act in question. No habit, however strong, robs his characters of this power; if it did, their acts would cease to be human. But Shakespeare's characters are essentially human, and the secret of their power is that his description of human life and character corresponds to our own experience, and our experience is that every human being is free. No man was more hopelessly enchained by his passions than Antony; yet he knew he could have freed himself if he chose, and that his safety lay in his doing so.

> " These strong Egyptian fetters I must break,
>   Or lose myself in dotage."
>   —*Antony and Cleopatra*, i. 2.

He did not break them, but voluntarily wore them until the end, and so lived and died " a strumpet's fool " (" Antony and Cleopatra," i. 1). Henry V. wasted long years in dissipation, and his companions believed his wild habits irretrievably fixed, but he corresponded to his better impulses, and " though the courses of his youth promised it not," (" Henry V.," i. 1)—

> " Never came reformation in a flood,
>   With such a heady current, scouring faults ;
>   Nor never Hydra-headed wilfulness
>   So soon did lose his seat, and all at once
>   As in this king."—*Ibid.*

The doctrine of moral responsibility is again enforced by Shakespeare's teaching on conscience. Its voice, with him, convicts the sinner of his personal guilt.   Thus Richard III. exclaims—

> "My conscience hath a thousand several tongues,
>   And every tongue brings in a several tale,
>   And every tale condemns me for a villain."
> —*Richard III.*, v. 3.

Thus, too, the murderer of the Duke of Clarence—

> "I'll not meddle with it; it is a dangerous thing, it makes a man a coward; a man cannot steal but it accuseth him; a man cannot swear, but it checks him; a man cannot lie with his neighbour's wife, but it detects him."—*Richard III.*, i. 4.

So, too, in the "Tempest"—

> "*Gonzalo.* All three of them are desperate; their great guilt
> Like poison given to work a great time after,
> Now 'gins to bite the spirits."—*Tempest*, iii. 3.

The examples quoted by Professor Caird furnish to our mind precisely contrary conclusions to those which he has drawn.   In Hollinshed, Macbeth was from the first a hypocritical, ambitious villain.   In Shakespeare, both Macbeth and his wife have good in them, and each step in their descent in crime is marked by the voluntary resistance to the pleading and stings of conscience, and by the bitter remorse consequent on each sinful act.

When the temptation to murder Duncan first suggests itself after the witches' prophecy, his whole being recoils at the suggestion—

> "Whose horrid image doth unfix my hair,
> And make my seated heart knock at my ribs,
> Against the use of nature."—*Macbeth*, i. 3.

He is, indeed, "too full of the milk of human kindness to catch the nearest way" ("Macbeth," i. 5), as his wife says. And though she, like a whispering fiend at his side, has overcome his repugnance to the crime, again his fears break out. They are, it is true, selfish human fears of the retributive punishment of his sin here. "For the life to come" "he is prepared to jump," but they equally prove the freedom and deliberation of his acts. After Duncan's murder, Macbeth manifests not only natural remorse of conscience, but a Christian sense of the guilt of mortal sin. He says of the grooms—

> "One cried, 'God bless us!' and 'Amen!' the other,
> As they had seen me with these hangman's hands.
> Listening their fear, I could not say 'Amen'
> When they did say 'God bless us.'
>   *Lady Macbeth.* Consider it not so deeply.
>   *Macbeth.* But wherefore could I not pronounce 'Amen'?
> I had most need of blessing and 'Amen'
> Stuck in my throat.
>   *Lady Macbeth.* These deeds must not be thought
> After these ways: so it will make us mad."—*Macbeth*, ii. 2.

So, too, in Dante's "Inferno" the maddening thought of hell is the incapacity to utter a prayer because the reprobate have forfeited the grace needed to pray.

Again, after the murder of the grooms, and before that of Banquo, the same conviction that he had voluntarily lost his soul is thus expressed :—

> (Have I) " Mine eternal jewel
> Given to the common enemy of mankind " (iii. 1).

And this sense of guilt works here upon the guilty pair apart from any apprehension of earthly retribution.   The murder was a success.   Duncan's sons were fugitive, and Macbeth was acclaimed king. All seemed fair without, yet within the criminal souls reigned blank despair.[1]   Lady Macbeth soliloquises—

> " Nought's had, all's spent,
> Where our desire is got without content ;
> 'Tis safer to be that which we destroy
> Than by destruction dwell in doubtful joy " (iii. 2).

And though she upbraids her husband for his melancholy, and tells him that " Things without remedy should be without regard ; what's done, is done " (iii. 2), his agonised reply expresses the state of her own mind.

---

[1] *Cf.* Bucknill's " Psychology of Shakespeare," p. 17.   1859.

> " Better be with the dead,
> Whom we, to gain our place, have sent to peace,
> Than on the torture of the mind to lie
> In restless ecstasy " (iii. 2).

Crime indeed leads to crime, but never necessarily. Throughout the downward course Macbeth recognises his increasing guilt. Banquo's ghost is but the reflex of his own inner agony, and after the slaughter of Lady Macbeth and her children, when in his disordered frenzy he is reputed mad, its cause is explained by his conscience—

> " Who then shall blame
> His pestered senses to recoil and start,
> When all that is within him does condemn
> Itself for being there ? " (v. 2).

And as his reign began by attending to the suggestion of the Evil Spirit, so it is consummated with the discovery that all his crimes have been but in vain, and that he has been duped throughout.

> " And be these juggling fiends no more believed
> That palter with us in a double sense ;
> That keep the word of promise to our ear,
> And break it to our hope " (v. 7).

With this portraiture of the soul's voluntary descent from crime to crime, its voluntary search for criminal opportunities, and all the bitter remorse proper only to the consciously responsible being, it is hard to see how Shakespeare can be regarded as denying freedom of will. He has, however, been vindicated in an unexpected quarter.

Modern necessitarianism is the modern offspring of Calvinism; and Milton, the Puritan poet, shows us how far Shakespeare was from holding the views now attributed to him. With every poet his work is a reflection of himself, and Milton, regarding himself as one of the elect, had, we are told, "a kingly intolerance for his fellows," and moved amongst other men with a sense of conscious superiority. The sinner with him must be essentially corrupt, the elect as essentially good. He would recognise, therefore, nothing of the strife between good and evil, of St. Paul's cry, "The good I would, I do not; the evil I would not, that I do," the very theme set forth with such pathos and power by Shakespeare in his sonnets, and throughout his plays. Milton therefore was dissatisfied with Shakespeare's "Macbeth," because in the king, notwithstanding his crimes, the conflict between good and evil was apparent to the last, and Milton thought of rewriting the play, as Professor Hales tells us, on Puritan lines.[1] He however contented himself with reproducing it in "Paradise Lost," where the same story is told. Man there yields to evil through a woman's agency, and loses all; for the first fall is, in its main feature, the type of man's most frequent transgressions. Now in Milton's epics is seen as nowhere in Shakespeare the necessary evolution of the sinner to

[1] *Nineteenth Century*, vol. xxx. December 1891.

his end, developed step by step through the inevitable force of the evil principle within him.   Satan
from the first could never have been aught but the
leader of the rebel host.   There was no weakness,
no hesitation before his sin, nor consequent remorse.
Even in his defeat he triumphs in his boasted independence.   " Better to reign in hell, than serve in
heaven."   Adam, on the other hand, is all weakness.
He loses all without a moment's misgiving, never
thinks of resistance.   He has not the will to say
" Nay ! "; and the feeling evoked by his fall is not
one of pity, but of sheer contempt.

Shakespeare's view of human nature is the opposite of this.   He has the keenest sympathy with his
fellow-creatures, above all with the sinner, though
coupled with abhorrence for his sin, and this is so
because he knew what he was himself.   St. Philip
Neri would exclaim when he heard of a terrible
scandal, " God grant I may not do worse."   So it
was with the poet.   Only a few of Shakespeare's
characters, Iago, Aaron, Goneril, and Regan, are
irretrievably, formally bad.   Even John and Richard
III. have a conscience.   The rest, Macbeth and his
wife, Antony and Cleopatra, display those traces of
goodness which show what they might have been
had God's image not been wrecked, and they so far
command a lingering regard.   Shakespeare's genius,
indeed, is seen in manifesting how the baser impulses within the soul may, and under certain
circumstances do, effect his ruin.   But these circum-

stances with him are the occasion, not the cause, as agnostics assert, of the fall that follows.   Speaking of Eve's excuse after the fall, Cardinal (then Mr.) Newman says: "And this has been the course of lawless pride and lust ever since; to lead us, first, to exult in our uncontrollable liberty of will and conduct, and then, when we have ruined ourselves, to plead that we are slaves of necessity." [1]

Professor Caird, again, tells us that with Shakespeare man is not to save himself from shipwreck "by timely good resolutions and persistent faithfulness in them, but by passing through the depths of self-despair and self-disgust." [2]   To our mind, Shakespeare insists explicitly on the very course of action the Professor cannot find in his teaching. For instance, Hamlet does not tell his mother to continue living with the incestuous king till she is weary of him.   On the contrary, he urges her at once to break with the occasion and she will be saved from the sin, for by repeated abstinence a good habit will succeed to the evil custom—

> "Refrain to-night ;
> And that shall lend a kind of easiness
> To the next abstinence ; the next more easy ;
> For use almost can change the stamp of nature
> And master the devil, or throw him out
> With wondrous potency."—*Hamlet*, iii. 4.

---

[1] "University Sermons," *Human Responsibility*, viii. 136.   1872.
[2] Ibid., 825.

Similarly Laertes does not tell Ophelia that her wish for Hamlet's company is irresistible, but on the contrary, that she is to keep away from " his unmastered importunity " (" Hamlet;" i. 3).

> " Fear it, Ophelia, fear it, my dear sister ;
> And keep you in the rear of your affection,
> Out of the shot of danger and desire."—*Ibid.*

Again, we are told how presumption prepares for a fall—

> " But something may be done that we will not ;
> And sometimes we are devils to ourselves,
> When we will tempt the frailty of our powers,
> Presuming on their changeful potency."
>   —*Troilus and Cressida*, iv. 4.

Again, with theological accuracy Hamlet describes the absolute dethronement of reason, judgment, sense, which consent to a guilty passion incurs.

> " What devil was't
> That thus hath cozened you at hoodman-blind ?
> Eyes without feeling, feeling without sight,
> Ears without hands or eyes, smelling sans all,
> Or but a sickly part of one true sense
> Could not so mope.
> O shame   where is thy blush ?" (iii. 4).

This expostulation would be meaningless were not the shame and blush supposed to be the result of a guilty conscience.

Gervinus quotes with approval Birch's saying

that Shakespeare "builds a system of morality upon nature and reason, a system independent of religious considerations, because he believed the laws of morality to be written plainly enough in the human heart."[1]   But Shakespeare knew of no divorce between religion and morality.   With him, on the contrary, the voice of conscience was the voice of God, and an act against conscience a sin against God, as has been abundantly demonstrated in the case of Macbeth.   Thus, too, the Duke in " Measure for Measure" instructs Juliet (as we have seen) on the difference between the sorrow to death after a fall, or mere self-disgust, and true contrition which has for its motive sorrow for having offended God.   So too Posthumus, in the passage already quoted, speaks of his conscience "being fettered by the gods " (" Cymbeline," v. 4), and of the satisfaction which he must make to them, before he can be fully acquitted.   This speech of his Bishop Wordsworth declares to be given as uttered by a heathen—purposely unchristian.   It is in any case undoubtedly the Catholic doctrine of repentance.

So again suicide is forbidden, not because it is an offence against society, or any merely human precept, but as a transgression of the divine law.

> "O ! that the everlasting had not fixed
> His canon 'gainst self-slaughter."—*Hamlet*, i. 2.

---

[1] Bunnett's trans., ii. 589. 1863.

And in " Cymbeline "—

> " Against self-slaughter
> There is a prohibition so divine
> That cravens my weak hand."—*Cymbeline*, iii. 4.

And Gloster in " Lear "—

> " You ever gentle gods, take my breath from me,
> Let not my worser spirit tempt me again
> To die before you please."—*Lear*, iv. 6.

Shakespeare's sense of the intrinsic malice of sin is seen again in his explicit recognition of the penalties inflicted by God.   He shows no trace of the modern sentimentalists' abhorrence of the doctrine of eternal punishment.   On the contrary, he states as explicitly as Dante himself the unending loss and pain consequent on one grave lapse. Thus Isabella protests that a brother had better die (a temporal death) once than a sister eternally. So too Mrs. Ford comments on Falstaff's letter : " If I would but go to hell for an eternal moment or so, I could be knighted " (" Merry Wives," ii. 2).   Claudio, again, speaks of the seven deadly (sins), and pleads that Angelo's would be the least :—

> " Why should he for the momentary trick
> Be perdurably fined ? "

And Isabella replies—

> " Is't not a kind of incest to take life
> From thine own sister's shame ? "
> —*Measure for Measure*, iii. 1.

And that shame would be, she said, an eternal death.

Thus a true conscience manifests the law of God, and any transgression of its precepts is sin. But to obey the law grace is needed, for Shakespeare is no more a Pelagian than a Calvinist. No man recognised more fully the corruption of our nature by the fall.

> " Our natures do pursue,
> Like rats that ravin down their proper bane
> A thirsty evil, and when we drink, we die."
> —*Measure for Measure*, i. 3.

And again—

> " Virtue cannot so inoculate our old stock,
> But we shall relish of it."—*Hamlet*, iii. 1.

Or again, the fight needed to master our evil inclinations—

> " Brave conquerors !—for so you are,
> That war against your own affections,
> And the huge army of the world's desires."
> —*Love's Labour's Lost*, i. 1.

And the one means by which this internal conflict is to be overcome is grace—

> " For every man with his affects is born ;
> Not by might master'd, but by special grace."—*Ibid.*

This grace gives always sufficient strength, but if neglected our weakness becomes apparent—

> " Alack ! when once our grace we have forgot,
> Nothing goes right ; we would, and we would not."
> —*Measure for Measure*, iv. 4.

Lafeu thus contrasts the office of God and that of the devil : " The one brings thee in grace, the other brings thee out " (" All's Well," v. 2), and yet how often temporal human favours are preferred to this divine gift.

> " O, momentary grace of mortal men !
> Which we more hunt for than the grace of God."
> —*Richard III.*, iii. 3.

Grace or divine aid is only to be obtained by prayer. In the scheme of Calvinistic predestination, of independent morality, or of modern necessitarianism, prayer has no logical place. Kant, in fact, said that the sight of a man on his knees praying, to a being who was neither seen nor heard, excited doubts as to his sanity. With the Catholic Christian prayer is the very element of his life, for his life depends on its inner communion with God. So it is with Shakespeare. He has fixed times for prayer. " Morning and evening he kneels in prayer " (" Much Ado About Nothing," ii. 1 ; " Merry Wives," ii. 2); before meals by grace (" Measure for Measure," i. 2); at departure or return (" All's Well," i. 1). Thrice each day, Imogen desires her lover's prayer. She would

> " Have charged him
> At the sixth hour of morn, at noon, at midnight,
> T' encounter me with orisons, for then
> I am in heaven for him."—*Cymbeline*, i. 4.

And this desire for intercessory prayer, which we have seen expressed in the invocation of saints and angels, is repeated through the plays with regard to those still living on earth. Ferdinand would know Miranda's name chiefly that he "may set it in" his prayers ("Tempest," iii. 1), and Hamlet asks Ophelia—

> " Nymph, in thy orisons,
> Be all my sins remembered."—*Hamlet*, iii. 1.

Thus prayer is the bond of union between man and man, as between God and man.

The attitude for prayer is that of kneeling as a humble suppliant. Portia, says Stephano,

> " Doth stray about
> By holy crosses, where she kneels and prays
> For happy wedlock hours."—*Merchant of Venice*, v. 1.

So Macduff to Malcolm thus expresses the sacrificial character of prayer—

> " The Queen that bore thee,
> Oft'ner upon her knees, than on her feet,
> Died every day she lived."—*Macbeth*, iv. 3.

In spite of the warning of Reformers against vain repetitions, and against prayers for the dead, Imogen says for Belisarius, supposed to be slain, " a century of prayers " ("Cymbeline," iv. 2) twice o'er, whilst she wept and sighed.

Prayer must be made "with fasting" ("Othello," iii. 4), with spiritual labour, fasting, and striving ("Measure for Measure," ii. 2).

Prayer even works miracles, for St. Edward cures the sick by

> "Hanging a golden stamp about their necks,
> Put on with holy prayers."—*Macbeth*, iv. 3.

Prayer obtains both the prevenient grace which preserves the soul from sin, and pardon after the fall—

> "What's in prayer, but this twofold force,
> To be forestallèd, ere he come to fall,
> Or pardoned, being down?"—*Hamlet*, iii. 3.

But prayer must be offered with faith and resignation to God's will, for, as St. Augustine says, "What He refuses to our prayers He grants to our salvation."

> "We, ignorant of ourselves,
> Beg often our own harms, which the wise powers
> Deny us for our good; so find we profit,
> By losing of our prayers."—*Antony and Cleopatra*, ii. 1.

Conscience, then, according to Shakespeare, is man's guide, God's law, his rule; and his free-will, aided by grace and prayer, are the means by which he masters his lower nature, and rises to better things. Such are the poet's ethics, and a further comparison between them and modern agnostic theories offers some instructive contrasts.

First, as regards the moral law, according to the moderns there is no fixed right or wrong. Kant's vaunted "categorical imperative" of which we hear so much is practically a phantom, for it is self-

2 C

imposed, and since man is autonomous, he can
charge or dispense himself, at will, from his own law.
Nay, not only can he do so, but according to the
necessitarians he must do so, when under the influence of overpowering temptation or, again, when his
character or destiny is, under the force of circumstances, taking its necessary development. What
stress of circumstances exempts man from the guilt
of murder, adultery, or theft, is left undecided, but
a true fellow-feeling with all that is human will
teach the careful, discriminating observer that our
complex life is "not to be embraced by any set
of maxims (that is, the ten commandments), and
that to lace ourselves up in such formularies represses
the divine prompting and inspiration which spring
from growing insight and sympathy."[1] Thus spoke
George Elliot, and the novelists who have followed
in her train have developed their plots on these
lines.

In the "Manxman" Pete leaves his affianced bride
in charge of Philip, his dearest friend. His trust is
betrayed. On his return from South Africa Pete
marries the faithless one, and discovers when too
late the treachery of which he was the victim; with
what result? True to the principle of modern
altruism and necessitarianism, Pete sees that he
should not stand in the way of his wife and her
lover, so he surrenders her to him, goes back himself
to South Africa, and the curtain falls on Philip and

[1] "Mill on the Floss," ii. 462, 463.

Kate descending the castle steps of Douglas arm in
arm, transfigured in the glory of the setting sun.
Charles Lamb said of the characters in Congreve's
comedies that though all were vain and worthless,
yet " they never offended his moral sense, because
they never appealed to it at all. They seemed
engaged in their proper element. They broke no
laws, no conscientious restraints. They knew of
none."[1] But our modern novelist goes further. The
heroine of to-day is not presented merely inane and
unprincipled, as a theme for the satirist's pen, but
she appeals to our admiration in her falseness and
shame, and in the depth of her degradation demands
the approval of our moral sense. " The source of a
good woman's fall," says Mr. Caine, is due not
" to the stress of passion, or the fever of instinct,
but because she is the slave of the sweetest,
tenderest, most spiritual and pathetic of all human
fallacies—the fallacy that by giving herself to the
man she loves she attaches herself to him for
ever."[2]

On Mr. Hall Caine's principles, Othello should
have handed Desdemona over to Cassio and returned
himself to Barbary. He adopted, however, a different
course, for he did not regard her supposed unfaith-
fulness as either " the sweetest or most spiritual of
human fallacies." Hear how he speaks. He could
have borne what affliction Heaven had pleased—all

[1] " Elia and Eliana," 185. 1893.
[2] " Manxman," 124. 1894.

kinds of sores and shames on his bare head—to be
steeped in poverty to the very lips, to be

> "A fixed figure, for the time of scorn
> To point his slow and moving finger at;
> Yet could I bear that too; well, very well;
> But there, where I have garner'd up my heart,
> Where either I must live, or bear no life,
> The fountain from the which my current runs,
> Or else dries up; to be discarded thence,
> Or keep it as a cistern, for foul toads
> To knot and gender in!"—*Othello*, iv. 2.

She is still beautiful, still has all her outward
grace, but what was gone in his eyes is her fidelity
and purity. These he loved; these are gone, and
their loss is irreparable.

> "O thou weed!
> Who art so lovely fair, and smell'st so sweet,
> That the senses ache at thee, would thou hadst
> Ne'er been born!"—*Othello*, iii. 2.

This is Shakespeare's constant teaching. Man
loves a woman because she is good, and because she
quickens and evokes all the good in him, for virtue
with Shakespeare is beauty, and sin a deformity.
Shakespeare's heroines thus represent the religious
sentiment, conscience, fidelity, truth. They are to
be wooed and won, not by an appeal to their lower
nature, but by reverence and sacrifice. They are
placed by man's side, as Eve was by Adam in Paradise,
to lead him to higher things. Where disordered
passion is pursued instead of true love, wreck and

ruin follow, as with Cleopatra, or, in a lesser degree, with Juliet. Another characteristic of Shakespeare's heroines is that they are essentially feminine, and are loved for that quality. The "new woman," when not corrupt, is engaged in a lifelong endeavour to unsex herself and become as far as possible a man. In such a metamorphosis Shakespeare would have seen only a hybrid or deformity.

> " A woman impudent and mannish grown
> Is not more loathed than an effeminate man
> In time of action."—*Troilus and Cressida*, iii. 3.

Portia indeed has great intellectual gifts, and performs marvellously her lawyer's part, but she evokes our admiration, not by her power in pleading or her matchless eloquence, but because she exerted these gifts and braved all danger for her husband's sake. She may put on man's attire, but she never divests herself of her womanly dignity and modesty, of her pledged affection, and of her high religious principles. Ophelia, on the other hand, has no striking mental qualities, yet she wins the affection of Shakespeare's most intellectual character, Hamlet, because of her innocence, simplicity, trustfulness, and the depth of her affection for him.

> " I loved Ophelia ; forty thousand brothers
> Could not with all their quantity of love
> Make up my sum."—*Hamlet*, v. 1.

And simple though she was, she could appreciate him.   He was all in all to her.

> " The courtier's, soldier's, scholar's, eye, tongue, sword,
>   Th' expectancy and rose of the fair state,
>   The glass of fashion, and the mould of form,
>   Th' observed of all observers, quite, quite, down !
>   And I, of ladies, most deject and wretched,
>   That suck'd the honey of his music vows,
>   Now see that noble, and most sovereign reason,
>   Like sweet bells jangled, out of tune and harsh ;
>   That unmatch'd form and feature of blown youth,
>   Blasted with ecstasy.   O woe is me !
>   To have seen what I have seen, see what I see."
>
> —*Hamlet*, iii. 1.

Again, it was the gentleness and sympathy of Desdemona which first captured Othello's heart, as his valour and renown mastered hers.

> "She loved me for the dangers I had passed,
>   And I could love her that she did pity them."
>
> —*Hamlet*, i. 3.
> Othello

And so we might go on page after page. Shakespeare would have us regard women as God made them, and he portrays his heroines with those special feminine traits which alone render them loving and loved.

Nor is his idea of man less lofty and true.   Man's nature is indeed complex and diverse.   If the soul can reach to heaven the body is but of clay, and has appetites in common with the beast.   Hamlet,

in one of his gloomy moods, puts both sides
before us :—

"What a piece of work is man ! How noble in reason !
how infinite in faculties ! in form and moving how express
and admirable ! in action how like an angel ! in apprehension
how like a god ! the beauty of the world ! the paragon of
animals ! And yet to me, what is this quintessence of dust ?
Man delights not me ; no, nor woman neither."—*Hamlet*,
ii. 2.

On his earthly side man is indeed of himself but a
"poor, bare, forked animal" ("Lear," iii. 4). But
he has that which gives him dominion over all the
lower creatures.

> "Men, more divine, the masters of all these,
>   Lords of the wide world, and wild wat'ry seas,
>   Indued with intellectual sense and souls,
>   Of more pre-eminence than fish and fowls,
>   Are masters to their females, and their lords ;
>   Then let your will attend on their accords."
>   —*Comedy of Errors*, ii. 1.

By his intellectual soul man is great, and that soul
he holds from God, and for his use of this gift of
reason he is responsible.

>   "What is man,
>   If his chief good, and market of his time,
>   Be but to sleep and feed ? A beast, no more.
>   Sure, He, that made us with such large discourse,
>   Looking before and after, gave us not
>   That capability and god-like reason,
>   To fust in us unused."—*Hamlet*, iv. 4.

Shakespeare knows nothing of man's evolution

from a brute, and he is wholly a stranger to the
doctrine of Professor Huxley, that "the cunning and
brutal instincts of the ape or tiger ancestors must
at times break out in any human being."   Man can
with God's help keep all God's law, and be ever
chaste, true, loyal, and just.   The modest and
chivalrous Macduff thus speaks when forced to
speak the truth about himself:—

> "I am yet
> Unknown to woman ; never was forsworn ;
> Scarcely have coveted what was mine own ;
> At no time broke my faith ; would not betray
> The devil to his fellow, and delight
> No less in truth than life."—*Macbeth*, iv. 3.

However coarse the poet may be at times in words
or jests, though who can say how much his writings
have been interpolated, no moralist was ever more
severe on vice.   Impurity, in his judgment, is allied
to murder, for both sins assail God's creative power.
The one "coins heaven's image in stamps forbid,"
the other "steals from nature man already made"
("Measure for Measure," ii. 4), and the affinity of
these two sins is again declared by Pericles—

> "One sin I know another doth provoke ;
> Murder's as near to lust, as flame to smoke."
> —*Pericles*, i. 1.

The contrast we have noted between modern
ethical teachers and Shakespeare in the moral law
is found also in their view of nature.   God made
the world, and " He saw that it was good," says the

ancient Scripture, and all men of the ancient faith believed this to be true. It is not so now. Men look at the same fair nature, the work of the all-wise and all-good Creator, but they survey it through the gloom of their own doubt or unbelief, and its fairness is lost. Consider on this point the reflections of Tennyson, the recognised teacher of higher things in this age. Nature, he says, is alike prodigal and improvident. Out of forty-nine seeds cast into the earth only one fructifies, the rest die barren. She cares indeed for the species or race, but she is "careless of the single life,"[1] and is absolutely indifferent as to the pain and misery of the many, provided only the type is preserved. Nay, she cares not for type neither. "I care for nothing—all shall go,"[2] she is made to say; as a proof see the fossilised remains of whole genera and tribes of birds, beasts, plants, cast as rubbish to the wind. What then can man think of nature's Lord! He

> "Trusted God was love indeed,
>   And love's creation's final law,
>   Though nature, red in tooth and claw
> With ravine, shrieks against his creed."—*Ibid.*

And what is man himself? In his weakness, ignorance, grossness, he fares no better; he is

> "A monster then, a dream,
>   A discord. Dragons of the prime,
>   That tore each other in their slime,
> Are mellow music matched with him."—*Ibid.*

---

[1] "In Memoriam," liv.   [2] Ibid., lv.

Now compare Friar Laurence's reflections on the same subject. He surveys the same universe; he faces the same difficulties—physical pain, growth and corruption, moral evil and sin, life and death. His is no utopian, rose-coloured optimism; he sees things as they are. But through the light of faith in his own soul, he can tell how in these apparent contradictions "one thing is set against another," evil ministers to good, poisons have a healing power, and death follows life.

> " The earth that's Nature's mother is her tomb ;
> What is her burying grave, that is her womb ;
> And from her womb children of divers kind,
> We sucking on her natural bosom find ;
> Many for many virtues excellent,
> None but for some, and yet all different.
> O ! mickle is the powerful grace, that lies
> In plants, herbs, stones, and their true qualities ;
> For nought so vile that on the earth doth live,
> But to the earth some special good doth give ;
> Nor aught so good, but, strained from that fair use,
> Revolts from true birth, stumbling on abuse :
> Virtue itself turns vice, being misapplied ;
> And vice sometime's by action dignified."
> —*Romeo and Juliet*, ii. 3.

Bishop Wordsworth finds these last lines hard to explain, and suggests as one solution the fact that it is a Romanist Friar who speaks, one who would hold that evil may be done for a good end. But the Friar is speaking of the physical, not the moral order. Virtue here signifies what is good, vile what is vile, in the material world, and the vilest things become valuable in ministering to a good purpose. The concluding lines merely repeat the sentiment already expressed. That this is so, is clearly shown in the conclusion of the speech, when the Friar shows that nature finds its counterpart in man, in whose heart also are two opposing principles, and who becomes good or evil as he follows his own corrupt will, or the grace of God.

> " Within the infant rind of this weak flower
> Poison hath residence, and med'cine power :
> For this, being smelt, with that part cheers each part ;
> Being tasted, slays all senses with the heart.
> *Two such opposed kings encamp them still*
> *In man as well as herbs, grace and rude will ;*
> And where the worser is predominant
> Full soon the canker death eats up that plant."
> —*Romeo and Juliet,* ii. 3.

And now let us inquire as to the cause of the prevailing widespread pessimism. Why, for instance, should the poetry of to-day be, as Mr. A. Symonds tells us, the poetry of despair; or the keynote of the age be heard in such tones as—

> " Our sweetest songs are those that tell of saddest thought."

Or this—

> " Tears from the depths of some divine despair."

And the answer is that with the endeavour to measure all things by human rule and gauge, and the rejection of any higher guide, no clue is left to solve the mysteries of life. Our teachers and poets spend their time in criticism, introspection, and analysis, and the result is nil.

> " Seek, seeker, in thyself, submit to find
>   For the stone, bread, and life in the blank mind."

The best they can hope for is thus expressed by Clough—

> " To finger idly some old Gordian knot,
>   Unskilled to sunder, and too weak to cleave,
>   And with much toil attain to half believe."

" Victorian poets," says Mr. Symonds, " have lost the spontaneity and the joyful utterance of the Elizabethan age." Like Iago, they are nothing if they are not critical; and the criticism is that of the philosophy and science of the day. Marvellous are the discoveries of science, but the ultimate results of its analysis are immeasurable realms of space, and endless epochs of time; and man is overwhelmed by the immensity and eternity disclosed to him. Philosophies innumerable spring up, but none survive a decade. There is more wealth now than was ever dreamt of in the past. This is the golden age, yet face to face with a plutocracy is a grim, menacing multitude, filled with envy and discontent, waiting only for the time to seize what others have. Political experiments—extended franchise, compulsory education, sanitary improvements, have all been tried. What is the product? The fear of a social upheaval unparalleled in magnitude and disaster. The distant rumbling of the earthquake may even now be heard. Such, almost in Mr. Symonds' words, is his summary of the world in which we live, and his only apparent escape from the gathering storm and darkness " is to retire from the world into an artificial paradise of art, and there among exotic fragrances and foreign airs to seek a refuge from the sombre problems forced upon him by the actualities of life." [1] Yet again, this as a fact he had tried. He was both the historian and the advocate of the heathen Renaissance, of the philosophy of pleasure; but he could not escape from the problems of death and doubtful immortality, " than which none others rack the heart of man in his impotence and ignorance more cruelly." [2]

To all this poisonous malaria and gloom Shakespeare supplies an antidote which is light and life. He does so, not by excluding the actualities of life, but by keeping us in the presence of the one infinite, personal eternal God, the first cause and last end of all things. For God with him is not a mere abstract principle or an architect outside his own work, or a world soul confined within the confines of the universe—his God is Adonai, the " I am who am," the King of Kings, the Lord of Hosts. He is all-seeing (" Richard III.," v. 1), has countless eyes to view men's acts, omniscient (" All's Well," ii. 1), knows

---

[1] "Essays, Speculative and Suggestive," vol. ii. 237, 238.
[2] Ibid., Appendix, 285.

when we are falsely accused (" Winter's Tale," ii. 1),
never sleeps ("Richard III.," iv. 4), reads the hearts
(" Henry VIII.," iii. 1), unravels the thoughts (" Hamlet," iii. 3), is our Father, cares for the aged, feeds
the ravens, caters for the sparrow (" As You Like It,"
ii. 3), the widow's champion and defender (" Richard
II.," i. 2), works in all His creatures (" Henry VI.,"
ii. 1), His sun shines on the court and the cottage
(" Winter's Tale," iv. 3), is just, rights the innocent
(" Richard III.," i. 3), the one supreme appeal (" Macbeth," iv. 3), guards the night (" Richard II.," iii. 2),
" an incorruptible judge " (Henry VIII.," iii. 2)

> " To whose High Will we bound our calm contents."
> —*Richard II.*, v. i.

> " To believing souls
> Gives light in darkness, comfort in despair."
> —*Henry VI.*, ii. 1.

Mercy is His attribute. " 'Tis mightiest in the
mightiest." God's mercy to us obliges us to be
merciful to our brethren (" Merchant of Venice,"
iv. 1). All human duties and obligations are founded
on our duty to Him. Kings and all in authority are
His deputies, stewards, ministers.[1] Man and wife
are united in Him.[2] And therefore marriage is indissoluble.[3] He is the God of armies.

> " O Thou, whose captain I account myself,
> Look on my forces with a gracious eye !
> Put in their hands thy bruising irons of wrath,

---

[1] " Measure for Measure," iii. 2.   [2] " Henry V.," v. 2.
[3] " Twelfth Night," v. 1.

That they may crush down with a heavy fall
The usurping helmets of our adversaries !
Make us the ministers of Thy chastisement,
That we may praise Thee in Thy victory !
To Thee I do commend my watchful soul,
Ere I let fall the windows of mine eyes ;
Sleeping, and waking, O, defend me still."
                                    —*Richard III.,* v. 3.

To Him alone victory is due.

"O God, Thy arm was here."—*Henry V.,* iv. 8.

Shakespeare's idea of the Deity is, then, that of an
all-wise, all-powerful, and all-good and loving God.
Doubtless he saw the difficulties that men feel in
the scheme of divine economy.   He can make Lear
complain in his bitterness that the gods make us to
destroy us like wanton flies.   Hamlet can regard
" this world as a congregation of pestilential vapours "
(" Hamlet," ii. 2).   The poet is not " God's spy."   He
bows his head to the inscrutable divine decrees without a moment's doubt of their justice.

"'The words of Heaven ;—on whom it will, it will,
On whom it will not, so ; yet still 'tis just."
                                    —*Measure for Measure,* i. 3.

But he does, as we have already said, find good in
evil, and a divine purpose in the pains and sorrows
of life.   The sufferings we endure are often the
remedial chastisements of our own sins.

" The gods are just, and of our pleasant vices
Make instruments to plague us."—*Lear,* v. 3.

And the calamities which befall the innocent are

not the cruel effects of a blind destiny, but are inflicted by God on His chosen ones to purify their
souls for Him.

> "Whom best I love I cross."—*Cymbeline*, v. 4.

So, too, when the pure die young it is lest malice
should pervert their understanding.

> "You snatch some hence for little faults ; that's love
> To have them fall no more ; you some permit
> To second ills with ills, each elder worse."
> —*Cymbeline*, v. 1.

Now, Shakespeare's knowledge of God is faith in
Him through Christ; and it is instructive in these
days, when our Lord is spoken of as a mere human
teacher, and His teaching is compared with that of
Mahommed and Buddha, to note the reverence, love,
and devotion with which our Saviour, the grace of
His Redemption, His Blessed Mother, and all that is
His, are treated by the poet.   Thus Clarence to His
murderers—

> "I charge you, as you hope to have redemption
> By Christ's dear blood shed for our grievous sin,
> That you depart, and lay no hands on me."
> —*Richard III.*, i. 4.

Battles, and suffering endured for Christ form the
Christian knight, the true Crusader.

> "As far as to the sepulchre of Christ,—
> Whose soldier now, under whose blessèd cross
> We are impressèd and engaged to fight,—
> Forthwith a power of English shall we levy ;

Whose arms were moulded in their mothers' wombs
To chase these pagans in those holy fields
Over whose acres walked those blessèd feet,
Which, fourteen hundred years ago, were nailed
For our advantage on the bitter cross."
—1 *Henry IV.*, i. 1.

And again—

"Many a time hath banished Norfolk fought
For Jesu Christ, in glorious Christian field,
Streaming the ensign of the Christian Cross,
Against black pagans, Turks, and Saracens ;
And, toiled with works of war, retired himself
To Italy ; and there, at Venice, gave
His body to that pleasant country's earth,
And his pure soul unto his captain Christ,
Under whose colours he had fought so long."
—*Richard II.*, iv. 1.

His country is dear to him, most of all, because she
produced a race of these Christian knights ; and he
contrasts England, once Catholic, free, and chivalrous,
with the degraded, enslaved country of his own age.

"This royal throne of kings, this sceptred isle,
This earth of Majesty, this seat of Mars,
This other Eden, demi-paradise ;
This fortress, built by nature for herself,
Against infection and the hand of war,
This happy breed of men, this little world,
This precious stone set in the silver sea,
Which serves it as the office of a wall,
Or as a moat defensive to a house,
Against the envy of less happier lands,
This blessed plot, this earth, this realm, this England,
This nurse, this teeming womb of royal kings,
Feared by their breed, and famous by their birth,

2 D

Renownèd for their deeds as far from home
(For Christian service, and true chivalry),
As is the sepulchre in stubborn Jewry
Of the world's ransom, blessed Mary's son.
This land of such dear souls, this dear, dear land,
Dear for her reputation through the world,
Is now leased out (I die pronouncing it),
Like to a tenement or pelting farm."—*Richard II.*, ii. 1.

The poet's faith is seen, last of all, in his death scenes. He fully realises the horrors of the throes of dissolution. He knows it as "a carrion monster, with its fulsome dust" and "vaulty brows" and "sound rottenness" and "detestable bones"; and he describes all this almost in the words of Job. He feels keenly the mystery of the

"Undiscovered country, from whose bourne
No traveller returns."—*Hamlet*, iii. 1.

Yet, with the Patriarch, "after darkness he hopes for light" again. Elze says that the word immortality only occurs once in Shakespeare, and then in reference to unending life on earth ("Pericles," iii. 2). But the equivalent in the adjective form is repeatedly given. We have seen how Macbeth speaks of his soul as his "eternal jewel"; how Isabel names sin "a death for ever"; and Hamlet tells us that the ghost could do nothing with his soul,

"Being a thing immortal as itself" (i. 4).

And so Poins distinguished between Falstaff's soundness of body and the need his "immortal part had of a physician" ("2 Henry IV.," ii. 2).

The poet's teaching as to a future state is, how-ever, far more clearly learnt from the lessons he inculcates as to the importance of dying well, than from the use of any particular term. And his teaching may be summarised in Edgar's words to the desponding Gloster :—

> " What, ill thoughts again ?   Men must endure
>   Their going hence, even as their coming hither.
>   Ripeness is all."—*Lear*, v. 2.

And that ripeness is obtained through the Sacra-ments of the Church. The acme of the Ghost's sufferings is reached, not in the fact that he had been foully murdered, but that the death-blow was struck when he was " unhousel'd, disappointed, un-anel'd" ("Hamlet," i. 5).   The intensity of Hamlet's vindictive purpose is seen in that he will not slay his stepfather when he is at prayer, but when he is

> " About some act,
>   That has no relish of salvation in it ;
>   Then trip him, that his heels may kick at heaven ;
>   And that his soul may be as damned and black
>   As hell, whereto it goes."—*Hamlet*, iii. 3.

So Hastings says :—

> " It is a vile thing to die
>   When men are unprepared and look not for it."
>   —*Richard III.*, iii. 2.

The horror of Beaufort's death was in his dying without one repentant sign.   Othello would not slay Desdemona when she was unprepared.   The same

truth is enforced by the care to provide a priest for
the condemned criminals, Abhorson and Claudio,
before they met their end; and while he calls
those

> "Fools of time,
> Which die for goodness, who have lived for crime."
> —*Sonnet* cxxiv.,

he yet recognises that a death-bed repentance, with
proper dispositions, does justify the soul. The
rule with him is: as a man lives, so shall he die.
The selfish, the brutal, the unfaithful Christian, die
without a sign of religion, often by their own hand;
without a hope, save some natural desire, such as Cleopatra's, of meeting Antony in the Elysian fields. The
consolations of religion, the hope that dieth not, the
prayers and the guardianship of angels, are reserved
for those who, at least at the end, have made their
peace with God. How could the Christian philosophy on life and death be better expressed than as
follows on Wolsey's fall and end :—

> " His overthrow heaped happiness on him ;
> For then, and not till then, he felt himself,
> And found the blessedness of being little :
> And to add greater honours to his age
> Than man could give him, he died fearing God."
> —*Henry VIII.*, iv. 2.

Again, how deeply Catholic is the dying speech of
Buckingham :—

> " You few that loved me,
> And dare be bold to weep for Buckingham,
> His noble friends and fellows—whom to leave

Is only bitter to him, only dying,
Go with me, like good angels, to my end ;
Make of your prayers one sweet sacrifice,
And lift my soul to heaven."—*Ibid.*, ii. 1.

Or to what creed belongs the description of the vision of the dying Catherine, the faithful Catholic Queen ?

" No ! saw you not, even now, a blessed troop
Invite me to a banquet ; whose bright faces
Cast thousand beams upon me, like the sun ?
They promised me eternal happiness ;
And brought me garlands, Griffith, which I feel
I am not worthy yet to wear, I shall assuredly."—*Ibid.*

We think, then, Shakespeare's moral teachings in direct opposition to those of modern growth. He made it his task to show " virtue her feature, scorn her image," and his characters, not the plot, are the aim of his drama. His characters show that the rule of man's life, and his way to perfection, is no shifting, vague, subjective standard of his own making, but the unchangeable law of God. Hence, in his eyes, right and wrong are always in necessary and essential antagonism ; and though full of tender compassion for human frailty, he exhibits no morbid sympathy with sin, nor regards its punishment as other than a retributive act of divine justice. As Coleridge says, he " has no interesting adulteries or innocent incests, no virtuous vice. He never renders that amiable which reason and religion alike teach us to detest, or clothes impurity in the garb of virtue." In his sonnets and dramas he forbids

> ". . . Fond
> Lascivious metres to whose venom sound
> The open ear of youth does always listen."
> —*Richard III.*, ii. 1.

His heroes are brave, good, and true. But their goodness is based, not on Puritan self-complacency, or, negatively, on the absence of temptation, but on self-conflict, waged and won for God's sake and through His grace.

In an age of doubt and despondency, single sentences of Shakespeare speak like the voice of conscience. Against unbelief, he warns us that " reverence is the angel of the world." The philosophy of the day is " excellent foppery." Against novelties he tells us "to stick to the journal course," and he never allows us to be " out of countenance with one's nativity," or to fear in the hour of darkness if our souls are prepared. " Ripeness is all." Hence he performs the poet's true function, the cleansing of the sick soul; and he does so with incomparable charm and power, not only by aid of his matchless genius, but because his mind is filled with the eternal forms of truth and beauty, and his ideals are divine.

INDEX OF NAMES

THE END

BURNS AND OATES, LIMITED, LONDON.